A Road Less Travelled

A memoir of a privileged life

Robin Knight

"Two roads diverged in a wood, and I – I took the one less travelled by, and that has made all the difference."
ROBERT FROST

Knightwrite Ltd

First published in the UK in 2011 by Knightwrite Ltd.

ISBN 978-0-9568770-0-0

Papers used in this book are natural, renewable and recyclable products sourced from well-managed forests and certified in acordance with the rules of the Forest Stewardship Council.

FSC
www.fsc.org
MIX
Wood from
responsible sources
FSC® C021018

Typeset in Adobe Garamond, designed and produced by Gilmour Print www.self-publish-books.co.uk

*To JK without whom
none of this would have been worthwhile*

Contents

Introduction

I was playing golf one day in 2010, and my partner asked me who I was writing this memoir for – myself, my family or a wider audience. I hadn't been asked this question before, but after a hole or two's thought I realised that I was writing for myself.

This is not meant to be a scholarly record but an account of one life mostly experienced in the second half of the twentieth century. In itself it is not an especially noteworthy existence, but already it is a life and a career that could not be repeated. The world has moved on. In that narrow sense this book is history. It is largely rooted in time and place but some distinct topics do recur – foreign correspondents, newsmagazines, communism and chance to name a few.

I have never kept a diary regularly but I have kept a lot of other things – letters, papers, magazines, photographs, cuttings and so on. They formed the core material for my research and without these props many more mistakes would have been made than, no doubt, have been made. It is amazing what tricks time plays with the memory.

I have been fortunate to have interacted with many prominent people over the course of the last forty or more years. That is one of the great privileges that come from being a journalist. When I began to work for one of the world's largest corporations in my mid-50s I saw first hand just how hierarchical most human organisations really are. It seems to be in our genes. Journalism is one of the few activities that, at least partially, tends to go against the grain and encourage access and interaction at all levels.

I owe a huge debt to my dear wife Jeannie, a loyal and doughty companion through so many of the ups and downs described in these pages. She endured my long and frequent absences on the road, put up with the many days I have spent at my computer researching and writing this book in the last 18 months and read every chapter as it came off the printer, often remembering important details that had passed me by.

My thanks are also due to Fred Coleman, my friend and one-time colleague, for taking the trouble to read and edit the manuscript, and to Ray Moseley for his sage authorial advice. Another friend dating back to university years, Hamish McRae, did me a great service by putting me in touch with Douglas Gilmour at Gilmour Print who oversaw the design and printing of the book. Any factual mistakes that appear despite their excellent efforts are entirely my fault.

The judgements, of course, are all mine. I have simply tried to tell it as I saw it and experienced it, without fear or favour.

Chiswick, London, June 2011.

1

Set Up in Tashkent

*"To travel hopefully is a better thing than to arrive, and
the true success is to labour."*

ROBERT LOUIS STEVENSON

By Soviet standards the day had gone well. Through a stroke of luck I had met and interviewed the second-ranking Muslim in the Soviet Union, visited a Muslim-run school and strolled around a museum displaying rare Muslim artefacts – all in a morning. The credit was down to a man called Zair who had introduced himself as my "guide" the evening before at the Intourist service bureau of the Uzbekistan Hotel. As Jean and I were leaving the museum, he announced that it was his 30th birthday and proposed that we go to a *chaikana* (tea house) on the outskirts of Tashkent to celebrate the occasion with some of his friends. In the circumstances it seemed churlish to refuse. So we went.

It was a decision with far-reaching consequences. On arrival at the run-down tea house we were met by three men and two women, all of whom claimed to know Zair and work for Intourist. But none of them seemed to know much about Tashkent or Uzbekistan. It quickly became apparent that we were the real guests at this "party." Two hours went by in desultory conversation, all of us reclining awkwardly on oriental cushions around a low table. We were plied with vodka which Jean did not drink and I sipped sparingly. Then we moved outside to a decrepit courtyard to watch pilaf being grilled on a greasy barbecue. My glass (in reality a small cup) was refilled inside and brought out to me. The vodka tasted the same but almost immediately I felt odd – dizzy and out of control. Briefly I went back inside the tea house, came out again and promptly collapsed unconscious on the ground.

A nightmare now unfolded which was to last for the next 30 hours until we finally staggered back to our flat in Moscow. Never did I feel more isolated or vulnerable in the three years we lived in the USSR. In the courtyard Jean tried to revive me for 40 minutes. Our "hosts" did nothing to help. Jean was then taken inside the tea house where two of the men made suggestive remarks and molested her. She ran outside screaming and found me vomiting into a tin bath. The two men followed her and tried to remove my jacket but she fought them off. In the light of our later questioning, it seems clear that the plan was to plant drugs on me. An empty old Intourist bus materialised from somewhere and Jean dragged me on board with the help of a couple of elderly Uzbeks who were passing by. On our way back to Tashkent the Intourist group sat at the back of the bus smirking and laughing.

Arriving at the hotel, the front entrance was barred although it was only 6.00pm. Our "guide" and his accomplices melted away as police appeared from the shadows. Only the intervention of a group of visiting American plastic surgeons in the hotel lobby area, who saw Jean banging on the closed glass door and forced it open, got us into the front lobby. Here we were hauled into the manager's office. For the next two hours three plain clothes and two uniformed policemen tried to get Jean to sign a prepared statement saying that I was drunk and disorderly. Earlier incidents during our tour in the Soviet Union involving foreign journalists giving police statements had shown that signing anything was a huge mistake. So she refused and refused, declined to let them take me away to a local hospital for "blood tests" and instead demanded time and again to be allowed to call the US embassy in Moscow 1,700 miles away to the northwest – only to be informed that none of the telephones were working.

Eventually Jean was allowed to take me up to our room, number 619. Here I spent the next twelve hours mostly unconscious, or vomiting, or teeth chattering or body shaking uncontrollably. Jean balled up a handkerchief and put it in my mouth to stop me biting my tongue. Later that night the telephone system miraculously recovered and Jean, having carefully written down her version of events, was able to call Moscow and report the incident to the embassy duty officer, a sympathetic and capable young second secretary called Anne Sigmund (later US ambassador to Kirghizstan) who immediately offered to send someone to Tashkent if we were unable to leave under our own steam. "She seemed to know what happened almost before I told her," Jean said later.

Next morning Jean began the chore of getting us on a plane to Moscow at short notice – a near-impossible task in the Soviet Union of those days. At first Intourist informed her there were no seats available "until the day after tomorrow." But in late afternoon, by which time I was feeling better, they relented. That evening, a Thursday, we boarded an Aeroflot flight and returned safely to our apartment on Leninsky Prospekt sometime after midnight. Never did that polluted, noisy flat with its massive steel-reinforced front door seem more welcoming or secure.

I had arrived in Tashkent from Alma Ata on the evening of 17th April, 1979, as part of a long-delayed reporting visit to Soviet Central Asia. I was 35 and ten weeks away from the end of a gruelling, if rewarding, three-year assignment in the USSR for my employer, the American newsmagazine *US News & World Report*. Jean, then 29, unusually was accompanying me as I had been unable to find anyone from the Moscow international press corps willing to travel with me – the normal practice at that time for foreign journalists moving around so-called "open" regions of the Soviet Union. Our intention had been to spend a few days in Tashkent before going on to Bukhara and Samarkand, and for me to write a piece about nationalism, Islam and Soviet control in the Russians' central Asian suzerainty. Unable to set up interviews in advance, I relied on Intourist, the state organisation that controlled foreign tourism in the USSR, to produce local contacts at short notice – never a straightforward matter in such a command-and-control society.

For months, even years, before this ill-fated trip I had been subjected to shrill attacks in the Soviet press about my reporting of "Soviet reality." As the time neared to pack up and leave for good, the attacks grew in intensity. Yet this seemed almost standard practice and no special cause for concern. Numerous American, British and French correspondents in that era found themselves targeted by the Soviets as their assignments drew to a close. As far as anyone could make out the aim was to smear and undermine the correspondent's reputation in the outside world as a "Soviet expert", inhibit his or her successor and rule out any second assignment – the Soviets always preferred inexperienced newcomers to returning veterans.

In such circumstances it was all-too easy to become paranoid so I had just ploughed on as usual, determined to continue doing the job I had been asked to do by my editors in Washington. In essence this was to convey to the magazine's solidly Middle America readership the reality, as far as that was possible, of everyday life in the Soviet Union sixty or more years after the 1917 communist takeover. Travelling outside Moscow was integral to achieving this objective, and in three years from 1976 I had made numerous fascinating excursions to the hinterland. Virtually every trip produced a story for the magazine, interesting encounters for me and an incident of some sort – but nothing serious or life-threatening. Some sort of risk-taking was built into the job; there was a limit to how defensive and cautious and suspicious of Russians one could be, particularly over a sustained period. In any case it was a key part of my remit to absorb and reflect local colour and to make contact. Given the prevailing cold-war atmosphere, professional curiosity alone was sufficient to make every western journalist vulnerable to deliberate traps – I knew that. Even so, the rare invitation to socialise with local people was much prized not least because the alternative – never to leave the western cocoon in Moscow – was so feeble and self-defeating.

The wider context played a part in my misadventure too. Ever since Jimmy Carter was elected US President in 1976 and started to emphasise human rights, Soviet-American relations had been on a roller-coaster ride. By April 1979 we were nearing the end of marathon and controversial negotiations to agree a bilateral treaty limiting nuclear weapons – the deal that came to be known (although never implemented) as SALT II. Meantime an aging and enfeebled Soviet leader, Leonid Brezhnev, was capable of no more than an hour's work each day and a power struggle was looming behind the scenes. One part of the Soviet hierarchy still favoured détente and began signalling this in early 1979 by relaxing Jewish emigration rules. A more hawkish element, probably led by the military and the KGB, viewed all agreement with the West in zero sum terms – if Washington supported a treaty, it must be bad for Soviet power and influence. Down at my "bootstrap" level, as one Soviet propagandist had charmingly placed me earlier that year, there was no consensus and local KGB types were free to play the field as they saw fit. The result was a rash of unsavoury incidents all over the USSR in the lead up to Carter's summit meeting with Brezhnev in June 1979, and afterwards. In Tashkent my unexpected lone appearance that April must have seemed like manna from heaven.

Back in Moscow the first order of business on Friday 20th April was a meeting with the emollient press counsellor, Ray Benson, and his aides at the US Embassy. Although Jean and I were British citizens, I was accredited in the USSR as a correspondent for an American publication and it was the Americans who went in to bat for me (although the British ambassador, Sir Howard Smith, did call and offer to help in any way he could). The American embassy's standard policy, the counsellor told me, was to protest incidents like ours vigorously. Had it not done so, I was told, this would be seen by the Soviets as an admission of guilt. In this case there was added pressure to speak out; the protest was being lodged on the personal recommendation of the feisty US ambassador, Malcolm (Mac) Toon, someone I had always respected. We were asked, however, not to talk about the incident publicly until the protest could be delivered to the Soviet Ministry of Foreign Affairs on the following Monday.

Inevitably, over that weekend, the story leaked and an enterprising colleague, Dan Fisher of the *Los Angeles Times*, called late on the Saturday night to ask me to confirm the garbled account he had unearthed. There was nothing for it but to ask my American colleagues to come round to Leninsky Prospekt the next day to hear my version, answer their questions and prepare for the inevitable media storm that would follow. Nothing before or since has persuaded me that this was the wrong course of action. When dealing with the Soviet regime publicity was by far the best defence for western correspondents and businessmen, however uncomfortable this may have been in the short run for their employers abroad and embassies in the Soviet capital whose overriding objectives, almost invariably, were to smooth things over.

Thus we embarked on our five minutes of fame. Over the next three days I was besieged by the Moscow foreign press corps. As far as I could I kept Jean out of the limelight but we were interviewed together on camera by all three US networks (one of which flew in a camera crew from West Germany), appeared on radio talk shows in Canada, the US, France and Australia and gave numerous accounts to print journalists, many of them good friends like Dick Beeston of *The Daily Telegraph* and the American David Satter of *The Financial Times*. Defending oneself against a charge of being drunk and disorderly is tricky, particularly in the absence of neutral bystanders. All I can say more than 30 years after the event is that not a single person we knew in the foreign community in Moscow appeared to think that the incident was anything other than a put-up job designed to discredit me. Such was the reality-based cold war mindset at every level in the late-1970s.

This initial barrage of front-page publicity all over the world produced some weird and wonderful coverage over the following few days. Most of the meaty stories in the US followed the wire services or *New York Times* accounts quite faithfully. Headlines were another matter. A kindly researcher in the *US News* library in Washington collected clippings of the incident for me, and later I spent a wet holiday in a hut on a hillside in Swaziland gluing them into three large scrapbooks. I still have them today. "Thugs run by Kremlin attack American couple" (*Martinsville, Indiana, Reporter*); "Newsman says Soviets hurt him" (*Winston-Salem Journal*); "Teahouse nightmare for US couple in Russia" (*San Francisco Chronicle*); "I was given a mickey, reporter says" (*Miami News*); "Drugged by Reds, US writer says" (*Quincy Patriot Ledger*); "Yank journalist claims drugging, attack by Russ" (*Milwaukee Sentinel*). Dozens of papers worldwide weighed in with editorials deploring the incident and what they saw as the latest Soviet assault on press freedom. Equally to the point, Craig Whitney of the *New York Times* (who had been put on trial by the Soviets and found guilty of libel on trumped-up charges in 1978) addressed the drink issue head on: "The difficulty of rebutting an accusation of public drunkenness makes it an attractive tool in a society where an official charge is usually taken as proof of guilt. Knight is known to diplomats and colleagues as a sober-sided professional and Mrs Knight is the librarian of the Anglo-American School in Moscow."

Before long the Soviets retaliated with a blast from *TASS*, the official news agency. Yuri Kornilov, a veteran hardliner with a bald head and a nasty temper who had taken aim at me several times before, was rolled out to respond. He was at his most tendentious and sarcastic. Apparently I had "staged a drunken brawl" in Tashkent which involved "smashing glassware and insulting waitresses." I was described as "the main character in a trashy detective story with anti-Soviet overtones" (probably the most heinous offence). Readers were told that I was a "scandalmonger (who) had long specialised in inventions about Soviet secret agents." I was, declared Kornilov, now fully ensconced in his lofty pulpit, "a zealous supplier of inventions about the Soviet Union." In other words, my "mad ravings" should be ignored. The piece, which ran throughout the Soviet Union and in such fellow traveller countries as Cuba and Vietnam, contained nine separate errors of fact. Among them was an allegation that I had appeared on *Voice of America* (one of the few radio stations that had not interviewed me) as part of a coordinated American plot to undermine détente. When *AP* and *Reuters* called for a comment I denied everything and said mildly that I thought Kornilov "could do better than this."

Propaganda blasts of this personal type were part and parcel of the background static of East-West relations in the 1970s as the Cold War rumbled on – and grist to the mill for me after three years of regular sniping. For Jean it was another matter. Each Soviet lie upset her more than the last. She has remained suspicious of Russians ever since and many times refused to return to Moscow. "It's sad that the second most powerful country in the world has to stoop so low just because it can't stand what an objective journalist like Robin writes about it," she observed in a letter home at the time. My reactions were more philosophic, but no less judgemental. "I'm tremendously proud of Jean and the way she handled the situation, and tremendously annoyed that it occurred at all," I wrote later to the foreign editor at *US News*, LeRoy Hansen. "I suppose it's a kind of warped tribute to the influence of the magazine that the Soviets feel it worthwhile to get at us this way. But I feel mortified that the magazine's good name should be dragged in the dirt. Of course I blame myself. But it is a vivid reminder just how vulnerable individuals here in Moscow always are." Later, to a friend in America, I added: "I always thought there were no limits to what the Soviets might try if you riled them enough."

Needless to say, the US Embassy protest to the Foreign Ministry went nowhere. "The Soviets offered a version of events which the embassy will not dignify by repeating," said the press spokesman, Jack Harrod, afterwards. In fact the exchange became a slanging match, with the Soviets upping the ante by producing a charge of misconduct against another US accredited reporter, Peter Hann of *McGraw Hill*. He was accused of causing $237 damage to a hotel room during a trip to Ashkabad, Turkmenistan – an absurd allegation which was dropped later. In Washington the State Department spokesman, Hodding Carter, issued a statement about Tashkent: "We deplore this action (which) undermines efforts for promoting understanding between our two countries." For my part I wrote to my minder at the Soviet Foreign Ministry, AK Voznikov, "to express my anger that such a staged event should ever have happened, particularly under the auspices of Intourist . . . The way my wife Jean was molested and pressured was totally inexcusable in a civilised society." Voznikov, a decent chap forced to work in an ideological straitjacket, sensibly never replied.

While all this was going on, *US News* remained curiously silent. Initially Roy Hansen learned of the incident through the State Department in Washington which had been in contact with the US Embassy in Moscow. I sent a telex message to Hansen once we returned to Moscow and, when the story broke, called him on the Sunday to warn him that it would be front page news the next day. Monosyllabic and terse at the best of times, he sat on the information. As a result no one called to see how we, and particularly Jean, were faring. And no one gave me guidance about whether to talk to the press or what to say if I did. Thus it was my decision to seek maximum publicity once my colleagues in Moscow knew of the incident. And when the tendentious *TASS* version of events appeared soon after, it was my decision to issue a rebuttal. Only five years earlier *US News* staffers had been forbidden to make any public statement about anything.

It was not until a full five days after the incident that Editor Marvin Stone and my former boss in London Joe Fromm (by then the magazine's assistant editor) actually contacted us – at 2.30am Moscow time, apparently after prodding by their respective wives both of whom had accompanied their husbands on foreign postings and understood what Jean – by then getting angrier and angrier at Washington's silence – was going through. Nothing much transpired as a result of this early-morning call and, it seemed to me at the time, Washington's attitude was "you got yourself into this mess, you get yourself out of it."

I could hardly complain. Of all the western correspondents I knew in the Soviet capital, I was left alone more by my masters than anyone else. Months would go by without any communication from anyone in a senior position in Washington. Mostly, the only regular contact was with the foreign editor's assistant who concerned herself with the minutiae of life such as the price of spare parts for our gas cooker or the amount of money we spent on toilet paper in the bureau. Marv Stone himself was a strong-willed, decent man well hidden behind a gruff exterior. Having cut his teeth as a wire service reporter in Asia after the Second World War, he joined *US News* in 1960 to cover the space race and worked his way up, becoming editor in 1976. His attitude to the magazine's half dozen foreign correspondents reflected his no-nonsense character. Once he selected you for a job, he left you alone to get on with it. Once you let him down, as he saw it, then it was rare to get back in his good books. He did not forgive or forget easily.

On this occasion, as I discovered later, plenty had been going on in Washington but Marv and Joe were reluctant to talk about it over the bugged international phone line. In the edition of the magazine prepared that week and issued on 30th April, Stone rode to the rescue with all guns blazing, describing me as one of the magazine's "most reliable, perceptive men in the field" and writing that "Robin and his wife Jean are exemplary in their personal lives." He followed this by stating that I had served *US News* readers well by reporting on Soviet "domestic truths," and that this had led to attacks on me almost from the start of my assignment. The editorial ended by arguing that my "refusal to back off undoubtedly played a part in the Tashkent incident." My first-person account of what had happened followed. It did not mince words.

The following week a deluge of supportive letters rained down on the magazine, flavoured by some inevitable (mostly communist-inspired or anti-British) scepticism. The great majority of the writers made it clear that they appreciated the way I had tried to describe Soviet reality in the preceding three years. I warmed, in particular, to one correspondent: "Robin Knight is a young man doing a great job – a man, and his wife, with ability, guts and determination. (In his report) he gave possibly the best definition ever printed in the public press of the lying, deceitful, untrustworthy and dangerous Soviet administration." When your back is to the wall, it's nice to have some supporters out front.

Revived by this show of support, Jean and I decided to live out our last few weeks in the USSR as we had planned. A couple of weekends after the incident we journeyed by train to Kiev with Michael and Joan O'Neill, good friends from the Irish embassy, for an uneventful tourist visit to the Ukrainian capital. I wrote my piece about Soviet Central Asia, reassured by Mac Toon's revelation at his regular briefing that incidents like mine occurred "weekly" when he lived in the Soviet Union in the mid-1960s. On his first Moscow posting in 1954, he said, things were so bad that "all US diplomats carried around a bottle of olive oil and a teaspoon and put the oil in the vodka before drinking." In theory this prevented any drug in the vodka getting into the bloodstream. Perhaps he should have told me this sooner! Editorials, mostly sympathetic, appeared in a number of US newspapers. An old friend and colleague in Moscow, Hal Piper of the *Baltimore Sun*, chose to run a long excerpt from the 1839 journal of the Marquis de Custine (a French nobleman) in his weekly column to emphasise how little Russia and the Russian character had changed in the intervening 140 years.

Around this time my strategy of high-profile, high-volume complaint received support from an unexpected quarter – James Angleton, the famed CIA master counter-spy, by then retired. A colleague in Washington bumped into him at a lunch and Angleton brought up my case, saying that if the KGB "got away unscathed with framing Knight, the official who arranged the incident would be promoted and there would be a repeat performance. If there is a serious, vigorous protest, the KGB official will be punished and there will be less chance of a repeat."

In the light of what followed it is a moot point whether promotion or demotion followed. First, I received a letter in mid-May from one of the Intourist "guides" stating that I had "undeservedly insulted a group of people who showed you hospitality, and caused harm to their official positions." Demanding an immediate published apology, the "guide" stated that, failing an apology, he proposed to go to court "with a request on behalf of myself and my colleagues for criminal punishable slander" – not an empty threat given the way the Soviet legal system had been manipulated the year before to prosecute and fine the correspondents of the *New York Times* and the *Baltimore Sun* for articles they wrote about a Georgian dissident. On advice from the US embassy, I ignored this letter and a follow-up telegram at the end of May. In New York the pro-Moscow *Russky Golos* magazine published quite the worst poem ever written, characterising me as "the big Yankee/ defiling hospitality/ (who) lost both shame and tact." *Literaturnaya Gazeta* weighed in by calling me "a simpleton who lost vigilance" – a rare touch of irony from a Soviet journal. Then *Izvestia*, the Soviet government newspaper, published a long story headlined "Gentlemen in Liquor." This piece of fiction was accompanied by a damning photograph taken from behind a tree of me being sick in the tea house courtyard, so confirming the staged nature of the whole incident.

At this point everything might have died down – even in the Soviet Union in 1979 there was a limit to the amount of anti-American bile Russian editors would publish – had it not been for the announcement that a summit meeting to sign the SALT II agreement would take place in Vienna in mid-June. This produced a mixed response in both Moscow and Washington, with opponents of détente staging more provocations and using my incident to buttress their case, and supporters of détente and summit meetings doing their best to ignore anything that seemed to call in question one superpower's ability to trust the other – in theory, a vital component of the SALT II deal.

The rash of SALT-related incidents involving KGB muggings, thefts, druggings and expulsions of foreigners eventually totalled nine and continued into July. It included US and Australian diplomats and American, French and German reporters as well as Jean and me. It also emerged that we had not been the first visitors to Tashkent to be victimised. Four years before an African-American trade official assigned to accompany a US exhibit in the city disappeared for a few days after forming a liaison with a local girl. When he resurfaced he was in traction in a local hospital allegedly suffering from venereal disease which, the girl claimed, he had given her. An East-West row ensued but was hushed up at the time. In my case the diplomatic reaction shifted like the wind. In Washington the veteran Soviet Ambassador, Anatoly Dobrynin, gave an audience to one of my colleagues in which he displayed an overwhelming insouciance about the harassment of journalists in the USSR coupled with a visceral hostility to *US News & World Report* and the US "military-industrial complex" which, he assumed, bankrolled the magazine. Meantime in Moscow Ambassador Toon concluded that the sooner I left the Soviet Union for good, the better it would be both for the Vienna summit and the future representation of *US News* in the Soviet Union.

Diplomats, of course, are paid to put their country's interest first and Toon's *volte face* from staunch defender to fence-sitter was no great surprise. His view, basically, was that the longer I remained in Moscow the greater the chance that I would be put on trial and the more likely that US-Soviet relations would be affected. The sooner I left, the greater the chance this problem at least would go away. I was not a diplomat. In my view if I left under a cloud my successor would likely pay a price throughout his assignment in Moscow and so would *US News* for years to come having given way to the Soviets under pressure. But this was not something I could decide alone. Marv Stone announced he was flying to Vienna to attend the summit and wanted Jean and me there regardless. In the event we conducted our own three-hour summit to discuss my future – Stone, Toon and myself – in a coffee shop in the Vienna Intercontinental Hotel.

Here the argument went back and forth with me, much of the time, an interested bystander. Toon, a four-time US ambassador and the son of a Scottish immigrant, was a good match for Stone. Both had served in the US Navy in World War II. Both were conservative and hard-nosed. Never one to give the Soviets the benefit of any doubt, Toon spoke his mind and was something of a lone straight-talker in the liberal Carter administration. By June 1979 he was nearing the end of his diplomatic career. In retirement he worked tirelessly to pursue Americans still deemed "missing in action" in the Vietnam War. Stories about his bluntness and outspokenness are legion. Also his love of martinis, his ego, his guts and the large dollop of common sense that he brought to all assessments of the Soviet Union. 'No comment' wasn't in his vocabulary.

For his part Stone had another six years to go before his editorship at the magazine came to a bitter, if lucrative, end sometime after the publication's sale in 1984. He then moved into government as deputy director of the US Information Agency in the Reagan administration. Although Toon and Stone shared many views about East-West relations and the Soviets, on this matter there was no consensus. Diplomacy and press freedom clashed, with no real middle ground. Eventually Stone turned to me and asked what I wanted to do. Toon then made it clear that while he wished me to remain outside the USSR, if I returned he would be supportive. I was determined to go back, both to avoid the impression I had been run out of town and also to do what I could to prepare the ground for my successor and to protect the magazine's good name. Stone sighed, looked heavenward and said, "Be it on your own head."

So I returned to Moscow for another three weeks and Jean insisted on accompanying me. It turned out to be a nerve-racking time during which we were subjected to low level harassment and made aware that we were under surveillance. For days on end loud pop music blared out of an empty apartment right next to our bedroom. Jean was hemmed in by two cars in a parking lot. Our Irish friends were pressured. I refused to drive anywhere, fearing another staged incident, and made Boris, the office driver, work overtime. No doubt under orders, since our staff routinely reported on our doings to their KGB masters, he often failed to turn up, causing added difficulties. But we survived and handed over the bureau as planned to our successors. Almost the last thing we did in

Moscow was to attend the 4th of July reception at the residence of the US ambassador. As we were leaving Spasso House Mac Toon came up to me, shook my hand and said that in my place he would have made the same decision that I had. I am sure he would have too.

Whether the incident harmed or helped my career is, as they say, an interesting question. The Editors at *US News & World Report* eventually let me know (by letter, naturally) that they were "very proud of you and very much impressed by the outstanding job you have done for us in Russia. There is a unanimous view that your reporting and writing on the Soviet scene has been unsurpassed. We saw the episode in Tashkent not as anything which discredited the magazine in any way. Far from it. It was seen widely here as evidence that we are doing a hard-hitting job of reporting Soviet reality." But later, as I languished in South Africa, second thoughts may have begun to creep in, and it was not for another four years that my star began to shine again. By then Tashkent had become a memory. Occasionally someone would recall the incident and ask me what *really* happened. But I resisted the temptation to sit down and re-examine the past – until now.

Even with the advantage of hindsight, the whole affair still seems pointless and counter- productive – yet sadly all too typical of the warped Soviet (and Russian) attitude to outsiders, critics and reporters which persists to this day. That I made mistakes is not in dispute. Looking back, we should never have travelled alone to central Asia, leaving Jean isolated when the trouble started, and instead waited until another western correspondent was able to accompany us. But time was not on my side with only ten weeks left in the USSR and we both wished to see Bukhara and Samarkand. So we went. I should also have been more suspicious of our original escort who must have been the first "guide" in Soviet history who did not know his way to the city war memorial. Perhaps I should have refused the tea-house invitation, yet I had no reason to reject it and good reasons to accept it. I was, after all, on a reporting trip, not a tourist jaunt. On our return to Moscow I should have visited the US embassy doctor immediately who would have checked me out to see what drugs had been used. A week after our return to Moscow my vomit-stained jacket was taken away for analysis in the West together with clothes worn by an American and Australian diplomat. Both men had been drugged in eerily similar circumstances in the Ukrainian city of Chernovsty the month before my incident, but the matter had been hushed up and only came to light after our incident. I never heard any more about the analysis. Above all, though, after three years in the Soviet Union, I should not have accepted a drink unless I had seen my hosts filling my glass.

Still, between the two of us we did a lot of things right. Jean held her nerve bravely and refused to be panicked into signing anything. She made contact with the US embassy as soon as she could, spelt out our situation accurately and succinctly and our plight was recognised quickly. Once the story leaked out I stood up for myself in public, rebutted the worst examples of Soviet lies and made it as difficult as I could for the Soviet allegations to stick. It helped enormously to have lived in Moscow for some years and seen how other, similar provocations against western journalists had been handled. Some people, and organisations, bent faster than others as the Soviet authorities well knew. I was fortunate to be supported by a tough-minded Editor, and a hardened diplomat who had seen it all before and was the last person likely to be taken in by Soviet propaganda.

Western reporters in the Soviet Union in my era were paid to take risks and were supported in their work, as previous generations had not been, by the 1975 Helsinki Accords which greatly widened the scope of possible reporting of Soviet "reality." But this raised the stakes too. For the first time western media representatives – print and electronic – covered human rights issues in the USSR in depth. As the harassment of Soviet Jews, internal Helsinki monitoring groups and minorities like the Lithuanians and Georgians grew worse, so did the newly sanctioned interest of western reporters in the situation. The result was an increasingly tense standoff between the Soviet authorities and western journalists throughout the 1976-79 period which had its expression in the many KGB-staged incidents, expulsions and tit-for-tat diplomatic denunciations which took place in those years. I was the victim of just one of many unsavoury events – less for my relatively low-key reporting of dissident affairs than for the spotlight that US News had been shining for the past three years on everyday reality in the disintegrating USSR.

On 5th July, 1979, we flew out of Moscow's decrepit Sheremetyevo airport for the last time – but not before we endured a final shakedown at customs which led to Jean handing over her engagement ring to the O'Neills, who had courageously accompanied us to the terminal in case of just such a situation. This little incident created a suitably sour final taste of Russia in our mouths as we circled above the marshy green fields and birch and pine forests stretching around Moscow – the last glimpse that we were to have together of a benighted country and city that had been our first home from home.

2

A Rootless Childhood

"Childhood shows the man, as morning shows the day."
John Milton

To be born in the middle of a world war the son of a professional soldier, to go to schools steeped in military discipline, to wear a naval uniform for five years, to grow up in a country seemingly resigned to austerity, authority and conformity – all this and more suggests an orderly, conventional middle class childhood of the 1940s and 1950s where the toughest personal challenges involved abiding by rules, passing exams and never questioning one's relatively fortunate place in the firmament. How wrong that impression is!

I was born on 10th June, 1943 when the tide of war was finally turning in Britain's favour, but victory was neither in sight nor yet conceivable. My mother had travelled from her parents' home on the Isle of Wight to a wartime maternity hospital on the mainland used by the wives of junior officers – a requisitioned country house belonging to a member of the Carreras family (tobacco magnates) in the Buckinghamshire village of Fulmer Chase, near Chalfont St Giles. Apparently it was a straightforward delivery. My father, then based in Salisbury, was not around at the birth, so setting a precedent that persisted throughout my childhood. Once my mother was discharged, she spent the night with her parents-in-law at their house in Walton-on-Thames. I cried continuously, Grandmother Knight did nothing to help, Grandfather Knight was disapproving and my mother had no idea what to do. Mercifully, the next day she was rescued by her mother, Grandma Heard, who took us back to the island and to her welcoming home at Newlyn in Shanklin. Here we all lived together until 1945 when my parents bought a cottage on the island at St Lawrence before the birth of my sister Susie at the end of the year.

Though I was not to realise it for many years, a framework for life had been established. The Knight family was large but it was not close. Indeed, today it might be called dysfunctional. Grandfather Arthur Knight, by the time of my birth a senior accountant with the Legal & General assurance company, was one of nine children of Thomas Crosby Knight and his wife Mary Ann. A family tree drawn up in the 1960s by Grandfather Knight's redoubtable sister Florence – interned at the age of 60 by the Japanese in north China in 1941; an article I wrote about her life is on http://www.theprow.org.nz/florence-knight/ – describes their great great grandfather William as an Essex sheep farmer in 1823. A distant relative and family historian, Tessa Adams, once told me that William actually was a shepherd who was born in 1783 and came from Papworth in Cambridgeshire.

Either way William's son, John Knight, moved to London as he is shown in the first-ever UK census in 1841 to be living in Carey Street off Chancery Lane, close to where he worked as a porter at Lincoln's Inn, with his wife Sarah Ann and two children. By the 1881 census my great grandfather, Thomas Crosby Knight (one of John Knight's seven children), is listed as having been born in the parish of St Andrew, Holborn in 1855. Thomas Crosby Knight went on to become a successful barrister's clerk. By his mid-30s he was prosperous enough to buy a large new house in the fast-growing west London suburb of Acton (23 Avenue Gardens, now 31 Avenue Gardens). He drowned in an unlucky ferry accident on the river Thames in July 1899, aged 54, and is buried in a family grave in Hanwell Cemetery. Seventeen years later his widow Mary Ann, then aged 60, also died in tragic circumstances when, according to a front page report in the *Acton Gazette,* she was hit by a "motor omnibus" while crossing Hammersmith Broadway in west London in May 1916.

Two of Grandfather Knight's five brothers were killed in the First World War and he, too, took part in the conflict. On a visit to Belgium in 1991 I found the headstone of one of the brothers, Cyril (after whom my father was named), in the evocative Ramparts Cemetery at Lille Gate, outside Ypres. A Private in the Royal Army Medical Corps, 2nd (London) Field Ambulance, Cyril was 19 when he was hit by a German shell on 4th April, 1915 while rescuing a comrade from a hospital ward which had just been hit by a prior incoming shell. John Percival Knight, the other brother to die, was killed in the March, 1918, German offensive on the Somme. He was 28 and a Lieutenant in the 7th Durham

Light Infantry. As the daughter of a schoolteacher at King's School, Canterbury, Grandmother Knight (nee Mount; she lost three of her brothers in the First World War) came from higher up the sharply defined pre-1914 social ladder – something she never forgot. The couple met at Henley Regatta (Grandpa Knight was a rower) before the First World War and had two sons, of whom my father (always known as Bob and born in 1917) was the elder by four years. The boys had little in common although they looked quite alike, and in future years I could count on one hand the number of times my sister or I met our uncle Peter or our two cousins. We were told they lived in Felixstowe, which sounded like the end of the earth. When Cousin Tim died from cancer in 2005 at the age of 55 and I attended his funeral in Ipswich, it was a revelation to learn of his larger-than-life character, his surrogate father, his globe-trotting career in the travel business, his first marriage to Pat and his second marriage to Dorothy Heng, a Singapore Chinese.

The Heard side of the family was little closer but rather warmer. Grandpa Heard also came from a large London family. Qualifying as a dentist prior to 1914, he moved to the Isle of Wight in the footsteps of an elder brother (also a dentist) who had opened a practice in Cowes. The pair supported each other, my grandfather often bicycling the 14 hilly miles between Shanklin and Cowes to help out during the difficult years of the First World War. History does not relate how he met and married his wife Charlotte Lake (born in 1888 and also from London), but my mother arrived in 1916 and grew up entirely on the island. Joining Lloyds Bank after school (she had hoped to go to university but funds did not permit it), she was working in the London headquarters of the bank as a secretary in 1940 when all the staff were evacuated to Salisbury. Here she met my Army officer father, freshly returned from two sensational evacuations from France the year before. They married in Salisbury on 30th August, 1941, in suitably austere circumstances. The waiters in the wedding hotel were on strike, there was no reception, the wedding cake was one-tier because of wartime rationing, petrol was very limited and the honeymoon had to be taken nearby at the oddly named Piddle Inn in the village of Piddletrenthide.

Early childhood memories are notoriously unreliable. My mother once told me that I saw the moon for the first time at Shanklin Cottage Hospital when she was giving birth to my sister Sue in December 1945. Maybe she was right – it's hard to know for sure. Moving on a couple of years, I can remember as if it was yesterday the morning I dropped a freshly boiled egg on the kitchen floor at our cottage at St Lawrence. A horrified silence ensued, penetrating even my youthful consciousness. This must have been in the harsh winter of 1947/48 when coal was rationed, we shivered by tiny fires, the snow piled up outside and public transport (we had no car) to isolated villages like St Lawrence ground to a halt. Eggs were rationed (this started early in 1940 and lasted, unbelievably, to 1954), powdered egg was the norm and my mother had given up one of her precious weekly quota of the real thing for my benefit. I can also remember the warmth of the spring and summer in 1948, wandering up the steep hill outside our thatched house to the Thomas-the-Tank-Engine railway line above it, picking primroses on the way, and the kindness of our young Dutch nanny Mia Sieberg who spent a year with us improving her English.

Sometime in 1948 I went to school for the first time – the first of six schools I was to attend during the next 13 years. A hole through the hedge led to Mrs Cox's nursery establishment next door. With a handful of other youngsters I began to learn to read and write and add up. No record survives of my progress, but for the vast majority of my schooldays I jogged along in the middle of every class, showing some aptitude for reading and writing but most of all for games, and cricket in particular. Teachers quickly divined that I would do much better if I tried harder but most of the time my mind was elsewhere – on the next break in lessons or the next innings or the next wicket. Life outside the classroom always seemed more interesting and "real" – an attitude that lasted at least until I was old enough to teach myself.

By far the greatest influence over me in these early years was exercised by my mother and Grandmother Heard. For a start, they renamed me. Father had been insistent that I was to be christened Robert, and I was. By the time he returned from the war I was the less formal Robin and remain so to this day. He was furious, and insisted on calling me Robert until I was about 19 or 20 when he gave up, reluctantly. It was with my grandmother that I first went shopping – to Mr Bound's Victorian grocery emporium in genteel Shanklin, all brown paint and wooden partitions. Everything for sale was on display on shelves high above me, to be collected by assistants using long stepladders before being loaded into brown or blue paper bags according to the purchase. It was my mother's side of the family who introduced me to cricket and classical music and choral singing (Grandpa Heard was choirmaster at St Paul's church in Shanklin for many years). Nearly 70 years later I can still dredge up the memory of my grandfather, jacket and glasses on, showing me how to bowl a leg break on the lawn at Newlyn. He had a distinctly round-arm action and could get the tennis ball we used to take an enormous twist away from the facing batsman on the little pitch we marked out by the spreading old apple tree in the garden.

My father remained a shadowy figure until I was six or seven. He had joined the Army in 1937. By 1939 he was attached to the 1st Battalion East Lancashire Regiment, based in Hollywood, Co. Down, and was sailing up Belfast Lough when he heard the declaration of war. Early in 1940 he volunteered to join the Commandos but was rejected because of a minor knee injury caused by playing rugby. "If that's your attitude then in future I shall volunteer no more and just do what I am told and go where I'm posted. This was the philosophy I followed for the rest of the war!" he recounted later in life. Soon after he was sent on a course to become part of a pool of young officers attached to a Corp HQ whose job it was to convey personal orders by motorcycle to commanders in the field from their respective commanders. Posted to northeast France in mid-March 1940 to join his battalion (part of 42 Division), he took part in the British rearguard action back to the beaches of Dunkirk before being evacuated successfully on 2nd June to Ramsgate on board a Medway steamer. He was one of 338,000 Allied soldiers to survive the 55 nautical mile voyage to England. A week later he returned with his motorcycle to France as a personal aide to Major General (later Field Marshal) Sir Harold Alexander who had been tasked with extracting the remaining British forces in western France.

The following 23 days must have been the longest, most dangerous, chaotic and exhausting of Father's long life. Standing on a quay on 17th June, he was present when the 20,000 ton *HMT Lancastria* was sunk by the Luftwaffe 11 miles off St Nazaire with the loss of some 5,000 lives – the single worst disaster in British maritime history. In a short memoir compiled later for the family he wrote: "The sight of the few oil-covered men who survived coming ashore was beyond belief. There was little that could be done for them. By this stage in the war one had become used to seeing the results of mass killing on the battlefield. But this was something new and far transcended any other experiences." Days later the French capitulated and a lawless interregnum ensued. On 2nd

July, with the evacuation of 215,000 Allied soldiers complete, Father removed the carburettor from his trusty Norton, fixed a padlock to the rear wheel, pushed the bike into the main dock at St Nazaire and was fortunate to get on to one of the last ships to escape French waters. On the way back to England he ceremoniously dropped the ignition key into the Bay of Biscay from the deck of the trawler that was taking him to Plymouth and safety.

For the next four years until D-Day Father shuttled around the UK between Salisbury, Newry and Folkestone, marrying, starting a home and learning about staff work in the Army (the basis of his post-war career). In June 1944, as a staff captain and part of 59th Infantry Division, he landed at Arromanches on D-Day + 4 (10th June, 1944 – my first birthday). He should have landed on D+3, but his sailing was delayed by dockers at Tilbury who refused to load vehicles as required. As he waded ashore under heavy German mortar attack, a fierce storm began. He survived, only to be stuck soon after in the middle of 'Bocage' country (very small fields with high hedges and deep drainage channels) near Carpiquet where he came under unrelenting German bombardment for the next five weeks until allied forces finally took Caen. During this assault he was bombed by the Canadian air force, a friendly-fire incident that caused "a distinct loss of morale" among the troops with him at the time. Eventually he joined HQ 59 Division, and later HQ 1 British Corps, as a staff officer as Allied forces swept through northeast France. Along the way he was a member of an advance party that discovered the headquarters of the Gestapo in Antwerp. It was another shocking scene that remained in his mind's eye into old age. "Mutilated bodies were everywhere, some hanging on meat hooks upside down, with torture equipment still attached."

When informed in January 1945 that he had been given a vacancy at the Staff College at Minley to train for higher command, Father was not displeased. It proved to be the end of his war as later he got a deferment of a posting to the Far East in the run up to the birth of my sister in December, instead returning to staff duties in Salisbury. Looking back on the conflict in 1996, he remarked: "The memory becomes faded as the years pass, but comfort there is in old loyalties. There was a bond forged in those years when all were united in common cause and everyone was relatively, and some amazingly, unselfish. Now we are all heroes. The fear, the inadequacy, the discomforts, the occasional horror and above all the boredom mostly forgotten. Reactions depend on the degree of exposure. I was lucky. My experiences never begin to compare with those less fortunate who were involved in bloodier battles."

It was during his home posting in 1945 that the cottage at St Lawrence was purchased. Almost immediately he was off again – despatched to the Middle East at the start of 1946 as Deputy Assistant Adjutant Quarter Master General (Maintenance) to HQ British Troops Palestine & Transjordan. The headquarters were sited in the King David Hotel. On 22nd July, 1946 Father was in his fifth floor corner office at the rear of the south end of the building when it took the full force of an explosion master-minded by the Irgun Zvai Leumi terrorist group led by Menachem Begin, the future prime minister of Israel. "There was a terrific bang followed by a strange calm. Lying on the floor I saw a view over Jerusalem I had never seen before. One entire outer wall of the office had disappeared," he recalled. With his assistant, who had also survived, he set about trying to help others. "Seeing photographs afterwards I was horrified to realise the width of the overhanging ledge along which I led people to safety. It was just hanging on by the steel pipes of the concrete with nothing below." Ninety-one people had been killed. Somewhat shaken, Father went off to Gaza to recover at an Army beach facility. Back on the Isle of Wight, Mother was sick with worry having heard of the bombing on the radio the day it took place and knowing that her husband was working in the King David. For three days there was no news. Then Father called to say he had survived. Apparently it had been impossible to phone before. Later he was awarded the MBE for his services in Palestine. For years afterwards we kept the towel railing that he caught hold of as he was hurled across the room, so preventing him exiting that office five floors up.

Father remained in Palestine until the end of the British Mandate, leaving in May 1948 for Egypt. Returning to the UK later in the year he was sent back to the East Lancashires, then stationed in Cumbria. I was five and Susie two and a half. For the first time we lived together as a family. Home was a rudimentary camp on Hadrian's Wall made up of converted wooden barrack blocks – the original design for the Maze prison 'H' blocks of Northern Ireland fame. Petrol rationing was in force and we had no car. So I was sent by bus to attend an unpleasant primary school in Carlisle a few miles away where bigger boys nicked my lunch and, by way of retaliation, Father arrived dramatically one day to inspect the kitchens. Then in 1950 he was posted to Klagenfurt in Austria as part of a training team located in the headquarters of the occupying British forces. With entrance exams to a prep school looming, it was decided that the best option for me was to become a weekly border at Ryde School on the Isle of Wight, spending weekends with my maternal grandparents. So off I was carted to boarding school at the tender age of six.

Unsentimental decisions like this one were part and parcel of the austere post-war world, particularly if you were an Army 'brat.' To this day I can remember the shock of being "abandoned" by my mother. So could she even in old age. But on the sink-or-swim principle, I had a choice – and thus began decades of enforced self-sufficiency that only really eased when I married. Ryde School was very ordinary. About the only thing I can dredge up from my memory bank now is standing behind a cricket net watching the older boys practising – that, and the ice-cold dormitory I had to sleep in at night. But it did its job, I passed my entrance exam and in the autumn of 1951 arrived at Cheltenham prep school. Why Cheltenham, I have no idea, except that it had military connections and was not Cranleigh, the public (private) school my father attended and disliked for the rest of his life.

My year at Ryde was not to be the last time I based on the Isle of Wight since a similar must-do situation arose in 1962-63, when I had to spend a year at Portsmouth Technical College learning Latin in order to be able to go to university, and returned to Shanklin at weekends. One consequence is that for the rest of my life I have tended to say, when pressed, that I come from the island although that is not strictly true. But where did I come from? It was a roots-type question that puzzled me for years as I grew up in a dozen different locations from 1943-67. As a child who knows no better, one side of me vowed to pursue an adult life anchored in community and long-term friends. Another side, rather belatedly, came to recognise that the sort of peripatetic childhood I experienced had its benefits and had left a lasting mark – not least in a kind of detached sense of belonging that lent itself to a roving international career.

It would be wrong to infer from this that my childhood was miserable or unhappy. Yet looking back it was oddly unfulfilling – rather solitary, rather narrow and rather unimaginative. It left its mark. Father never seemed to relax at home and always found my questions, and wish to engage in discussion, wearying. We had many arguments, with my mother usually acting as peacemaker. Television only arrived with Queen Elizabeth's coronation in 1953. We rarely went on holidays as a family, and never went to the cinema or theatre or out for a meal. Much of this, of course, reflected the make-do-and-mend era after the war and our comparative lack of resources. As a family we were not poor, but the budget must always have been tight and there was rarely any spare cash. At home in the school holidays I would read voraciously or dig the garden or calculate cricket batting and bowling averages *ad nauseam*. In some of the places we lived, such as Seaview on the Isle of Wight, I devised obsessive solitary pursuits such as collecting driftwood or arranging "shot-putting" competitions with myself on the beach opposite the house we were renting using large stones I had found. Visiting my Knight grandparents by myself (they would never invite Susie and me together), I would organise marathon golf putting competitions with myself on Grandpa Knight's pristine lawns (by then he was living in retirement at West Clandon in Surrey). Holiday after holiday I would return to the latest place called home and realise that I knew no one beyond the hedge. Susie faced a similar, if different, challenge; until she was 13 she was fated to move everywhere with my parents and even to be taught by my mother for a time. My return home was always greeted like the relief of Mafekeng despite my enduring desire for a brother who could play cricket.

While my parents were living in Austria in 1950-52 in an attractive requisitioned house on the edge of the beautiful Worthersee in Carinthia, I made my first trip abroad and learned to ski and swim in the lake and even to count in German thanks to the earnest efforts of the lederhosen-clad Josef, our Austrian factotum. Twice a year in the school holidays all the children of officers serving in Austria who were being educated in the UK travelled out to their families by train, escorted by friendly if ineffectual guardians from the WVS (Women's Voluntary Service). Chaos was the name of the game from the moment hordes of excited youngsters (mostly boys) got on a train in late afternoon at London's Liverpool Street station. At Harwich we boarded a ferry for an overnight crossing of the North Sea to the Hook of Holland. On arrival in the Netherlands early next morning we scrambled on to the so-called Medloc train, arriving at Klagenfurt in southern Austria the following afternoon. It was a point of honour that no one washed during the entire 48-hour trip and I also recall endless pillow fights, charges up and down train corridors and general youthful mayhem. The return journey when the holidays were over was always sadder and quieter.

One of these trips back to England was to have lasting consequences. It must have been in the winter of 1951 that a huge storm blew up one night in the North Sea while I was on the ferry. Virtually every child on board was horribly sick, except me. Sneaking up to the main deck and crouching behind a lifeboat to see what was going on, I noticed that the ship was stationary in the churning waves, close by what appeared to be a wallowing four-masted sailing vessel straight out of the 19th century and tales by GA Henty (a favourite author at the time). The ship turned out to be the venerable *Pamir,* built in 1905. Earlier in 1951 she had been brought back into service as a training vessel for the reviving German marine industry. Now she was in trouble (*Pamir* was eventually to sink in the South Atlantic in a hurricane in 1957 with the loss of 80 lives). After standing by for hours until help arrived, we reached Harwich late but unscathed. I was enthralled by the whole experience and that moment decided to go to sea. Somewhat taken aback, my father began scouting around, hit on the Nautical College, Pangbourne, and put my name down, assuming I would soon recant. But I persisted, arriving at the NCP five years later.

Before then I had Cheltenham prep school to navigate. In 1951, the year I arrived, The Junior, as it was known, was an orthodox middle class feeder establishment for 175 or so boarding and day boys mostly destined to go on to the Senior School across Thirlestaine Road. The main building was Edwardian and the facilities pre-war rudimentary. From the start I seem to have regarded learning here as an optional extra to the real business of the school – playing sport. Almost all my memories of Cheltenham revolve around physical activity of some sort – roller skating, ferocious cricket games in the playground, batting nets with a weird red-haired master called Mr Brack who tied legs together to prevent you taking too big a stride forwards, competitive tennis and hockey matches on bumpy pitches, sports days and boy scout camps in places like North Wales (where I discovered how to roast a joint of meat in a biscuit tin). I also learned to play a musical instrument and eventually became leader of the 2nd Violin section in the school orchestra overseen by the long-suffering Mr Coleridge.

In my last term at Cheltenham in the summer of 1956, aged almost

13, I kept a diary. By then I was a prefect. The main benefit of this exalted position, I noted wisely in the diary, was that now I could listen to BBC Radio's 'Sports Report' in the prefect's room each Saturday evening. My avowed aim for the term was to become captain of the 1st XI which I did, rather than to win a much-needed scholarship to Pangbourne, which I failed to do but still did well enough to avoid having to sit any other entrance exam. Already I was developing some analytical, if not reportorial, skills. "Chapel today – not a bad sermon" I wrote on one occasion, followed laconically by "Terrible results in Latin and Maths prep throughout this term." Another day I recorded that a crucial cricket match had been "a very great strain," ignoring the fact that I had taken 6-26 with my fastish leg breaks. In July I went to Stratford to see a Shakespeare production for the first time: "It was magnificent. We sat on the balcony and heard and saw perfectly." I failed to mention what the play was or who was in it. The following week I was sent off with another boy to conduct a survey of rail and bus facilities in Cheltenham. With a bow in the direction of similar assignments in journalism in the future, I reckoned it was all "wizard fun."

Individuals from that era are a hazier memory. One who stands out is Sebastian Walker, a good friend who became a leading children's book publisher. Sunday after Sunday his mother would entrance us boys at chapel in the Senior School with her extraordinary hats – large concoctions of straw, fruit salads and flowers. Sebastian's sister, Mirabel Cecil, would later be my deputy editor on *Trinity News* at Dublin University. Seddon, Wise, Byas and Tomlinson peer half-remembered out of the 1956 1st XI cricket team photo. Mike Shortt, later to join me at university, was already a human calculating machine with a penchant for laying gambling odds. Yet he had nothing on a boy called Humphrys who caused much hilarity by lying on shelves and counting into the millions for the fun of it. About the only teacher who remains clearly in my mind is Mr Wheeler, a talented games player who took an interest in my future career and kept in touch when I moved on.

For most of my time at "The Junior" the school operated on a threadbare basis typical of the postwar era. Rationing limited menus. The weekly sweet allowance at the College tuck shop was down to a single bar of Fry's cream chocolate per person. Dormitories were barely heated. Hot water was strictly limited. Socks were darned and redarned, and uniforms handed down from child to child. Given the prevailing fuel shortages, excursions into the wider world were major events – one good reason for joining the Scouts who at least managed to organise camps in distant outposts of the realm like Shropshire. Today "The Junior" is unrecognisable. The 2009 Yearbook stretches to 145 glossy colour pages. Girls and boys intermingle. There are more than 100 members of staff. Lively reports written by the children describe school visits to places like Normandy, Paris and the Alps. After-school activities now include cookery, Mandarin and calligraphy.

I rarely stood out at Cheltenham, jogging along in the middle of the pack and avoiding prominence until my last year. Then I began to crave some recognition – in this case, the captaincy of the school cricket team. I must have rubbed a few people up the wrong way because, in a letter to my future overseers at Pangbourne in January 1956, headmaster Hugh Clutton-Brock describes me as "a nice boy who has had rather a difficult character because he did not find it easy to take criticism. But this has improved a great deal recently. Naval discipline is exactly what he needs." With equal prescience, given what was to ensue in my mid-teens at Pangbourne, he also described my father as being "rather ready to rise up in arms when his son is criticised on reports!" In a second letter in June that year Clutton-Brock added that I was "not really a scholar . . . he is no more than a sound Common Entrance candidate . . . he is a likeable boy and a useful athlete. At the same time he is a person who has a very good opinion of himself. A little naval discipline will do him no harm."

That September I began to discover what Clutton-Brock had in mind. Except, perhaps, for a period forty years later when I was unemployed no transitional episode in my life has left a stronger mark than my induction into the NCP and all its peculiar ways and traditions. Within a couple of years of arriving at the College on the back of a bursary provided by Shell Tankers Ltd and help from my grandparents, I knew I had made a big mistake. My essentially curious, questing character (not for nothing was I known at home as 'Twenty Questions') simply did not fit into a Services-style command-and-control environment. Nor did that independent streak of mine align easily with an institution that valued military-style teamwork and unquestioning acceptance of authority. But by then it was too late and I remained at Pangbourne for a full five years, enduring endless brushes with those in charge during my middle years. Looking back, maybe Clutton-Brock was on to something; I am sure the naval discipline did me some good. But the NCP as it was then structured – narrowly focused on preparing teenagers for careers at sea in the merchant and royal navies, run on a shoestring, stuck in a 1930s time-warp and culture, and staffed by too many aging time-servers – almost entirely failed to get the best out of me until it was very nearly too late.

Classroom life at Pangbourne in those days concentrated on the basics plus some maritime subjects (I am the proud owner of 'O' level certificates in Navigation and Seamanship). Whole areas of human learning such as music, drama and art were ignored. External stimulus in the form of visiting personalities was largely non-existent. The school's leadership was unimaginative, remote and perpetually short of resources. The wider educational context simply reinforced this situation. Entry requirements into the Merchant Navy were so low that anyone from the NCP qualified automatically unless he was totally idle. The consequence was a prevailing lack of academic ambition. Only when Dartmouth began to insist on two 'A' levels for officer entry to the Royal Naval College in the mid-1950s did the governors at Pangbourne react, building a study block and two divisions (houses) – architecturally woeful, but a statement of intent. Despite this lethargic environment, some of my contemporaries thrived and went on to have illustrious careers outside the naval arena. Several, like me, managed to get into university even though the lack of Latin instruction weighed heavily against anyone wishing to take an Arts degree.

All that said, in 1956 the NCP was still serving its core function to prepare teenagers for the British merchant navy as defined at its establishment in 1917 by the Devitt & Moore shipping company – something it had ceased to do a decade later. Britain remained an important maritime nation in the mid-1950s and most cadets, as we were known, were at the College because they wished to follow seagoing careers. Naval-style ship training routines left over from the pre-war era set the tone. Marching dominated our everyday lives as did early morning runs, cold showers, working parties, endless uniform checks and shoe cleaning, daily morning "divisions" and evening "quarters" on the parade ground Most Sundays there was a parade, ceremonial inspection and march past by the entire school. Bugles dictated the rhythm of this regimented existence, waking you up (reveille), summoning you to parades and meals and marking sunset. Before lunch we were made to groan through 20 minutes' vigorous PT (physical training) or to stand at ease on the parade ground trying to decipher the meaning of obscure flash signals transmitted from a dim lamp by a cadet standing on the roof of a distant building. It was all play-acting, even if it did have an underlying purpose.

Life in Port Jackson, the first year division (then based at Croft House) to which all newcomers were assigned, was competitive and designed to weed out the weak, which it did. After a year of "Ackers" – runs of a mile or more anywhere on the 240-acre campus high on a freezing hill overlooking the Thames valley – and being shouted at and pursued around the place by three intimidating Petty Officer instructors from the Royal Navy who held your feet to the fire, anything afterwards seemed a cinch. At the river Thames, the nearest Pangbourne came to the sea, ancient gigs and whalers were still in use, with the instructors showing us lower deck tricks such as how to tap weevils out of ships' biscuits as we rowed. We even learned how to heave a lead standing at the end of a high diving board. Swimming took place in the polluted river, until one blissful summer afternoon in 1958 when the annual mile-long King George V swim for charity coincided with the appearance of a dead cow floating down the river towards Pangbourne lock.

Still in diary mode, I kept a record of my first term at the NCP. I was just 13. A typical entry for Monday September 24, 1956, soon after I arrived, goes like this: "After we got up we all had to go for a half mile run. Apparently this happens every morning except Sundays. After that you are sprayed with cold water (shiver). Breakfast as usual in the house. Then we cleaned our shoes, were inspected by the cadet captains, marched up to the College and sent to our form rooms. We had three lessons before break and two after. Before lunch we had PT; I must be more efficient. Games in the afternoon. I played one half of rugger as there were too many boys. Two more lessons after this. Then we had an hour's prep – I couldn't remember anything by that stage! Marched back down to Croft House, had tea and then had half an hour silent reading (I read *The Daily Telegraph,* which was allowed). Prayers after this. We turned in at 9.00pm"

Much of the character of the NCP at the time came from the odd collection of teachers and retired naval types on the staff. The nominal head of the school was the Captain Superintendent, Commander Hugh Skinner when I arrived and later Captain AFP Lewis, both former Royal

Navy officers. Skinner was rather obviously cruising downhill to retirement, exceptional only for his penchant for strolling airily around the campus accompanied by a black Labrador and two pretty teenage daughters. Lewis was more old-school authoritarian and committed to shaking things up in a backward-looking way. His blinkered approach nearly capsized the school, and only the appointment of the College's first civilian headmaster, Peter Points, in 1969 was to save the day. A low-key director of studies, Kenneth Topliss, led the academic staff. He, too, was on the verge of retirement. So were many others one of whom, Philip Davey, taught me a lot about spin bowling. Philip had played for Somerset against the 1930 Australians and bowled his looping off-breaks to the great Don Bradman. He was a fount of cricket wisdom, but less good on geography. Another of the same ilk was the English teacher Desmond Walker – once a fine sportsman, but by the time I came across him past his peak and enormously overweight. Several younger people did begin to liven up the staff as the 1950s wore on including Lionel Stephens and Richard Norris (then an outstanding centre forward for the England hockey team). Yet even as a boy at the school one sensed too many of the staff were going through the motions – post-war tiredness and ennui, quite possibly, but also the consequence of working in such an undemanding milieu.

My salvation at Pangbourne, as at Cheltenham, was found on the games field. Harried by the ever-demanding instructors, the most memorable of whom was called Tiger Knights ("Knight's your name is it?" he bawled at me soon after I arrived at the school. "Well, you've got something to live up to here."), and ceaselessly targeted by aggressive cadet officers (prefects) who instinctively mistrusted my go-it-alone mentality, I retreated from their naval-driven values to more straightforward pursuits like cricket, hockey and squash to prove my worth. Eventually I became a rare triple colour, playing in the 1st XI cricket team for three years (two as captain), the hockey team for three years (getting an England schoolboy trial) and even making the 1st XV rugby team as scrum half for a season in 1960. Somehow it was typical of my relationship with my rugby-mad father that the one time he journeyed south from Preston (our home at the time) to see me play, I injured a shoulder in training the day before the game and could not turn out.

In most other respects, at least until my final year, I was a misfit at

Pangbourne – something confirmed by my stormy school reports, copies of which were kindly retrieved from the basement of Devitt House in the 1990s and sent to me by one of the reporters! From 1956-58 they are unexceptional apart from repeated whines from my mediocre housemaster, RC Aitken, that I was "selfish in outlook" (Lent 1958), "much too prone to ask 'why'" (Summer 1958) and "opinionated" (Winter 1958). In 1959 open warfare broke out.

That April my father wrote to Shell Tankers to inform the company that I had decided not to go to sea because I did not want the same sort of "uncertain" life he had led. This was partially true. "He is thinking of a profession as a career after a period at university," my father stated confidently, then added: "In this he may be too ambitious." The College was upset, fearing it might lose Shell's patronage. Whether this letter had any effect on my report for the summer term 1959 will never be known. At any rate, when it arrived it turned out to be a prize example of academic overkill, and most probably libellous. The Executive Officer (Number 2 in the College's naval hierarchy), Lt Cdr Ronnie Hoyle (a friend of Aitken's who I rarely encountered), complained that I was a "loudmouthed, complaining braggart" who offended College servants. Aitken weighed in, stating that I was "wasting my talents" and grumbled all the time. Skinner, who was retiring, called me in for a stern lecture. After discussing things with me, Father responded by firing off a broadside to Skinner criticising the "uncouth and ill-mannered statements" in the report and noting that Hoyle and Aitken had made no attempt to contact him or to talk to me in person. He ended by saying: "Robert is a great credit to Pangbourne wherever he goes . . . many senior Army officers have commented most favourably on his modesty, manners, behaviour and comportment."

At the root of this stand-off was a personality clash between myself and my irritating housemaster RC Aitken. A small man in every way, Aitken was quite unable to handle a fairly typical questioning, individualistic, but not malevolent, teenager. In effect, he never tried and instead preferred to blame others for his difficulties, especially me. Fatally, he never won my respect, and he knew it. Yet over the following two years a kind of truce was brokered. Eventually I was promoted, but given no direct responsibility, and largely left to go my own way. The result was a miraculous blossoming which concluded with my winning numerous academic prizes in my final year, gaining a couple of 'A' levels, going from strength to strength on the sports field and, for the first time, making my own choices in life. By the time I left the College aged just 18 in the summer of 1961, Captain Lewis felt able to write: "He can look back on a very successful College career. I hope he will get to university from where he can choose himself, and in slow time, the career most suitable to his talents."

In other ways, too, this is a chapter with a happy ending. For the next 26 years I had nothing to do with Pangbourne and never returned to the College and put the place firmly out of my mind. Then, one day in 1987, the phone rang and Lionel Stephens (still teaching at the school) asked me if I would help the OP Society to put out its annual magazine; the previous editor had died suddenly. I agreed, and so began a second, more enduring and more worthwhile relationship with this unusual institution. In 1987 I joined the OP Society committee. In 1994 I became a governor of what was by now Pangbourne College and remained one for the next 15 years. From 2003-07 I was chairman of the OP Society and then its President from 2008-12. Along the way I met, and befriended, a wide circle of interesting and decent people who otherwise would have passed me by.

Today I can look back and assert with absolute confidence that in the six decades since I first marched up the Prince of Wales Drive in September 1956 Pangbourne has been transformed entirely for the better. It now offers 400 plus boys and girls (at a high price, it is true) a unique educational package including academic and sporting excellence, distinct and enduring values and residual naval discipline. Interestingly, it is the pupils who have repeatedly insisted on retaining the naval uniform, the Marching Band and the Guard. Money, as ever, is in short supply but even so the campus has been vastly improved by a far-sighted Board, the academic and support staff is unrecognisable, around 80% of the pupils go on to university, arts and drama are of a very high order and a succession of outstanding civilian headmasters has given inspirational leadership for more than 40 years.

My parents, both still alive in the 2000s to observe the culmination of this unexpected rapprochement with an institution they, too, were always ambiguous about, no doubt heaved a sigh of relief when I reached the end of my time at the NCP in 1961. Their life caravan, and my home, in the meantime had trundled on from Austria to Camberley in Surrey, Luneburg in Germany, Hong Kong, Seaview in the Isle of Wight and (twice) Preston in Lancashire. The summer I left Pangbourne they moved again, to Malaya where my father had been appointed deputy commander of the 28 Commonwealth Infantry Brigade based near Malacca. Effectively, that was the end of our conventional family life together.

Childhood, for me, consisted of a series of constantly shifting relationships, people and places. Individuals came and went from my life – like Judge Philip Ingress Bell, onetime Conservative MP for Bolton East. A friend of my father's from service together in France during the war, Philip sought out things we had in common despite our 43 year age gap. On the golf course at Lytham he spent hours trying to persuade me to qualify as a lawyer and go into politics. Another unlikely teenage influence was one of my father's batmen (personal servants) – Gordon Milne, later to play football for Liverpool and England as a wing half before managing Wigan, Coventry and Leicester and teams in Turkey and Japan. Six years older than me, Gordon was doing his national service (abolished in 1960; I avoided it by two years) at Fulwood Barracks – the Lancastrian Brigade training centre for new recruits commanded by my father. Already on the books of Preston North End just down the road where his father was the club trainer, Gordon was the first person I related to in any depth and at any length from a different social background. Open-minded, courteous and helpful, he made a huge impression at the time although he can't have been more than 22. The Morrison family in North Berwick generously invited me into a different world again – Scottish, wealthy, rooted in faith and community. Garth, a friend from the NCP, was to go on to a distinguished career in farming, scouting, the National Health Service and as Lord Lieutenant of East Lothian for which he was knighted by the Queen. My boyhood hero, the cricketer Colin Cowdrey, epitomised for me how sport at all levels should be played – hard but fair. It was no surprise later in life that, with Ted Dexter, he devised the MCC's "Spirit of Cricket" initiative. Another unlikely influence was Grandpa Knight – a world class gardener, who taught me all I know about plants and trees and pruning without my realising it, and took me to my first restaurants to eat lunch.

Looking back, I really have little to carp about although it often felt different at the time. By the age of 18 I could write clearly, I was reading widely and I was learning to educate myself. I could sail, ski, ride a horse and play several sports to a decent level. I had experienced life abroad and learned to cope on my own. Nothing is perfect, and my roots in community were very shallow, but I had had a reasonable start in life. I wish I had received a more rounded, liberal education, but in the 1950s this was easier said than done. The basic groundwork had been laid and now it was up to me to build on it.

3

Creating a Future

*"A university should be a place of light, of liberty,
and of learning."*

BENJAMIN DISRAELI

The question was – what to do next after ten years' enforced confinement at fee-paying schools in Cheltenham and Pangbourne? On balance, no one would have described me as exceptional. Aged just 18, I was open-minded, curious, evolving and ambitious. I left the NCP in the summer of 1961 with a couple of modest 'A' levels, some academic prizes and lots of kudos on the sports field – but with no obvious defining talent and no real sense of direction.

A career at sea was out, that was apparent. So was the military; my father had long since pronounced me quite unfit for a regimented life in the armed services. He was right. But his next idea, that I acquire a "professional" qualification, fell at the first hurdle. One scorching summer's day in 1961 we met up in London for an interview he had arranged with a firm of accountants. I was wearing my heavy No. 1 naval uniform, and the stiff white collar grated into my neck all day. The accountants were located in the City in a stuffy old building with rabbit warren offices, creaking floorboards and brown-painted walls little changed since Victorian times. I had no idea why I "wanted" to be an accountant which put a bit of a damper on proceedings. Matters were left hanging, and we repaired to a nearby pub to consider the next move. Clearly, accountancy was a long shot. Other "professions" – medicine, the law, banking, stockbroking – held equally little appeal. It all pointed one way. I would have to get in to a university, not least to put off the terrible day of reckoning.

In 1961 less than 5% of my age group in the UK went to university. A slow expansion had begun, and that same summer Sussex University became the first of a wave of new universities to open its doors. But getting accepted remained a tough call. No one in my family had ever gone to university. Moreover, Pangbourne rarely sent students direct to university and had no academic reputation worth the name, while I was proposing to do an Arts degree which in those days meant having at least an 'O' level pass in Latin – a subject that was not taught at the NCP. My qualifications in Seamanship and Navigation seemed unlikely to be accepted as alternatives. On the other hand, provided I could wriggle in somewhere, I should be able to fund my way through a three or four year degree course thanks to the generous university grant system then in place, some parental assistance and the occasional job in the long summer vacations.

The immediate challenge was to pass Latin 'O' level and to improve my 'A' level grades in History and English Literature. Nominally, I came from the Isle of Wight which fell under the auspices of the Hampshire Education Authority of the time. Suitable arts courses (and grants, since my father was now based abroad in Malaya as part of the Commonwealth Brigade) were on offer at the oddly named Portsmouth Technical College. Come that September I enrolled in this hitherto unknown institution for a year with the goal of passing the necessary exams and finding a university that would accept me the following autumn. It meant, in many ways, a wasted nine months but at the age of 18 and with nothing better on the horizon this seemed less of an issue than my missing Latin qualification.

Thus it was that in October 1961 I found myself boarding with Mrs Hugman (the plump, and impecunious, widow of a naval officer) in a large "garden" flat in Southsea, and sharing a room with a monosyllabic chemistry student from a grammar school in Nottingham. I made a few friends, rejoiced in my escape from uniform and began to think for myself for the first time. Latin proved a cinch thanks to the grounding in the language I had received at Cheltenham; I ended up translating Winnie the Pooh to amuse myself and gained a 95% pass at 'O' level. Mostly, though, it was a maturing interlude. During the winter months I played hockey for Havant at the weekends, discovering the rough-and-tumble differences between school and adult sport. In the summer I caught a ferry back to the island on Friday nights, stayed with my grandparents and played cricket for Shanklin and the Isle of Wight – earning a few headlines in the local newspaper for my batting. Trad jazz in smoky clubs was the fad of the moment and my memory of that year is full of the sounds of Acker Bilk and Chris Barber and their hybrid music. Girls entered my life and continental Europe opened up. During the summer of 1962 I hitchhiked and took trains through France and Italy with a chum called John Goble and spent six weeks living in a hostel at Rome University on ten shillings (50p) a day – enough to buy a bed, breakfast, a bowl of pasta and fruit in the evening – and exploring all that this magic city, later to be my home for a couple of years, had to offer.

Early in 1962 I began pestering universities. This was the year before the central clearing system for applications to universities in Britain and Ireland was invented. Huge amounts of time in the winter evenings had to be spent form-filling for individual applications. If one was lucky, the occasional interview followed. Spurning Oxford and Cambridge on the pragmatic grounds that I was unlikely to get in and did not have the time to apply to dozens of individual colleges, I alighted on Durham, Leicester and Queen Mary's College (London University) as reasonable prospects. Durham responded first, offering an interview at 9.00am one cold winter's morning. A marathon overnight journey by train from Portsmouth to Durham was followed by a dismissive 20-minute session with a bored, half-awake academic. No offer followed. I was all-but resigned to provincial obscurity at Leicester when my Latin teacher at Portsmouth suggested Trinity, Dublin. I had barely heard of the place let alone been to Ireland. But it sounded prestigious and different – and, most important of all, did not require an interview. So I applied, and sometime that Spring a letter of acceptance arrived in Southsea. I was offered a place on the university's four-year General Studies course – the lowest rung on the TCD academic ladder, but a degree course nevertheless.

Trinity in the 1960s, and for many decades before that (less so since), was a unique academic institution whose essential character only improves with the passing years. Journeying to Ireland in October 1962 on the overnight Hollyhead-Dun Laoghaire ferry in the company of noisy, stout-drinking navvies, young girls with lilting accents returning home after an illicit visit to Liverpool, intimidating-looking priests in heavy black cassocks and wet-behind-the-ears English students like myself, I knew instinctively that a very different cultural landscape lay ahead. How different became apparent almost the moment I got off the ferry train in central Dublin. The smell of burning peat in the smoky city air, the dominant feel of a bygone era, the dirty elegance of decaying Georgian buildings, the sharp tang of the Liffey, the unintelligible cries of urchin newspaper boys, the shabby bustling street life, the threadbare clothing and the relative (compared to England) poverty of so many people – all offset by their instant friendliness and welcoming mien – struck me like a blast of fresh air. I fell in love with Trinity the first time I entered the university through the famous covered octagonal passage, past Porters' Lodge with keys hanging on every wall, past notice boards festooned with College information and into the grandeur that is Front Square. Here was a real university with fine buildings, impressive statues, age old cobblestones, a world famous library and nearly four hundred years' of mostly illustrious history (TCD dates from 1592) – all to be found on 42 acres of prime real estate right in the centre of a European capital city. No more than 3,000 students attended TCD when I arrived (today there are at least five times more) – but each year a quarter of a million tourists would tramp across Front Square on a quest to see the ancient Book of Kells. It was more than enough to banish all thoughts of Leicester from my mind for ever.

Lest I be accused of gilding the lily, other less attractive aspects of southern Irish life in the 1960s gradually became evident. By no stretch of the imagination could Dublin be termed a "swinging" city as defined in the 1960s. By 10.00pm on weekdays the centre was silent apart from pubs and drunks and police sirens. Irish society was deeply inward-looking and hardly changed since independence in 1921. Conformity dominated cultural life to such an extent that a Trinity production of Dylan Thomas's 1954 play *Under Milk Wood* was still controversial, if hugely popular, a dozen years later in 1966. An obdurate Roman Catholic Church held sway, upholding seriously conservative values regardless of the reforming thrust of the Second Vatican Council. Books such as James Joyce's *Ulysses* and JP Donleavy's *The Ginger Man,* and innumerable films, were banned or butchered by an official censorship board. State-run television (still in its infancy) was sycophantic and tightly constrained. Contraceptive advertisements in imported English newspapers had to be covered up and pregnant teenagers were forced abroad for help.

Most amazingly to this typically skin-deep Anglican, the profoundly reactionary Catholic archbishop of Dublin, one John Charles McQuaid, had erected a *cordon sanitaire* around the University of Dublin, as TCD is known formally. Each Lent he would solemnly preach a nonsensical fire-and-brimstone sermon prohibiting Catholic attendance at the university. By the time I got to TCD about a quarter of the students were Catholics who had managed to elude McQuaid's clutches despite the threat of excommunication. Nevertheless the university remained a Protestant outpost in a sea of Catholicism – almost the last relic of the centuries-old Anglo-Irish ascendancy in Ireland. The futile and self-defeating ban on Roman Catholics was finally lifted in the 1970s, and thereafter Trinity began its inevitable transformation into a fully Irish university with close financial and educational links to the Irish state which was how it was bound to be. It had only taken 50 or so years since Irish independence.

By contrast Trinity in the early 1960s was a microcosm of what Ireland would become – tolerant, relaxed, secular and part of the pan-European liberal value system. Students arrived from all over the place and in particular from Ireland south and north, England and Scotland, the US and English-speaking countries in Africa. It was anything but a political institution, and played a marginal role in public life in the republic. Yet it hardly led the way as an educational establishment either, being too self-absorbed, unchallenging and impecunious. For students, the need to compete academically was virtually non-existent – learning was 'there to be enjoyed for its own sake' went the prevailing mantra. Socially and athletically the pressures were somewhat greater – TCD still rated. Student unrest was virtually unknown and focused largely on internal issues such as the role of women in university bodies. In any case, students were treated as adults and had vast freedom to do as they pleased – academic work was only a backdrop. For some, mostly the 600 or so English students, this was an invitation to a life of partying, pubs and plagiarism. But others unearthed life-changing opportunities, particularly those with a creative or sporting bent. Looking back now, my main sentiment about Trinity is one of enormous gratitude – for allowing me the space to be myself, for showing me diversity, for stretching me, for giving me the chance to study in depth for the first time and for introducing me to Ireland and the Irish. I was a guest in another country – a guest, indeed, who came from a nation with a bloodstained 800-year relationship with my hosts to live down. But not once in the next four years was I made to feel in the least unwelcome.

Having absorbed the splendour of Front Square that first day, I made my way to the accommodation office and so began my years at TCD. The university had arranged digs for me and even selected a room mate. For the first year I boarded with Mr and Mrs Reynolds and four other students from England in distant Rathmines for three pounds ten shillings a week in a nondescript guesthouse which reeked of boiled cabbage. Three of my fellow inmates, Peter Bowles, Clifford (Tiffy) Gould and Ivan Pawle, had been at school together at Haileybury. My easy-going room mate on the ground floor, Tom Baker, came from Radley. We formed a disparate group. Tom and Ivan were immediately drawn deep into Trinity's creative world while Peter and Tiffy confidently concentrated on cars and and the fair sex while I played hockey and nervously contemplated my first year exams. Mr Reynolds, an Andy Capp figure forever clad in a filthy vest and braces with a half-smoked fag drooping out of the corner of his mouth, idled the day away perusing the horse racing pages. His wife cleaned house, shopped and cooked awful fried breakfasts of huge slabs of charred bacon and cindered sausages as well as a greasy meal in the evening for any of us strong enough to face it. Trinity was a nine-penny bus ride away, down Rathgar Road on which all the essentials of Irish life could be found – pubs, bookies, pawnbrokers, banks, estate agents and shops selling basics such as newspapers, milk and the ubiquitous peat briquettes.

Right from the start I was determined to transfer to an honours degree if the chance arose. Before too long it did. By a stroke of great good fortune I was assigned a tutor who took a genuine interest in me, pulled a few strings behind the scenes and within days had my name added to the 30 or so first-year history and political science honours degree students. David Thornley was to become a lasting friend, but at this early stage I knew nothing about this mercurial, brilliant, flawed, inspirational man. In 1964 he became the youngest Fellow in Trinity's long history. In 1978, having blazed like a meteor in the cloudy skies of Irish public life for a few short years, and having been extinguished just as quickly by its limitations, he died aged only 42.

David was born in England to an Irish republican mother and an English Socialist father. His mother returned to Ireland with her children during the Second World War and seven years later in 1951, aged 16, David won a place at TCD. By the time I arrived at Trinity he was carving a stellar academic reputation for himself in the world of 19th century Irish politics and winning the loyalty and respect of successive

1 Great Grandfather Thomas Crosby Knight (1845-99). 2 Grandfather Arthur T Knight at the start of World War One possibly in his garden at Lebanon Park, Twickenham. 3 Great Aunt Florence Knight aged 52, Tientsin, China, 1933. 4 Me aged a few months in 1943 with Ma in the garden at Newlyn, Shanklin, Isle of Wight.

5 *Granny and Grandpa Heard with Susie and me at Newlyn in 1953.* 6 *Most of the Knight family at White Ness, West Clandon in 1954.* 7 *In 1956 aged 12 at Cheltenham Prep School.* 8 *Marching in the Founder's Day parade at the Nautical College, Pangbourne, July 1960.*

Opposite: 9 *Taking part in an England Schoolboys hockey trial 1960.* 10 *My tutor at Trinity, Dublin, David Thornley.*

9

10

11 *TCD Front Square as it looked in 1966.* **12** *Stanford University central campus in 1967.*

13 *Dudley Doust with a young Seve Ballesteros in about 1980.* *14* *Our wedding day April 8th, 1972.*

15 Leninsky Prospekt, Moscow, in April 1977 (No. 36 left background). *16 My first US News & World Report cover story – Oct. 24, 1977.* *17 Near an oil well on a visit to Surgut, Siberia, in February 1978.*

Opposite: *18 At the Shcharansky trial in Moscow in 1978 – David Satter of the FT is interviewing Shcharansky's mother. Kevin Klose of The Washington Post to the rear.*

19 *Reading Pravda together for the AP photographer after the Tashkent incident in 1979.* 20 *US Ambassador Malcolm (Mac) Toon.* 21 *Posing in South Africa for the magazine – in July, 1981.*

generations of students. Short and pugnacious (he loved boxing), trenchant, exuberant, challenging, informal, amusing – David was all of these things. He enjoyed the company of students, drinking with many of us at 'The Lincoln' outside Back Gate on Saturday nights together with his long-suffering wife Petria. His tutorials could be events in themselves and invariably made one think. In 2008 a book of essays in his memory called *Unquiet Spirit* was published in Dublin by his daughter Yseult. Painfully honest, it charts David's later rise to television stardom, entry into Irish politics and subsequent decline into alcoholism and early death. He never produced the great academic work his intellectual gifts suggested he could and, in the end, a series of catastrophic misjudgements about the IRA sullied his reputation. As one of the essayists in *Unquiet Spirit*, the well-known Irish broadcaster Rodney Rice (a Trinity contemporary), put it: "He had self-destructed in his frustration at his lack of achievement at the point that should have been the pinnacle of opportunity for such a dynamic mind."

This tragedy lay well into the future. In 1962, for whatever reason, David spotted something in me that he liked and backed me. This was rash, but entirely typical. Outstanding at seeing people in the round (he was a mass of contradictions himself, being an ardent Irish republican, a staunch Catholic who believed in divorce and contraception, a libertarian and a socialist all at the same time) David was forever searching for new ways to bring his subject matter alive. The secret of his appeal lay in his openness and lack of dogmatism. He was never doctrinaire or overbearing and should one of his students come up with an interesting or provocative idea, he would always give it his full attention. Alone among the small coterie of history and political science professors I knew at Trinity, he invited interesting contemporary personalities to address his tutorials. Learning, for him, was a joint activity in which conventional boundaries were there to be expanded and age-old truths subject to rigorous re-examination. All of this was deeply appealing to me.

When John F Kennedy came to Ireland in June 1963, David invited me to his rooms overlooking College Green to watch the open-topped presidential cortege drive through huge crowds in central Dublin – a generous gesture and an unforgettable moment for a 20-year-old as Kennedy looked directly up at us as he swept by. Like everyone alive at that time I recall, as if it was yesterday, where I was when I heard the news of the president's assassination in Dallas five months later – in the kitchen of our flat, listening to the early evening news on Irish radio. When I edited *Trinity News* David gave generous support in terms of time and contacts, once arranging a meeting with the affable future Irish prime minister and lover of numbers Garrett Fitzgerald, then lecturing in economics at the Catholic-approved University College, Dublin – a contact that was to stand me in good stead years later. Such inclusiveness and generosity was enormously encouraging to someone of my non-Irish background.

Later, after I graduated, we remained in touch and on occasional reporting visits to Ireland I always made contact. David was never less than incisive and always prepared to be quoted by name. On one memorable occasion we were lunching in the Shelbourne Hotel in 1970 in the middle of a sensational trial involving Charles Haughey, another future Irish prime minister, and others. Haughey and his pals had been accused of attempting to import arms illegally into Northern Ireland on behalf of the IRA. David at that point was the country's leading current affairs television interviewer and had been taking a tough line on the scandal. One of the defendants, Neil Blaney, began taunting him across the dining room. David got up and ostentatiously rearranged our table so that his back was firmly turned to Haughey and his fellow conspirators. You could have cut the atmosphere with a knife. Great drama, and a valuable insight for a young foreign correspondent into the heightened tensions by then coursing openly through Irish political life.

David also made it clear to me that I would have to work hard to justify my promotion. On an honours course at TCD in the 1960s there were only two exams that mattered – a weeding-out hurdle at the end of the first year, and Finals after the fourth year. In between, undergraduate students were expected to do little more than attend lectures and tutorials and write a few term essays. At my first lecture with the dry-as-dust, chain-smoking mediaevalist (and mistress of the put-down and obscure Latin texts) Dr Jocelyn Otway-Ruthven, she pulled off her annual trick of announcing that one-third of us new arrivals would not be around by the end of her course. I took her at her word and tried hard to get to grips with *Stubbs' Select Charters* and make sense of her dreary renderings of the life of long-dead Irish notables such as Brian Boru. Other members of the faculty were easier to warm to – the Beethoven look-alike TW Moody with his quip that 'history is the past'; FSL Lyons (a future TCD Provost) who introduced me to the horrors of famine in 19th century Ireland; and the eccentric Junior Dean RB McDowell who lectured on 18th century European history when the whim took him. McDowell talked so fast that no one could take notes, wore a pork pie hat, scarf and overcoat winter and summer and wandered across Front Square muttering to himself. Forever the butt of student pranks, McDowell loved Trinity deeply as an institution, and this affection eventually conveyed itself even to the most louche, disruptive, idle students of whom there were many.

Outside the lecture room I began to relax and play – hockey, cricket, golf, pubs, parties. By modern standards my generation at university was well off. Credit was non-existent, but two weeks in Corfu cost £80 and a new car could be bought for £500 – about what it cost to be a student at TCD for a year. Given a generous grant by the Hampshire/Isle of Wight Education Authority which covered fees, board and lodging (and even paid my ferry ticket to Dublin), plus a bit of support from my parents (by then in Malaya) and the occasional summer job in London, I never felt short of money. Living costs in Ireland were no more than two-thirds those in the UK and by my second year I had acquired a car (a Mini), a part-share in a rented flat behind the US embassy in upmarket Ballsbridge and the resources to entertain girls to a pub meal at 'The Old Stand' in Exchequer Street where Maurice, the friendly barman, controlled student misbehaviour with a world-weary shrug of the shoulders. Sometimes we indulged ourselves and went upmarket, ordering kidneys and bacon accompanied by a glass of red wine at The Shelbourne Grill. How privileged we were when one compares this to the parlous financial situation students find themselves in today!

First-year exams successfully navigated, and Otway-Ruthven mercifully consigned to the past, I branched out in 1963-64. In my second year I got into Trinity's hockey team and won my colours, something I repeated the following season before retiring in my fourth year to concentrate on exams. Several members of these TCD hockey teams went on to play at international and Olympic level. Games and pitches were rough by English standards, and Trinity was always struggling to be competitive in the top echelon of the Leinster League. Yet in both my years in the 1st XI I toured England and played successfully in teams that beat Oxford and Cambridge, once having my finger broken deliberately at Fenner's by a future pillar of the MCC

'Spirit of Cricket' campaign. In 1965 I won an Irish Under-23 trial. Sport at this level is all or nothing, and in the end I felt I had to make a choice between training and study. This involvement with Trinity hockey nevertheless was to have one enduring consequence. Late in 1963 someone on the undergraduate weekly *Trinity News* asked me to write up short reports of the games in which I played. The first one, a 200 word effort, appeared on 21st November, 1963 under the stark headline "Mills Cup flop." I seem to have been consistently hard on the forwards, of whom I was one, that season! From these humble beginnings, so typical of the chance opportunities thrown up by student life, began a near 50-year odyssey through the world of journalism and corporate writing.

Within a year I advanced to sports editor on *Trinity News* and my photo was appearing above a by-lined column. From sports reporting I branched into news reports, profile writing, features and analysis. By the start of the summer term in 1965 I had been elected Editor (or Chairman as the position was known) in succession to Jefferson Horsley (later a leading Lib Dem in the west of England). Jeff had upset the *Irish Times* earlier in the year by opposing a decision of the Board to confer a degree on Sean Lemass, the Irish prime minister of the day. My very first editorial, therefore, was a column defending freedom of the press. Other editorials that term covered such diverse topics as whether or not women should be able to speak and vote in the main university debating society ("Not every male conversation is enhanced by female intervention"), the finances of *Trinity News* (they needed shoring up through the use of an external advertising agency), student value-for-money, and the competence of lecturers. A last editorial in late-May robustly argued that most Trinity students "seem to live in a state of inertia unrelieved except for a brief hiatus around exam-time . . . Too few people in this place are giving value for money."

Trinity News was fun and introduced me to something new which I seemed good at. On publishing days I would trot along to a nearby printers under the creaking old railway bridge in Pearse Street and enter a Dickensian world of cynical typesetters who had seen many student editors come and go, slabs of filthy black metal letters (all inserted upside down into a plate), huge rolls of paper and windows thick with the grime of decades. For all its amateurism *Trinity News* had external impact as part of a capital city culture, being quoted frequently and having its articles reproduced in Irish national newspapers. That inhibited none of us. Editorial meetings usually turned into meandering debates which left the editor to decide and take the brickbats. By far the greatest feedback came from students complaining that they had been libelled by items in the paper's gossip column. Attacks on academic dignitaries were commonplace but the authorities ignored them, probably in the hope the paper would implode. In fact *Trinity News* flourished, and in 2001 celebrated its 50th anniversary with a weekend's carousing in Dublin to which all past editors were invited. Many, including myself, *The Independent's* Hamish McRae and Rodney Rice of *RTE*, had gone on to high-level careers in journalism.

As the somewhat conservative tone of my editorials suggests, Trinity was no hotbed of radicalism in 1962-66. In a very real sense we were a transitional generation. No one ever offered me drugs and I knew no one who took them – most of us were too busy drinking, smoking and gambling. We dressed quite smartly until jeans began arriving circa 1964. Bouffant hairstyles and stockings were commonplace among the girls, and the contraceptive pill did not cross the Irish Sea until at least 1963. The word "stress" was never mentioned although "alcoholic" and "debauched" may have been. The Beatles took Dublin by storm late in 1963 when I was induced to attend my first and last pop concert. Tickets cost ten shillings (50p) for a balcony seat at the Adelphi cinema in O'Connell Street, and the hysteria after the first of two shows was so great that the Fab Four were unable to leave the stage. Mostly, though, a student's social life was built around impromptu bottle parties in Trinity, more formal dances in private homes in and around Dublin and Saturday night dances at Dublin rugby clubs where the music was raucously belted out by livewire Irish showbands and the girls loved our English accents. For once in modern history the North of Ireland was quiet, the Irish economy was expanding, jobs were on offer and wider concerns, like the Cuban missile crisis in 1962 or the growing conflict in Vietnam, had yet to stir up the Irish student body. When a group of IRA supporters blew up the iconic Nelson's Pillar in O'Connell Street in March 1966 to mark the 50th anniversary of the 1916 Rising, no one was more surprised than the southern Irish. In the Dublin watering holes I frequented the episode was regarded as a joke or a prank. Sadly, it was far more than that, and proved to be the harbinger of sustained terrorist violence in Ulster in the decades just ahead.

At this point the reader may well inquire why we students were so passive. Many possible explanations spring to mind nearly 50 years later, but perhaps the key is that Ireland was so peripheral to world events in the early 1960s – and self-centred. Most of us at Trinity, whether Irish or British, came from conventional, middle class backgrounds and we were having a good time – the first post-war generation able to say this. None of us was cause-oriented; even demonstrating against apartheid and visits to Ireland by South African rugby teams (as David Thornley did) seemed vaguely cranky though it pains me to write this today. Instead the order of the times, as one of my contemporaries later wrote, was "low key hedonism."

In my second year I moved into a top floor flat at 27 Raglan Road in the leafy inner Dublin suburb of Ballsbridge. I was lucky. Most Trinity students were forced to live in remote suburban digs or in College for the first couple of years, but as my parents were based outside the UK and Ireland, and I had no home to go to during the long vacations (which lasted no less than 30 weeks out of 52 each year), I was allowed to rent a flat. Through this gaping loophole others followed, and over the next three years I shared the flat with a number of people who became friends for life – Alastair Bond (later my best man), Peter Bowles, Adrian Naughten, Mike Shortt. Others seemed to come and go and sleep on the floor for varying periods. In 2006 about 50 of us (with wives, husbands and partners) returned to Trinity for a happy 40th graduation reunion weekend. It was good to see Raglan Road unchanged. Yet one doubted students could afford to live in the area any more. Even in the mid-1960s we squashed in so as to be able to pay the rent. In one bedroom there were three beds alongside each other. In a second room there was a single bed – the focus of endless masculine competition. Somehow we avoided too much squalor, too much housekeeping and too many complaints from the neighbours. Girls came and went with dizzying frequency and not until my final year did I form a lasting relationship. Up and down sand hills on Brittas Bay beach, at dances that lasted to dawn, in my Mini on drives in the beautiful Wicklow Hills, on vacation trips around Ireland, at the annual Trinity Ball in College, the chase went on. My heart must have been broken half a dozen times in four years, but one learned. Life was there to be lived.

My 21st birthday came and went in the summer of 1964, an event I celebrated together with three co-hosts (also celebrating their 21sts) at a memorable dance in the ballroom of the Central Hotel down the street from 'The Old Stand.' Sister Susie came over to Ireland for the occasion. During my fourth year I abandoned hockey and student journalism and studied intensively, night and day. It was worth the effort. Finals in September 1966 involved a marathon test of stamina and memory in the form of eleven long handwritten papers that had to be completed against the clock in six days. I emerged with writer's cramp, five first class grades (all in politics) and six upper seconds (all in history) and graduated later in the year with a 2:1 and a place in the top ten of my history year group — not a bad result after my somewhat chequered beginning. Unfortunately, I never did see Dr Otway-Ruthven again to inform her of my success. But on a visit to Dublin a year or two later I was able to toast David Thornley in suitable style and thank him for the opportunity he engineered for me.

Out of the blue during this final year at Trinity I received a letter from the Rotary Club in Shanklin on the Isle of Wight — theoretically my "home" town. The writer, a Mr Jack Young, wanted to know if I was prepared to put my name forward for a Rotary Foundation Fellowship to study anywhere in the world in the academic year 1967-68. It was an attractive proposition, but a very long shot. In between going through the milk run of interviews with prospective UK employers visiting TCD, I filled in a Rotary application form and waited. Three rounds of interviews against other candidates from the Isle of Wight, Hampshire and southern England followed in the Spring vacation of 1966. I came through, a generous all-inclusive grant of $4,900 for the year was offered and then it was up to me. Objective to a fault, I decided that after four years in the Irish mist I wanted to study in the sun and targeted universities in California and Australia. It was not smooth sailing. Melbourne University informed me that Rotary Scholars usually had little time to study, while Stanford University replied that PhD candidates were favoured. Then my luck turned and Stanford decided to widen its graduate foreign intake in the political science school for the 1967/68 academic year. David Thornley wrote me a glowing testimonial and soon after "by unanimous decision of the faculty" I was accepted — by one of the world's leading universities, with no money worries and the chance to earn an MA at the end of the year. It was a marvellous opportunity that was to change my life.

The only fly in the ointment was the need to find something to do in the meantime. My imagination rather let me down, and instead of going to France, as I should have done, taking any job I could find and mastering the language, I migrated to London and a make-weight position with Haymarket Press, a publisher of glossy magazines and trade directories set up a decade before by one Michael Heseltine. The nine-month experience was boring, but not entirely wasted. I learned that I was a hopeless telephone salesman. I acted as bag carrier for a friend of Heseltine's – Chris Chataway (Olympic athlete, television presenter, Tory MP and later cabinet minister; he had lost his parliamentary seat in the 1966 general election and was marking time by opening doors for Haymarket). And I wrote and published spuriously erudite commentaries to flesh out quarterly salary surveys produced by Neil Crichton-Miller's Graduate Appointments Register, another arm of the growing Haymarket empire. Sharing a flat north of Hyde Park with three Trinity contemporaries, slogging into work on the tube, counting the pennies, analysing enviously the salaries on offer to well-qualified graduates (the mid-1960s saw a post-war peak in graduate recruitment by industry and the professions), I realised, perhaps for the first time, just how competitive it was out there.

In folklore mythology the summer of 1967 is remembered as the "Summer of Love" when Procol Harum's haunting 'Whiter Shade of Pale' spent six weeks at No. 1 in the hit parade, hippiedom reached its zenith and the culture of free-love took the land by storm. Life seemed rather more humdrum in Lancaster Gate. With much regret and many backward glances, I returned to earth after the halcyon Trinity years. Yet the descent was not to last too long or go too far. In May Susie married her Army officer fiancée, Tom Brodie of the Black Watch, at a splendid wedding in central London. Three months later I resigned from Haymarket and helped my mother and father move south from Lancashire to Norfolk. Father had retired from the Army at the age of 50 to take a job managing student accommodation at the new University of East Anglia. For the next 43 years my parents lived in a Jane Austen look-alike house in the village of Mattishall, eleven miles from Norwich, until my mother died in 2010. At the start of September, I drove down to Heathrow and boarded a glamorous-looking BOAC aircraft bound for San Francisco and the start of my American adventure.

Nothing had quite prepared me for the USA as it was in 1967. I had never studied American politics or history. The Vietnam War was still a somewhat remote issue in the UK and Ireland. The dissent welling up on every US campus had barely rippled across the Atlantic. The huge generational gulf and political divide which erupted into open social warfare the year I lived in California never had a counterpart in Britain for all the later rewriting of history. Nor did the acute political and racial tensions in American society that led to the assassinations of Robert Kennedy and Martin Luther King Jr. and the decision by President Lyndon Johnson to stand down during the momentous 12 months that lay ahead. It was a truly historic year – one that had lasting impact on American society. Even at the time I knew that I was privileged to be given a ringside seat, while for me personally the consequences were to endure for the next three decades.

By no stretch of imagination could my day-to-day American context – Stanford and Rotary – be described as being at the cutting edge of this enormous social upheaval. The Leland Stanford Junior University, to give the full sonorous title, had been founded in 1891 by a Californian railroad tycoon and named after his deceased young son. Attractive, low rise yellow sandstone buildings with red-tiled roofs and elegant, cool cloisters stood cheek-by-jowl with palm trees, green lawns and sparkling fountains under azure skies to give the central area of the 8,000 acre campus a country park feel. When I attended Stanford it had around 11,000 students, the great majority from white, well-to-do (the fees were sky-high) and conservative American backgrounds. About 40 per cent were graduates. By the late-1960s the university was already one of the world's leading teaching and research institutions and was well on the way to becoming the hub of the emerging Silicon Valley complex. Unrest involving sit-ins and demonstrations directed by an outspoken student leader called David Harris (then dallying with the folk singer Joan Baez) had bubbled up in 1966, stimulated by the US civil rights movement and growing student opposition to the draft and the war in Vietnam. Yet it was gentle stuff compared with the mutinous ferment going on 40 miles to the north in Berkeley, home of a polarized and radicalised campus of the University of California.

Met at the airport by John Donegan, a 50ish crew-cut lawyer and leading light in the Palo Alto Rotary Club in his large and impressive American automobile (the first I had ever seen), I was soon introduced to some of the day-to-day luxuries of US life in the late-1960s – freshly squeezed and chilled orange juice at breakfast, colour television, air conditioning, ritzy golf clubs and lazy barbecues by the pool. The Donegans lived in some style in Portola Valley astride the San Andreas Fault in a sprawling wooden house on stilts in the dry, brown foothills behind Stanford. As soon as I entered their home they let me know that their Ford Mustang was mine for as long as I needed it. A week or so later the forceful Joan Donegan marched down to the university's somnolent accommodation office and stirred things up. So it was, a day or two before the Winter term began, that I found a billet in a room at the back of a garage attached to a professor's house just a three-iron from the lush rolling fairways and impressive old oak trees of the Stanford University golf course.

That done, Mr Donegan informed me that I had only one Rotary obligation in the year ahead – namely, to visit Rotary Clubs and make post-prandial speeches about England. This came as a bit of a surprise since I had never made a public speech in my life or been told that this was part of the deal. Yet it turned out to be one of the most rewarding parts of my year in America, introducing me to different people and taking me all over California (even, on one occasion, co-piloting a two-seater plane to an evening meeting in an old gold mining town in the Sierra Nevada mountain range and, on another, playing golf in Santa Rosa with Charles Schulz, creator of the Charlie Brown and Snoopy cartoon strip). Along the way I learned how to relate to an audience and, as campus tensions rose, act as a kind of student emissary to my somewhat conservative, small town audiences bemused by their offspring's' rejection of everything they held dear. In all I was to make some 25 speeches in nine months – great training, and the source of many unexpected insights and experiences as America tore itself apart. Beyond this, Rotary left me alone. Fees and student living costs were met promptly and I became one of 38,000 graduates from some 100 countries to benefit from the organisation's Ambassadorial Scholarship programme (as it is now known) between 1947 and 2009. Though I had little to do with Rotary in subsequent years, largely because of the roving nature of my career, I tried to take any opportunity that came my way in future to broadcast the value and generosity of the Rotary programme which truly did shape my life and career.

Initially my academic focus at Stanford was directed to completing a Master's degree in Political Science in one year – half the time normally allowed for such a course. Having spent four years at Trinity, and written innumerable essays, I discovered that I could avoid taking set-piece exams, instead writing lengthy research essays each term on subjects that I was studying. Eventually I was to compile nine such papers during the year and sail through to my Master's – a very proud moment. Most of my topics involved international politics and, particularly, communism. It may seem that I was consciously equipping myself for my future reporting career, but in reality it was just a coincidence which stood me in good stead. I was helped enormously by three outstanding members of the Stanford faculty. Michel Oksenberg taught contemporary Chinese studies with a verve and wit and tenacity that inspired his students to get to grips with China's alien political system, culture and behaviour. He was later to serve as President Carter's National Security Council adviser on issues involving China and East Asia from 1977-80. Robert North was an expert on the causes of international conflicts such as the Cuban missile crisis. He introduced me to quantitative analysis of things like population and resources as a means of determining attitudes and perceptions related to state behaviour – another useful tool for the future. Jan Triska, a Czech émigré with an open, friendly personality and an independent mind, taught courses on Soviet foreign policy and the politics of communism. To him I owe my lasting interest in Eastern Europe – at the time a neglected backwater for most west Europeans of my generation.

Studying at Stanford was more solitary and less discursive than at Trinity. Most students, even the graduates, tended to receive knowledge and recycle it. Time after time I would find myself the only person in a seminar raising a point or challenging an assumption. My American contemporaries mostly regarded me as a European cynic in sharp contrast to their innate optimism. In 1967-68 this optimism expressed itself strongly in a widespread campus belief that students could change society for the better – violently if necessary. The Stanford Research Institute, a body that received half of its funding from the US Department of Defense for classified work, was targeted day after day by student protestors. The naval ROTC (Reserve Officers' Training Corps) building was burned to the ground, and the office of the president of the university destroyed. A later history of this period at Stanford describes "a campus bristling with rancour." Certainly it was a campus riven with division and deeply suspicious of authority and hierarchy. But it was also rather poorly led by limp-wristed academics unsure how to handle the mass rebellion on their hands.

Stanford in 1967-68 also epitomised three fundamental shifts going on in US society in the late 1960s over the role of and attitudes to blacks, women and youth. When I arrived the university had no more than 100 students of Afro-American heritage. Less than one-fifth of the student body was female, thanks to a decades-old resolution limiting women's enrolment and enforcing tight living restrictions. Youth, despite the effect of the post-1945 baby boom, still counted for little, not least in elections, and much of the syllabus on arts degree courses had barely changed in a generation. Assuming I was swapping a rather traditional academic environment in Ireland for the cutting edge of modernity in California, I was somewhat taken aback to discover that most of my new student colleagues were convinced of the need for radical change if not outright revolution on the Stanford campus. To begin with, there was an almost exhilarating novelty to the proceedings as sit-ins took over buildings and governance meetings were forced on to reluctant faculty heads. But before long, and certainly by the end of 1968, the Stanford campus had become dysfunctional – the scene of wearying social mayhem that went nowhere and was to bring the university to its knees (and police intervention) a couple of years after I left.

In theory, I might have remained isolated from all this in my garage back room. But two factors drew me in. Each night, as part of my Stanford "experience," I was generously given a free meal by an undergraduate fraternity – a social organisation represented on most American campuses and usually defined by Greek letters such as Phi Beta Kappa or Phi Sigma Alpha. It was in such a body of 60 or so all-male students that the most intense discussion took place in the evening around the dining tables about campus issues, race issues and above all the raging Vietnam conflict. Usually my evening in the fraternity would begin by watching the early evening CBS news read by Walter Cronkite who my fellow students trusted like a family member – the first and almost the last time I (or most others) saw real, uncensored combat in colour on primetime television. The impact was profound, not least on those fraternity members facing military service in Vietnam on graduation in a year or two. We had a fight in one class after a professor defended the war. Another time a Navy man in the fraternity melodramatically "resigned" his commission during dinner.

Several of these fraternity members became my friends. I was staying with one, Terry Ross, at his home in Los Angeles over the Thanksgiving holiday in November 1967 when President Lyndon Johnson made his dramatic, and totally unexpected, announcement on television that he would not stand for re-election and instead would devote his time during the coming year to finding a way to bring peace to Vietnam. So deep was the alienation from the political process felt by the Ross family that no one would watch the presidential broadcast with me – and no one believed me when I relayed what Johnson had just said. The following Easter five of us drove south to Mazatlan on Mexico's west coast through the striking Sonora desert in my trusty Mercedes 190 (bought for a modest sum from a Palo Alto car dealer friend of the Donegans). Every one of these 21-year olds would be in the military within a year.

The other factor which drew me into the heart of student life was the *Stanford Daily*, a student-run newspaper of a quality and scope that TCD could only dream about. Mostly the paper was staffed and run by students taking journalism courses but on arrival I presented myself to the editor, explained my background and he roped me in. As a result I covered a wide range of one-off campus and non-campus events in my spare time. These included interviewing a returning American Red Guard from Beijing and a Peace Corps volunteer from Thailand, profiling a Berkeley protestor, analysing racism in England and the end of the British Empire, and even explaining how Leland Stanford's efforts in 1878 to show that a horse's four legs are off the ground at the same time when it gallops had led to the prototype of the moving picture. Most interesting to me were several pieces I was able to file on a special (by-) election held in November, 1967, in nearby San Mateo County for the 11th Congressional District. This propelled a hitherto unknown Vietnam veteran and peace activist called Pete McCloskey to national prominence and was one of the first clear examples of students in the US swaying a vote. McCloskey won the election as a Republican and went on to enjoy a long career in Congress, challenging Richard Nixon unsuccessfully for the Republican presidential nomination in 1972 before becoming a Democrat.

My three terms at Stanford passed like a flash. It was not all heads-down study. I played many rounds of golf on the fine university course where Tom Watson and Tiger Woods honed their games, once getting as near as I ever have to a hole in one. I acquired a lively, curious American girlfriend with a penchant for picnics and literature. I tried to teach my fraternity friends how to play seven-a-side rugby. At weekends I visited

San Francisco in my Mercedes, once seeing the frenetic Little Richard in manic action and on another occasion crossing the famous Golden Gate Bridge to sample the wines in Napa valley. At Christmas in 1967 I was skiing with the hospitable Grant family in the snowy Rockies. The following June I drove their Austin Healey car through the magnificent Yosemite National Park and by Lake Tahoe to Reno to stay with friends of my sister. Then I moved south through the desert to Las Vegas, watching shooting stars in the sky as I slept by the roadside, before going on to the Grand Canyon and back up to Longmont in Colorado. There I joined forces with a friend who was on his way to rejoin the US Naval Academy at Annapolis, and we rumbled across the Great Plains of Kansas, through industrial Ohio, up to Niagara Falls and down to New York and Washington DC. By mid-July my MA had materialised, my money had run out, I had nowhere to stay and my visa was expiring. It was time to return home and begin a career.

It's said to be bad manners to quote oneself, but a journalist writing a memoir may be forgiven the occasional solecism. I looked back at my American sojourn on several occasions at the time – in a thank-you speech to Palo Alto Rotary Club the week before I left Stanford; in an unpublished essay written before I left New York; and in a long article that appeared in *The Illustrated London News* in December 1968. Not surprisingly, the speech was the most effusive. "These past ten months have been the most incredible of my life," I began. My first speech to the club had taken place just after the murder of Dr King. My farewell followed the murder of Robert Kennedy. "This has been a year in which each one of you has had to question very basic beliefs about the American Dream . . . It has affected me too . . . I shall remember the year above all else for the mental and political questioning it has involved and for the way for me it has helped so much to bridge the gap between nations and men, their minds and their ideologies. Thank you very much Rotary."

In the private essay I described the year as "the time that I first began to face up to, and relate to, the world outside university." Trinity, I felt, had allowed me to develop at my own pace "in an atmosphere of consent and harmony." In contrast Stanford had shown me "the turbulent waters of national and student politics and helped me to come to believe in the immorality of American actions" in Vietnam. My American odyssey, I reckoned, had "brought home the bitterness of racialism (sic) . . . Race and Vietnam are so similar," I concluded. "To start to solve either question the powers-that-be have to admit one thing – that a gigantic, appalling, catastrophic mistake has been made. On the one hand this mistake has condemned 20 million people to think of themselves as a beleaguered, hated group whose only salvation lies in violence. On the other, it has led to a major war, half a million men in arms and $40 billion a year being squandered in the barrels of guns fired in defence of democratic freedom." My tone in the *ILN* article was somewhat less apoplectic. Yet the conclusion was equally bleak. Even on Stanford University's "gilded youth" campus where the sun never set and nothing was lacking, unrest and rebellion had become profound and enduring, underlining "just how deeply unsettled present-day American society has become."

4

Reality Dawns

*"Choose a job you love, and you will never have
to work a day in your life."*

CONFUCIUS

I was 25 and the rest of my life could no longer be avoided. Arriving back in England in 1968 during the "Summer of Love" and the "Age of Aquarius," it was easy to believe that a rewarding and fulfiling future, hopefully in journalism, lay ahead. For once the British economy was expanding, there were jobs aplenty, society was relaxing, I had a valued higher degree from one of the world's leading universities in my back pocket and my self-confidence was brimming after a testing and eye-opening year in the United States.

It did not take long to bump into reality. While still in America I had approached the *Financial Times* seeking a job on my return. An encouraging letter in reply outlined a position on the foreign news desk – one of the traditional graduate routes onto the paper. With a spring in my step, soon after flying back to London I attended an interview in the old *FT* headquarters in the City. What a let down! The "offer" remained "on the table," but only provided I went away and spent two years in obscurity on a provincial newspaper. I left the building furious and outraged. Apparently the "Father of the Chapel" – the diehard representative of the National Union of Journalists on the paper – had objected to the *FT* employing someone "straight out of university." In vain did I protest that this was untrue. The NUJ's neanderthal grip on hiring and firing in Fleet Street was total in the late-1960s, and no management would challenge it. So the "offer" had been modified. Ever after I viewed trade unions with a degree of antipathy. The NUJ was one of the worst of its kind. Not content with blocking the introduction of computers and forcing a closed shop on management, it discriminated against graduates who had the temerity to specialise or achieve a higher degree. It was also deeply hypocritical. A few years later, now employed on an American newsmagazine, I applied for membership on the grounds that one day I might need to work on a British newspaper. By then I was beyond the reach of this self-serving organisation, and it accepted my application at once. Such were the values of the time – half forward-looking and half firmly rooted in the past – which married "swinging London" and "the white heat of [technological] revolution" with obsolete, avowedly restrictive and quite unreasonable employment practises.

Just about resigned to missing out on a worthwhile career in journalism, I looked elsewhere and was offered a consultant-type toehold in banking. Days prior to starting work at American Express, and spending my time going round Europe assessing the efficiency of AmEx operations, I chanced upon a three line advertisement on the front page of *The Times* (still in its traditional format) for a local hire to work in the London office of an American newsmagazine. Several hundred others saw the same ad and, like me, applied the same day. Not for the first time, I was lucky. The bureau chief, a live-wire American by the name of Joe Fromm, spotted something in me and offered me the job. The magazine was called *US News & World Report* and I had barely heard of it, let alone read it. Years later Joe recalled that he chose me because "I was impressed by your promise at our first meeting . . . you were pretty brash but you fulfilled my expectations."

US News, as the magazine was generally known, could only have existed and flourished in a vast continental country like the United States. Founded in 1933 by a man called David Lawrence, and headquartered in Washington, DC, its basic premise was to explain, analyse and interpret the previous week's news – and to look ahead. In this endeavour it was aided, above all, by the provincialism of American newspapers. The emphasis, as editor Marvin Stone put it in 1978, was on "pure, hard information with no frills, no nonsense and no distractions." The publication billed itself as neither liberal nor conservative, avoided advocacy, spurned "soft" topics such as the arts and sport (unless there was a business dimension) and made a positive virtue of its sobriety. A core feature was called "News You Can Use" – an early stab at consumer journalism, focusing on such topics as ugliness (23.8.76) and insect stings (10.5.76). "We are not entertainment, we are not pop-journalism" Stone asserted proudly on one occasion.

U.S. News & World Report
WASHINGTON

HYDE PARK 4643

72·NEW BOND STREET,
LONDON, W. 1.

September 19, 1968

Mr. Robin Knight
Several House
Mattishall
Dereham
NORFOLK

Dear Mr. Knight:

    I am happy to inform you that we have decided to go ahead with the appointment of a British journalist as editorial assistant in my office and I feel that you are qualified for the opening.

    If you will phone my secretary we can arrange another interview when we can discuss the final details, including salary.

    I am looking forward to what I hope will be a long, interesting and mutually beneficial relationship.

Yours sincerely,

Joseph Fromm

JF:nc

Such a parody of rectitude could not, and did not, exist anywhere in Europe. Much of the United States, too, was beyond the publication's reach including the liberal eastern seaboard and *avant garde* California. Instead *US News's* heartland was that vast stretch of territory known as "Middle America" – small-town America, suburban America, Rotary Club America, the Midwest – and the growing army of well-heeled retirees in sunshine states like Florida and Arizona. By the time I turned up at the end of the 1960s, the readership was around 1.75 million and the magazine was stuck at the "dead centre of inertia" in Stone's brutal assessment made a decade later once he had taken over from Lawrence and his heirs. An aging group at the top was proving reluctant to change the formula or innovate in any way, few of the staff was aged under 40, almost nobody was female or black – yet America was reinventing itself by the day and all the old cultural and societal certainties were under pressure.

I knew none of this when I signed on the dotted line in London – and I doubt if anyone in Washington knew that I had joined the magazine. A curious double standard applied which meant that I was not employed out of America but out of London – a local staffer on local wages who went unlisted on the masthead and was excluded from the magazine's pension and profit-sharing plans, not to mention its unique employee shareholding scheme which Lawrence had set up in 1962 when he concluded that his children had no wish to follow him into the newsmagazine business. A bloated news department staff of 220 – about three times that required at *The Economist* – including 11 foreign and eight domestic bureaux produced 60,000 words a week. A typical issue consisted of 80-100 pages and might include 18 articles, eight "newsletter" pages and a couple of foreign stories skewed heavily towards an American audience and American interests. "World Report" it was not. In fact the only recognised non-American on the staff was a banking guru based in Switzerland who Lawrence (then in his eighties) was convinced had the inside track with the "gnomes of Zurich."

The magazine's working culture was built on initials and an almost unquestioning, top down ethos. A caption on a report of an advertising sales meeting in 1978 gives some of the flavour: "JPD & JMT seem intent on what SJK has to say. Behind them: AJ". Employees were forbidden to make outside speeches. Few articles carried by-lines. Opinion columns did not exist. The writing was little better than routine wire service stuff – two-sentence paragraphs, no adjectives, sparse description and sparser colour. Photographs were black-and-white, postage-stamp size. Covers often consisted of horizontal lists of articles; not until the late 1970s were any images or drawings used. On the road a correspondent was supposed to fend for himself. Even the use of an interpreter was frowned on, let alone that of a fixer. Telex costs were kept to a minimum and often articles were filed by airmail. Reputation-wise, the magazine ranked highly with insiders in government and business, less so within the journalistic fraternity which knew it as "Snooze". External awards were few and far between. Still, the circulation rose steadily in the 1960s and the critics were shrugged aside. The more one got to know the company, the more it resembled a sect.

Despite all of this, or maybe because of it, the staff was enormously loyal to Lawrence and respected him for his achievements as a pioneering newsman who had built a career, and a publishing empire, since the 1920s on news and information about government. His opposition to the New Deal and the civil rights movement, and his support of Senator McCarthy's anti-communist hearings and of the Vietnam War, tended to be explained away. I met him once, in 1970. By then, three years before his death at the age of 88, he grunted and squinted and came across as a bit of a spent force behind his large oak desk. Small talk was never his thing. After inquiring about life in London, a city he loved, the conversation petered out. Years later I found myself overseeing the upkeep of a wooden seat that he had had placed in Mount Street Gardens in memory of his wife near his favourite London watering hole, the Connaught Hotel. The pigeons loved it.

Such career-threatening responsibilities lay well into the future. For the moment my first task was to come to terms with the London bureau of *USN&WR* at 72 New Bond Street. To be kind, it was an odd set-up. Joe Fromm presided with a light touch supported by a second American correspondent (shortly to return home and not be replaced) who spent as much time as he could in London's art galleries and theatres; a jack-of-all-trades named John Harvey-Lee who breezed into the office each evening after a day's teaching to cut and file newspapers; a devoted (to Joe) unmarried secretary in her mid-30s; a mysterious Swiss gentleman in a camel overcoat who acted as the magazine's European advertising manager, and his glamorous German personal assistant who was married to a racy Japanese businessman called Jimmy.

This disparate community existed in silos. Each day Joe would drive in from his home in Highgate, jauntily walk to work past the overbearing US Embassy building on Grosvenor Square, arrive in the office around 11.00am, lunch leisurely at the Connaught or the Garrick Club with government ministers, officials and diplomats and then pound away on his typewriter in the afternoon and evening. His wife Gloria mostly went her own way up in Highgate. These were the last days of the post-war American journalistic raj in London. Foreign correspondents like Joe were top-of-the-range models living well, travelling first class, dining first class and earning first class. Joe's indulgences included a saturnine driver called Mr Waite, who was rolled out to carry him around on "official" occasions, and a horse he bought for one of his daughters that had to be shipped back to the US at company expense when he finally returned home. It was the first oil price shock in 1974 that marked the end of this era. Subsequent American reporters in London endured a 30-year slide in their status until, by 2005, even *Time* magazine had given up chauffeurs and expense-account lunches while the *New York Times* was making its correspondents file three times a day.

Joe himself could not have been friendlier or more supportive to a young whipper-snapper like me. Born in the Midwest in 1920 and a true child of the Depression, he made his way on his own merits, beginning his career on a paper in Indiana during Roosevelt's New Deal era. Ever after his political views were conservative Democrat. During World War II he somehow contrived to serve as an ambulance driver with British forces in North Africa, later becoming a captain in the Indian Army. Joining *USN&WR* in 1946, he was based in Asia until 1957 when he was transferred to the UK. For the next two decades – "the happiest years of my life, professionally and personally, an idyllic life indeed" – Joe was in his element. Bustling around London, always smartly dressed in suits from Henry Poole of Savile Row, dark hair and military moustache carefully trimmed at Trumper's of Mayfair, he never stopped networking and inserting himself into the heart of the British Establishment. At the same time he carved out a wider role, helping to found the (International) Institute for Strategic Studies, becoming chairman of the AACL (Association of American Correspondents in London) and eventually being awarded the OBE by the British government for his services to Anglo-American understanding. Great Britain had no greater friend in the US press corps in London in my era, and I acquired a generous mentor who opened many doors that otherwise would have remained firmly shut to a novice like myself.

To Joe I also owe whatever skill I developed in "seeing" a newsweekly story, the crucial significance of the introductory paragraph and the importance of clear, concise writing. Joe was not, however, a fluent or nuanced writer himself. Most of his copy was of the black-and-white, wire service variety. He was also prone to sweeping generalisations that opened him up to criticism and, sometimes, ridicule. On leaving the UK in October 1974, for example, he put his head on the block by announcing in a by-lined piece that "a revolution is well under way" in the UK before going on to highlight the rise of some peripheral and eminently forgettable vigilante organisations. *US News* liked the sharpness and one-two-three flow of his copy and Joe flourished, becoming the third-ranking journalist on the magazine as well as a major shareholder. Even in retirement at the age of 90 he was still attending lunches and dinners in Washington, sharing ideas, taking part in government seminars and adding his two penny worth.

To begin with I contributed mostly to anonymous round-up pages in the magazine, particularly one devoted to the activities of US companies abroad and another to business around the world. Everything I sent in was rewritten heavily, and it was a rare week when I spied even one of my phrases in a published article. Gradually I started filing one page (750 words) stories – again heavily subbed – on British topics such as London's victory over smog, racial integration in English schools, the royal family and changes to the UK welfare system. It was unusual to report or write more than one article a week, and sometimes weeks would go by with little or nothing to do. By the spring of 1970 this meagre diet had begun to pale so I reopened negotiations with the *FT*. Somehow Joe got to hear of this, and within weeks I had been despatched to Washington for a six-week trial stint to see if the powers-that-be considered me suitably qualified to join the International Staff. After some mind-numbingly tedious days rewriting others' copy, living in a gloomy hotel near the office and wandering around the humid city alone at weekends, I was accepted and became a full member of the magazine's staff. At 27 I was at least a dozen years younger than practically every other reporter on the staff and my payslip reflected this – just $9,330 (£3,660) in 1971. Working for *US News* was never to be the road to riches.

On the other hand, in the words of Pepper Martin, the foreign editor in 1970, I had been given "a passport to see the world." A crusty sort of a fellow who had lived life to the full, Pepper was part of a near-mythical generation of American foreign correspondents who made their names in Asia in the 1940s and 1950s. He remained foreign editor until 1978 and died in 1993. As he also pointed out, it was a good time to be joining *US News*. Circulation was rising (it broke the two million mark in 1974). The pension plan had $12 million net assets. The profit sharing plan was worth more than $5 million. Pay rises were generous. Anyone over the age of 30 who had been on the staff for five years was entitled to own stock in the company. The foreign staff was expanding and I would turn out to be one of the first of many younger hires. Meantime plans were being hatched to build smart new headquarters and to invest in computer-based production technology which, by the end of the decade, led the American magazine publishing industry into a new era.

Back in London the pace of life picked up. The 1970 general election produced several stories and I was allowed to pen a suitably sceptical profile of of the charmless Edward Heath. Late in 1970 Joe, never a great traveller, decided that my education in Ireland qualified me as an expert on the North and packed me off to Belfast to begin the magazine's long-running coverage of "The Troubles." For the next six years I shuttled back and forth, mostly to the much bombed Europa Hotel until it could be hit no more and closed its cardboard front doors (the glass had long since been blown away) for the duration of the violence. It was always an uncomfortable assignment for me – life on a tightrope, never sure that anyone in the province accepted me as an impartial observer given my origins and professional background. More times than I care to recollect a contact in a mean Belfast back street would challenge my credentials. In 1972, when over 500 people were killed in a single year and Northern Ireland seemed on the verge of meltdown, I made eight visits to the province. Each one had its distinctly nerve-racking moments. The temptation to remain more or less safely in my hotel room and rely on the telephone was never greater. But I'm glad to report that the lure of the real and authentic always prevailed.

US News quite quickly adopted a weary, hands-off detachedness towards the whole Irish imbroglio ("Irish vs Irish – Why They Keep Fighting" was the give-away headline on a two page spread in October 1970), and never bought the irredentist Irish-American line that it was all about Irish unity and British "exploitation." By and large it proved to be a conflict without heroes. Some decent and brave people did cross my path. In particular, I recall surreptitious meetings in out-of-the-way places with a variety of intermediaries working for peace. There were some memorable moments such as attending Sunday service in the Rev Ian Paisley's vast church and hearing him thundering on about "papist plots" to his gullible congregation as they thrust large denomination banknotes into his collection buckets. At Stormont, the seat of political power, pin-striped British officials tried to keep up the appearance of normality, often by taking one to lunch at some hideaway country rendezvouz as far removed from the violence as possible. But the lasting impression looking back is of small-minded people relentlessly pursuing small-town aims while the store burned down around them. Violence was never going to drive the British out of Northern Ireland in the 1970s, but it certainly destroyed the middle ground and made compromise next-to impossible.

Other highlights of the time included a Concorde test flight across the Atlantic and back one Sunday, a succession of stories about the sorry state of British labour relations as the number of working days lost to strikes rose to a record 24 million in 1972, and a sobering trip to Ebbw Vale in 1973 to investigate post-industrial poverty in the UK. One evening in 1970 I attended a reception in London hosted by the Foreign Press Association and met my first Russian – a curious little ferret who masqueraded as a diplomat, smelled of radishes and alcohol and had a squat wife with dyed henna hair cascading down to her ample backside. Within days my new friend had invited me to lunch in a nondescript restaurant in Notting Hill. He was to spend many hours subsequently pumping me for my non-existent "inside" information about the British government. When 105 Soviet officials were ordered to leave the UK by the Heath government in September 1971 for "unacceptable activities," my contact was among them.

Reflecting the airline schedules of the time, I had been designated the magazine's Africa correspondent in 1970 on the pragmatic grounds that it was simpler to fly to Africa from London than from almost anywhere else. At the end of 1971 I made my first trip to the continent – six gruelling weeks on the road that took in South Africa, Rhodesia, Ethiopia and Israel just before Christmas and produced my first by-lined articles. Many more visits followed in the years ahead and I was to come to love the wide open spaces of Africa, its friendly people and their inate optimism – for all the woes that roving correspondents like me were obliged by events to report.

Explaining decades later in an era of instant communication just how I went about my business in those far-off days takes some doing. The summer of 1974 offers a good example since, for once, I kept a diary. In July-August I spent two months in Portugal, Angola and Mozambique charting the revolution in Portugal and the subsequent collapse of the Portuguese empire in Africa. The two-week spell in Angola was typical. A nine-hour flight from Lisbon to Luanda was followed by my arrival in the middle of the night at a down-at-heel, insect-infested hotel. I spoke not a word of Portuguese, had a meagre allowance to hire an interpreter and knew no one. A bitter black-white taxi strike was underway. The hotel air conditioning had collapsed. Promised mail from London and Washington had not arrived. The phones were not working. I woke up after my initial night in town with a badly swollen right eye – a victim of the first of many vicious mosquito assaults.

After I met the local fixer – a genial barrel of a man called Mike Chapman who ran a stringer service and had one of the few functioning telexes in town – things began to look up. Over the next ten days unrest erupted all over Luanda. A curfew was imposed, demonstrations broke out and there was violence, yet the atmosphere on the ground remained remarkably relaxed – to the extent that Chapman and I and two other journalists hired a car, drove to the scene of a protest march and survived to tell the tale. I began to make useful contacts. A vehicle I acquired broke down on the outskirts of Luanda, stranding me at a second-hand clothing market in one of the poorest sections of the city as dusk fell. Then a friendly African arrived from nowhere and unearthed a taxi. Signs appeared in shop windows stating 'Real freedom involves respect for the opinions of others." No one bought it, and the unrest continued. I purchased a stamp worth 33p from the hotel. The man who sold it produced a pot of glue which he applied liberally to the envelope to stop workers in the main post office peeling the stamp off and reselling it.

An anti-government demonstration right outside my hotel one day turned nasty and ended with the police and army firing into the crowd. Many people were killed and injured. Later that same day (July 15) black troops in the Portuguese army mutinied. Wandering around Luanda with a German television crew in the evening, we ran into a crowd of whites menacingly surrounding three blacks in a car, and a hysterical white woman distraught that a white policeman had been killed by a black soldier who had run amok. At a funeral for the victims of the demonstration next day, our car was circled by Africans who noticed the 'Impresna' (press) sign plastered all over it and happily answered our questions. Then we were told to leave in a hurry; someone had objected to our presence. Later I met with the Portuguese military spokesman in Angola – a charming gentleman who was part of the radical officers' movement which had earlier overthrown the Salazar dictatorship. Commandante Martins a Silva averred that it was time for revolution in

Angola too – not the usual bland military briefing! A few days later I tried to fly to the oil-rich enclave of Cabinda only for the small plane to develop a "technical condition" in mid-air and limp back to the airport. I suspected the "condition" was due to the fact that novice passengers on board (there were many) jumped up in unison to gawp out of the right side cabin windows as we circled Luanda – a sudden shift of weight which caused the plane to dip and roll violently.

All this time *US News* was conspicuous by its silence. This hands-off stance was replicated at Japan's *Asahi Shimbun* newspaper. One evening I bumped into its correspondent (a London acquaintance) on a bench by the harbour. He was composing one of those laborious Japanese leads – all about cherry trees and blossom and the beauty of Luanda's horseshoe bay as the sun went down. Any reference to the lively situation developing around us had to wait for the sixth paragraph. *US News* was really no better. It wanted nothing from me that week, or the next. I moved on to Mozambique and posted my Angola story by snail mail. It appeared in print six weeks later, reflected little or nothing of my adventures and by then had been overtaken by events.

This sort of thing took some getting used to. Throughout my early career with the magazine its detached, offhand attitude to foreign coverage demoralised its correspondents abroad. True, not all of them made much effort to get to the cutting edge of the situations they were reporting. Yet most did. Rarely was this frontline effort worthwhile as all colour and life were drained out of one's files by dull-witted rewrite merchants back at base who had trouble seeing "beyond the Beltway," as anywhere outside Washington DC is known. Yet the magazine was quick to boast about its representatives overseas, claiming in mid-November 1974 that "so far this year our (foreign-based) staff has dispatched more than two million words and travelled almost 200,000 miles to be on the spot when news was breaking that is significant to Americans." Not until the ownership of the magazine changed in the mid-1980s, and a more imaginative editing team was installed towards the end of the decade, did things buck up. One day in 1987, to my amazement, I received a call requesting more pizzazz in something I had written. It was like being released from a corset. By then I had been strangled in the chains of wire service prose, style and attitudes for nearly 20 years.

One answer to this frustrating situation, I concluded early on, was to develop interests beyond 72 New Bond Street. A prime example occurred in the autumn of 1968 and was to have all sorts of consequences. In the final Test match of the summer at the Oval cricket ground in London the South African-born mixed race cricketer Basil D'Oliveira scored 158 for England against the visiting Australians. His reward was to be omitted from the MCC party to tour South Africa later that year. A national outcry ensued, a member of the tour party fell out through injury, D'Oliveira was included belatedly – and the white-minority South African government led by prime minister BJ Vorster refused to allow D'Oliveira into the country of his birth on the grounds that his selection was a political plot master-minded by South Africa's enemies. Furious MCC members led by the ex-England captain Rev David Sheppard (subsequently Bishop of Liverpool) and a young psychoanalyst called Michael Brearley (yet to make his Test debut; later he captained England most successfully in the 1970s) demanded a special general meeting (SGM) of the club to discuss the matter. I had been an MCC member since 1963 thanks to a friend of my father who noticed my enthusiasm for the game and put my name on the waiting list. With about a hundred other members I responded to an advertisement in *The Times* seeking support for an SGM. Then I became de facto organising secretary of the "rebel" group one of whom was a television administrator called Peter Lewis. His mini-skirted secretary, Jean Sykes, whom I met in a pub in Knightsbridge opposite Harrods one Friday evening after work, was to become my loving partner for life.

All this lay some distance in the future. That autumn the argument over sport with apartheid South Africa raged on. In October I attended a disagreeable meeting at Lord's as note-taker for our group. It had been billed in advance as an "informal" gathering. In the event the MCC president, former prime minister Alec Douglas-Home, flew down from Scotland to attend, along with the full committee. We realised very quickly that the entire event had been staged to get us to drop our demand for an SGM and/or to separate Sheppard and Brearley from the rest of us. A succession of false claims and half-truths was made by Douglas-Home and his reactionary co-conspirator Gubby Allen, once a Test player himself but by then an authoritarian *eminence grise* at Lord's. There was no meeting of minds and we broke up further apart than we started. It was only too apparent that the autocratic MCC committee was out of its depth, knowing nothing about the reality of life in South

Africa and little about politics. Two months later an acrimonious SGM was held in the assembly room at Church House in London attended by about 700 MCC members. One boorish speech by the committee or its supporters followed another, the chairman of the meeting made no attempt to be impartial and Douglas-Home thought it "inappropriate" to speak. Our group won the argument hands down but lost heavily when the postal votes of backwoodsmen not present at the meeting were included in the count. All in all, it was a peculiarly English farce.

In retrospect no one came out of this sorry saga with honour. Douglas-Home, a noted appeaser before World War II, gave deeply disingenuous advice to the MCC committee. The leading lights on the committee (Messrs Allen, Gilligan, Aird and Silk) were bent on preserving sporting ties with South Africa at all costs. Lord Cobham, a former president of the MCC who had been told informally by Vorster earlier in 1968 that D'Oliveira would not be welcome, failed to convey the warning clearly to the club. The secretary of the MCC, SC Billy Griffiths, lied to journalists and failed to pass on the Cobham warning to the full committee; indeed, the very existence of the Cobham message was suppressed by Allen from his colleagues. David Sheppard was informed by Cobham of Vorster's warning, but failed to share this information with his group, even when the MCC committee was taking us for a ride. Mike Brearley wavered behind the scenes. Even the ever-resilient Basil D'Oliveira blotted his copybook by preparing to accept a lucrative offer to step aside from the tour made by a calculating South African businessman. The full truth about Vorster's warning, and the MCC's subsequent behaviour, dribbled out months later in the spring of 1969. It was the final straw. England would not play South Africa at cricket for a generation. At Lord's resentment simmered for decades. Not until 2010 did the MCC committee turn the other cheek and put a beautiful charcoal drawing of David Sheppard on display in the pavilion, as befitted a former England captain.

To be involved in such a national brouhaha, even at the margins, was something of an revelation so early on in my post-student life. My support for the MCC "rebels" had its roots in what I had seen and debated in the United States earlier in the same year. Three years on, I was able to judge things for myself when I visited South Africa for the first time at the end of 1971. Nothing I saw or heard then, or reported in a four-page spread in *US News*, made me feel that I had taken the wrong course in supporting Sheppard. The article that appeared under my name leant over backwards to be "balanced" – so realities such as street curfews in black areas, biased courts and the imprisonment of prominent churchmen on trumped up charges of terrorism were juxtaposed by editors in Washington with the number of homes built by white taxpayers for blacks (350,000 in 36 townships). There was no real relationship of course; a few new homes in a few townships was a sop that fooled no sentient black South African. Yet the article did make clear, in unambiguous terms unlikely to have gone down well with most *US News* readers, that the price of apartheid was getting higher and higher – and it already included many human rights abuses, the undermining of the rule of law, a slowing economy, widespread black poverty and increasing international isolation.

It was through the D'Oliveira affair that I met an American-born journalist in London who was to become one of my closest friends – Dudley Doust, once of *Time* magazine but in 1968 a freelancer struggling to make a living on the sports pages of *The Sunday Times* where he compiled a sports news column called 'Inside Track.' Driven and inquisitive, Dudley unearthed the fact that I had contact details for all the MCC rebels, and so began a lifelong association that was only to end with his untimely death in 2008. Among other things, he proved to be my entrée to some great sporting occasions. It was Dudley who took me to the Albert Hall to watch Joe Bugner battling in the ring and it was Dudley who took me to Wentworth to observe the young Seve Ballesteros escaping from the trees. It was also Dudley and his English wife Jane who gave me somewhere to stay at the top of their house in Greenwich when a flat I was living in was sold from under my feet in 1970. In return, I introduced him to Lord's and cricket – a game that was to fascinate this lifelong baseball fan sufficiently to stimulate him to write a perceptive biography of Ian Botham and two outstanding collaborative books with Mike Brearley.

Over the course of a 40-year career in British journalism, Dudley set new standards for in-depth sports reporting. It was a scandal that his peers in the business never recognised his achievement with a suitable award while he was alive. With his caterpillar eyebrows, penetrating stare, unruly hair and American drawl, everyone in golf or boxing or cricket or national hunt racing (his main specialities) knew and trusted him – a rare achievement for any journalist in Britain. This trust was not built on sycophancy but on Dudley's deserved reputation for persuading people to explain in detail a truth about their sporting endeavours, good or bad. In *The Ashes Retained*, to give one example, Dudley compiled a brilliant reconstruction of Derek Randall's epic 150 in the 4th Test of the 1978/79 series that remains celebrated years later for its meticulous command of the facts, organisation and relentless drive to discover why.

We argued endlessly, mostly about politics; Dudley was somewhat to the left-of-centre. But we usually kissed and made up – no one ever had a smooth relationship with him. Dudley was forever "the grit in my shoe, always challenging and debating and demanding to be right – a wonderful, decent, liberal human being" I wrote to Jane after his death. He kept his political views out of his reporting and scrupulously described things as he found them. Dudley also had a gift for friendship with the most unlikely people, not least in deepest Somerset where he lived for the last three decades of his life. I shared a by-line with him in 1968-69 on several cricket-related stories for *The Sunday Times,* and once interviewed him for a *US News* feature about Americans living abroad. Typically, he pulled no punches, declaring, "I don't like American values" and claiming that life in New York was "dehumanizing." That said, Dudley remained a true American to the end, emphasised by his unswerving devotion to democratic ideals, human rights, freedom of speech and freedom of the press.

As Dudley came into my life so did another unusual character of a rather different hue – John Biffen, then a young bachelor Tory MP making his way in parliament. On returning to England I had joined the Bow Group and made contact with the editor of *Crossbow* magazine, Simon Jenkins (later editor of *The Times,* chairman of the National Trust and a *US News & World Report* columnist). One day Simon called and said that a ghost writer was needed for a column Biffen had agreed to pen in the *Daily Sketch*. This seemed inherently improbable; John was definitely not tabloid columnist material, being sensitive, nuanced, modest and diffident. Yet he needed the money and wanted the exposure, so he had agreed to become the *Sketch's* answer to the raucous and opinionated Woodrow Wyatt in the *Daily Mirror*. I signed up at once, and visited John in the House of Commons one evening a month to hear him pronounce on a range of subjects neither of us knew much, or anything, about. The paper never gave the columns any prominence and within six months the experiment ended. But I remained friendly with John for years to come.

The son of a Somerset tenant farmer, Biffen was the classic post-war 'scholarship boy made good.' After Cambridge, he got into parliament at a famous by-election in 1961 and remained there until 1997 when he received a life peerage. He died in 2007. Along the way he served in the first two Thatcher governments, including five years from 1982 to 1987 as an able and popular Leader of the House. Politically, he was never easy to pigeon hole. Suspicious of ideology, he changed his mind often. At various times he was a supporter of Enoch Powell, a radical Tory reformer, a Europhile and a Eurosceptic. Essentially, John was his own man, and he made and kept friends across the political spectrum. To my mind he had a romanticised view of England and the English, but I always felt his heart was in the right place. A good example was his principled opposition to Thatcher's poll tax plans in 1990 taken, he told me, because of the tax's probable impact on the poor.

John took his time to decide whether he liked someone or not, but once he decided he did he remained true to you even after, as in my case, a decade apart. For a number of years I drove up to his Oswestry constituency in the summer to spend the weekend with him and to captain his cricket team against a local side. Totally disorganised prior to his marriage late in life, he never had any food or even soap in his converted barn home and lived a hand-to-mouth existence. On one occasion Enoch Powell, surprisingly lively and amusing in person, and his long-suffering wife Pam, who cleared up behind him, came to lunch on a rainy Sunday. We spent the afternoon haring through churches and cemeteries in Shropshire – a characteristic Powell leisure activity made treacherous by his manic driving but remarkable by his ability to decipher and explain the most obscure Latin text on a memorial. Biffen, always an attentive constituency MP, was in his element, knowing every back road and every vicar in the county. Once John's column-writing days at the *Sketch* ended we lunched together regularly at *US News's* expense, and he would pass on political titbits. I rarely learned much of interest to an American audience until, one day in October 1986, he let slip a bombshell just 48 hours after the event to the effect that Margaret Thatcher had known nothing in advance of Ronald Reagan's dramatic proposal at the recent Reykjavik superpower summit to eliminate all nuclear ballistic missiles. The prime minister, John told me gleefully, was

"incandescent with rage." By that stage he had grown weary of Thatcher's
imperious ways and was moving to his infamous, if celebrated, "semi-
detached" status in the Cabinet and eventual ejection from government
after the 1987 general election.

Many other new and interesting types came into my life for the first
time during these early years at *US News*, especially government
spokesmen, diplomats and politicians. At Downing Street, to which
American correspondents in London traipsed faithfully each Wednesday
morning for a background briefing session with the spokesman of the
day, I encountered a series of larger-than-life exponents of the black art
of "off-the-record" briefing. In those days the press secretary occupied
the ground floor room on the right of No. 10. A dozen or more of us
would enter Downing Street by the front door, gather around the
photocopier outside the press secretary's office and wait to be ushered in
at 12 noon precisely. Then we would select fold-up chairs from a pile in
the corner, circle around the spokesman sitting in his armchair or behind
a desk in front of the curved window, and take out our notebooks. "Off-
the-record" did not mean recalling from memory afterwards anything
that was said but simply not attributing any statement to any source.
Depending on who was giving the briefing, there might be some sort of
preliminary statement followed by questions. Unlike the dealings with
the British lobby, these proceedings rarely degenerated into
confrontations and resembled a seminar more than anything else. Some
of the press secretaries actually looked forward to our sessions as a grown-
up antidote to the antics of the UK press. Others could barely contain
their boredom. As a newcomer, I skulked at the back of the group and
watched silently for some months before venturing a question. It was all
too easy to reveal one's naivety or lack of knowledge in such a battle-
hardened troupe.

Trevor Lloyd-Hughes, the first press secretary I dealt with at Downing
Street and a former lobby journalist himself, was on his way out when I
arrived – a victim of prime minister Harold Wilson's growing paranoia.
He knew he was on the transfer list, yet kept strictly to the script. Still,
mutual relations were cordial. His successor, Joe Haines, could not have
been more different, making it clear as soon as he arrived in 1969 that
"there are no votes in America." The result was that the US lobby was
downgraded – which meant that he often failed to turn up. Partisan, and
a paid-up member of the awkward squad, Haines never went out of his

way to cultivate Americans even when transatlantic divisions over the Vietnam War were at a peak. Many of us came to rely on his deputy, the suave, ever-courteous Henry James, to explain British positions and to smooth the waters. Haines was to return to Downing Street in 1974 with Wilson. But before he did we enjoyed four years' adult treatment at the hands of Donald Maitland, prime minister Edward Heath's inspired choice to run the Downing Street communications machine. The pint-sized Maitland, even shorter than Joe Fromm, was a career diplomat and mandarin par excellence known for his dry wit and command of detail. He was also a forensic briefer who believed in "getting the facts out" rather than spinning them – perhaps the last Whitehall spokesman to do so. For a time he tried, and failed, to conduct lobby briefings on-the-record. This won him friends among American journalists who were never comfortable with the nod-and-a-wink style of briefing usual in London and always had their editors in the United States on their backs demanding attributions to the anonymous quotes emerging from Downing Street.

Various politicians, too, crossed my path in these early days. With Joe Fromm I attended formal interviews with both Wilson and Heath in Downing Street. The former was vague and distracted, the latter clinical and emotionless. Joe monopolized the questions and I supervised the tape recorder. Over in Ireland I was on my own with successive leaders including Brian Faulkner in the North and Charlie Haughey in the South. The latter, unfortunately, knew of my association with David Thornley following our encounter in the Shelbourne Hotel dining room. As he wished to appeal to Irish Americans for support in his efforts to pressure London for concessions in the North, he consented to an interview. It was not a success. An ultra-pragmatist who was later shown to be up to his eyeballs in dubious financial deals, Haughey believed in telling audiences what they wanted to hear. This made interviewing him tricky since one had wildly contradictory statements to go on. Fixing me with a beady eye, he ended our session by saying "Mr Knight, you may think you have command of the facts but I have command of the detail." He was right; Haughey knew where every skeleton in Ireland was buried.

On another level the US ambassador to the UK at the time, a billionaire publisher called Walter Annenberg, proved a generous, if overpowering, host at his splendid residence at Winfield House in Regent's Park – my first taste of such high-level entertainment. On the other hand he never had any useful insights to share. For that I often turned to another American in London – the opinion pollster Robert Worcester who had recently relocated to Britain and was making a name for himself as one of the all-time great networkers in British life. Bob was far more than that, however, and it was his carefully researched work on the challenges facing the many US banks arriving for the first time in the old-style City of London of the early 1970s which brought us together. Over the years Bob was to prove a wonderful contact – informative, balanced, gossipy and perceptive all at the same time. To him I owe my membership of the prestigious Anglo-American organisation known as The Pilgrims which he chaired with panache for many years.

For all the career opportunities presented by my new position, it took me sometime to settle into a pattern of living. For about 18 months I rattled around, sharing flats with friends, sampling what London had to offer, making new connections and gradually coming to realise that I was a journalist rather than a student and that the rest of my life had finally begun. On summer weekends I played cricket in the Thames valley for an exotic outfit called the Frederick Pickersgill Memorial XI named, it was claimed, after a Yorkshire tax collector. The core of the team was a dozen or so people five to ten years older than me who had been at Oxford University together in the mid-1950s and were friends of Michael Sissons, one of the leading London literary agents of the day. Some of them had real claims to fame, such as Paul Wheeler, a canny left arm bowler/diplomat turned television dramatist; the well-known BBC journalist Richard Kershaw, with whom I often opened the batting; an earnest industrialist called Jonathan Fry (grandson of CB Fry), who bowled stratospheric left arm lobs; the lawyer John Gold who stood behind the stumps more in hope than expectation; and the unforgetable John Nagenda – "poetry in motion" as he modestly described himself and his military-medium bowling. John played for East Africa in the inaugural 1975 cricket World Cup and went on to become media advisor to the Ugandan president Yoweri Museveni, earning a dubious place in history by defending Idi Amin.

Early in the 1970s Pickersgill acquired a home "ground" near Abingdon – in reality little more than a seeded ploughed field with a small, bumpy square in the middle adjoining a stream next to the Sissons' fine-looking mill house. Like many in the Pickersgill milieu at the time,

Michael's relationships were unstable, and he soon moved out of the mill. Yet Pickersgill stayed on at Marcham in spite of the wicket and played there for a number of years, even acquiring a rudimentary pavilion with the help of a grant from the MCC. At some point Johnny Gold was dragooned into becoming the full-time groundsman, while wives and partners were drafted in to provide teas. Colourful characters came and went, most alarmingly a blindingly fast West Indian bowler called Ossie Gooding, who terrified the wits out of helmet-less village batsmen in the Thames valley, not to mention the Pickersgill slips. My own playing record was patchy; I always maintained that the basic conditions were against my cultured style of play, but enjoyed the eclectic company. The glorious summer of 1976 turned out to be something of an *annus mirabilis* including my only century (against Private Eye XI) and a batting average above 40 as the sun shone endlessly at Marcham, pitches quickened and shot-making rather than self-defence became a reasonable proposition. In the event it proved to be my swan song as an active cricketer although I did manage a few games later in exotic locations such as central Moscow and a cinder track outside Rome.

By 1971 I was also the proud owner of a house – a three bedroom "Victorian working man's cottage" as the title deeds disdainfully described it, located in a quiet side street adjoining Chiswick House in west London. Fed up with endlessly seeking new flats and flatmates, I hit on Paxton Road after pounding the pavements at weekends and sending letters to everyone in the road to find out if anyone wanted to sell privately. One person did – a woman who lived in Portsmouth who had inherited No. 35 on her mother's death. A sale was concluded just before Christmas 1970, and the freezing, unmodernised house was mine for £6,750. The timing was excellent – house price inflation was about to erupt. Forty years later a similar house in the same road was sold for £750,000. Much needed to be done, however, to make the classic terrace building habitable, including knocking down internal walls, installing central heating and building a proper kitchen. My finances were strained to the limit. But eventually the work was done just in time for the biggest upheaval, and most significant event, in my life so far – marriage to Jean in April 1972.

At that point we had known one another for a couple of years. But the path of true love never runs smooth. In theory we were edging to marriage as early as the end of 1970. But then I became a fully-fledged foreign correspondent, always on the move and socially unreliable, while Jean decided to escape her family in Ealing and see the world. Joining BOAC as an air stewardess (despite the airline's confdent prediction that the work would not suit her), she spent six months flying back and forth across the Atlantic and elsewhere. The job soon paled, and one happy autumn day in 1971 I was in the tiny back garden at Paxton Road when she turned up unannounced and told me she was resigning from the airline. One thing followed another, and on a wet and windy April day in 1972 we were married in Kensington at Christ Church, Victoria Road, followed by a short honeymoon in Cornwall. Then off I went to Norway to cover a North Sea oil story. Marrying Jeannie is something I never regretted. It was the start of a long, happy and close association which was tried and tested in many places by many situations. As I was to discover more times than I care to recall, I had found a true and loyal partner who enhanced my life in every way.

The following year, 1973, saw other firsts. Prime Minister Heath took on the coalminers, the UK plunged into a three-day work week and my new wife and I sat shivering around the dining table in Paxton Road under candlelight. Strikes were endemic and provided a steady diet of alarmist stories for the magazine about the "embattled island." The logjam at the top of US News broke and Marv Stone took over as editor with a mandate for change. Stone, I sensed, was nobody's fool and abrasive with it. We met for the first time that autumn, when Jean and I flew to Washington for two weeks "home" leave, and presumably left a positive impression. We then took advantage of an obsolete US News perk and sailed back to England on board Queen Elizabeth II. Early in 1974 Marv decided that he wanted Joe Fromm back in Washington as his senior analyst of strategic and international affairs. Joe and his family went reluctantly. Subtle and not so subtle applications to replace him rained in on Stone who ignored them all, took Joe's advice and appointed me the new London bureau chief at the age of 31. It was a rare honour as well as a massive boost and a fortunate second chance, given that the year before I had turned down a move to Bonn. So I became one of the few Brits ever to head an American news bureau in London, as well becoming the youngest bureau chief in the US lobby and easily the youngest bureau chief the magazine then employed abroad.

Joe left London in September 1974, and the following 18 months proved to be hectic, challenging and fulfilling. No one replaced me in the bureau, so I was on my own. Soon after Joe departed his secretary resigned. The 1974 devaluation of the dollar led to budget cuts – no more car parking under Hyde Park, no more lunches at the Connaught, no more travelling first class, no more cost-of-living increases and a pay freeze for a year or so. Work demands piled up under the new-broom Stone editorship. I covered stories in the Mideast for the first time, spent weeks in Portugal as the post-Salazar revolution there reached a climax and journeyed again to South Africa and Ethiopia. Several of my analytical pieces carried my byline, I began to cover pan-European issues, and for the first time I was trusted to conduct on-the-record question-and-answer interviews with luminaries such as Sir Bernard Lovell of Jodrell Bank fame, who talked about the relationship between science and money, and the think-tank insider Brian Crozier who assessed the Soviet challenge in Africa. In all, I contributed 68 stories in 1975, including a dozen two or three pagers filed from outside the UK.

Marv Stone had visited Europe in 1974 and held a meeting of all the European bureau chiefs in London. There were six of us present and one of his messages had been to expect cutbacks. He also took me aside and told me not to dig in too deep in London – he had plans for me elsewhere. Beyond that he gave nothing away; Marv always liked to keep people off balance. Late in 1975 the other shoe dropped. A letter from Pepper Martin wanted to know, in terms that made it clear that I had no choice, if I was prepared to go to Moscow. The magazine had opened a bureau in the Soviet capital early in 1974, deeming that Cold War conditions had eased sufficiently to make such a costly investment worthwhile. But much of the intervening period had been given over to the practicalities of getting a bureau up and running. Now Washington wanted someone in Moscow for three years who was going to be productive, get around the country and file every kind of story for the magazine week in week out, undeflected by the difficult local conditions.

I remember vividly coming home that evening and sitting down with Jean (by then back working at the ITA in her old job) and trying to decide what to do. It was one of those turning points in life. If we went to Moscow it meant a huge upheaval for us both and a permanent lifestyle change. In all probability, we would become part of the international caravan of foreign correspondents moving around the world from assignment to assignment for the next 10-15 years before being returned to "base" in the US as our 50s loomed. If we refused to go it would be the end of my career with *US News*, with no guarantee of anything comparable in journalism. We had youth on our side, no children or family ties that made it hard to leave England and were both up for an adventure. Quite quickly we got behind what was a rare opportunity. No one we knew had even been to Moscow, let alone lived there, and we spoke not a word of Russian between us. But you only live once. There were plenty of hard times to come in the USSR, but the years I spent there were to make my career, cement our marriage and provide memories and experiences that live with me to this day.

Being *US News*, though, there was a catch. I was supposed to go on working in London as bureau chief while learning Russian with Jeannie in the evenings. It was a mad idea, and we suffered agonies together as our diligent but hard-to-understand Russian language teacher, an orphan exile from Siberia named Alexander Fainstein who had been allowed to emigrate from the USSR earlier in the 1970s as part of the small Jewish quota, struggled to make headway with our weary, uncomprehending brains. Throughout the hot summer of 1976, even on holiday by the sea in Pembrokeshire, a Russian grammar book was never far away, along with a dictionary and a set of written exercises to complete. Alex persisted, we learned by rote and the more Russian we absorbed the harder the language seemed to become. Something of a watershed occurred when we discovered that in Russian there are two distinct words for each verb in English, depending on the tense being used. What we needed was a total immersion course and no distractions. But *US News* lacked the resources to offer such an option. So we did our best, sold our cars, rented out Paxton Road, said our goodbyes to colleagues and friends and, in late September 1976, as the shadows were lengthening across the cricket square at Marcham, turned our backs on England for an indefinite period and flew off to Moscow.

5

Russian Roulette

"It is a riddle, wrapped in a mystery, inside an enigma."
WINSTON CHURCHILL ON RUSSIA, OCTOBER 1939

As though it was yesterday I recall waking up early one autumn morning in Moscow in an enormous, curtainless bedroom on the 11th floor of the cavernous Peking Hotel – it served no Chinese cuisine and little edible food – and hearing the rumble of tanks rolling along the inner ring road just outside the building. It was October, and the Soviet Army was practising for its annual 7th November military parade in Red Square, a couple of miles away. Nothing to that point had driven home to me quite so clearly that the Cold War was now more than a catch phrase, and that Jean and I were committed to spend three years of our lives in the ideological heartland of this worldwide struggle.

By late-1976 the East-West freeze which had polarised the world for three decades was showing signs of thawing, at least at a geostrategic level. Détente had been formalised when the Helsinki Accords were signed the year before. A new US president was shortly to take office, determined to improve superpower relations. Disarmament agreements were in the air, and across Europe there was rising expectation, in the wake of the deal in Helsinki, that the Iron Curtain might be raised a chink before very much longer. Foreign journalists, in particular, seemed to have been promised better working conditions in the USSR. The reality on the ground was to prove rather different. Indeed, the whole of our three years in the Soviet Union was to be shaped by old-style high decibel Cold War rhetoric, confrontational Soviet behaviour, unrelenting Russian suspicion of the West and westerners, and countless provocative incidents designed to send a no-change message to the long-suffering Russian people – with hindsight, almost the last gasp of Soviet communist paranoia before the whole wretched edifice collapsed a decade or so later.

As far as US-accredited journalists in Moscow were concerned, the stage had been set only a month or so before I arrived in the USSR when the weekly *Literaturnaya Gazeta* launched an extraordinary attack on American correspondents, presumably in an attempt to discredit them and warn Russians to shun such unreliable characters. Three named American reporters based in the Soviet capital were said to be part of a vast, global CIA-run spy network which used foreign reporters as its core building block. One of the journalists, Alfred Friendly Jr. of *Newsweek*, tried to hit back by suing for defamation in a Soviet court but got nowhere and left the country. The accords, it was clear, were going to have little immediate positive impact on deeply ingrained Soviet attitudes to the likes of me regardless of what had been pledged on paper in Helsinki.

Through my studies at Stanford I was not unprepared for this truculence and hostility. Nevertheless, nothing in my previous career had quite equipped me for the depth and persistence of the animus. Until we arrived in the USSR I had only worked in relatively benign developed or developing countries. I was used to people answering the phone, being responsive and helping with the everyday challenges of a foreign correspondent's life such as booking planes and hotel rooms and hiring translators. Yet in Moscow the context proved to be utterly different and remained so throughout my assignment. Western journalists were tolerated within strictly defined limits, and only because the Soviet authorities saw advantage in having their own representatives masquerading as reporters in our societies. To the men in the Kremlin or the woman in Gorky street, to the mid-level official in Leningrad or the *dezhurnaya* (floor monitor) in a hotel in remotest Siberia, a western journalist was a class enemy, to be handled with extreme caution.

It took time for all this to sink in, which was just as well as the longer one remained in the USSR, the more wearying and antagonistic the system tended to feel. First impressions of Moscow in 1976 were of a grey, drab, down-at-heel sort of place set apart from the mundane by memorable extravagances such as the Kremlin, Red Square and St Basil's cathedral. Seven or eight massive, cockroach-infested skyscrapers, modelled on the Empire State building in New York and erected in the Stalin era, ringed the compact central core of the city like watchtowers. There were almost no individual houses, and virtually everyone lived in anonymous high rises built since 1945. Public transport was a distinct plus – frequent and reliable – and the Moscow Metro was (and is) a tourist attraction in itself. But no accurate plans of Moscow or, indeed, of the USSR could be acquired for love nor money. Instead foreigners, and some Russians, relied on maps produced undercover by the CIA in the early 1970s – one of the most effective pieces of public relations ever dreamt up by Washington.

Getting around was difficult for other reasons. Unexpected driving hazards proved to be numerous; it was fortunate that the *US News* bureau possessed a car and employed a driver. Behind the wheel, as one learned the hard way, it paid to be wary of the devious traffic police who hid behind trees wielding speed guns and jumped to the centre of roads to levy hefty on-the-spot fines. Just as often, these guardians of the "law" would control traffic lights manually, always on the look out to switch the signals abruptly when a *bolshaya shishka* (big shot) approached at speed in a curtained ZiL automobile. Traffic regulations can only described as obtuse, and the *razvorot* (left turn) system on the broader city streets was probably unique. Even on major thoroughfares smoke-belching, khaki-coloured delivery trucks trundling along at 20mph tended to monopolise the entire road, oblivious to anyone else. At night many car owners (their numbers were beginning to creep up as we arrived) drove on sidelights despite the dimly-lit streets and took home their windscreen wipers, batteries, spare tyres and wing mirrors to prevent theft.

Few petrol stations or garages existed; foreigners usually took their cars to Helsinki once a year (a round trip of 1,100 miles) for a service, braving the eerie, deserted no-man's land between Soviet and Finnish border posts close to Vyborg. To drive anywhere beyond a 25-mile range from the centre of Moscow required specific permission on each occasion from the Foreign Ministry. Our car had a unique, easily identifiable American journalists' number plate and surly, jackbooted policemen wielding truncheons like a conductor's baton would often strut into the middle of the major roads exiting the capital and wave us down to make sure our travel papers were in order. Just in case any westerner circumvented these ogres, stopping on all major highways out of the Soviet capital anywhere between the countless glass and concrete security checkpoints which lined such arteries was banned. Movement inside the city presented fewer problems, but even then some areas were off-limits to us – we never knew exactly which ones.

Nothing, in fact, was quite what it seemed. Stores in Moscow had window displays, but were largely empty of things to buy. Foreigners were allowed to import household goods duty free, but only once during a three-year assignment. A hefty bribe was required to clear all consignments, however legitimate, through customs. Our main source of weekly produce came from a couple of basic supermarkets selling imported western products of varying quality and availability. However, to purchase anything you had to possess 'D' coupons acquired for hard currency from the *Vneshtorg* (foreign trade) bank where we all had individual accounts. These *beriozkas* (there were others that sold items like tourist souvenirs and electrical goods) were dotted anonymously around the city and to get past the guard at the door you needed a foreign passport. Soviet citizens were banned although there were ways round that; our staff, for instance, were for ever pressing to have most of their wages paid in 'D' coupons. On one occasion we bought a painting from a well-known Russian artist and paid for it with a refrigerator acquired from the electrical *beriozka*. Apartment blocks inhabited by foreigners – there were around 5,000 of us living in the Soviet capital in 1976 – were guarded round-the-clock, winter and summer, by uniformed and armed militiamen. Allegedly, this was to protect us from crime but in reality to check on all Russians brave enough to try to enter. And so it went on. Either one adapted to this surreal, but carefully calibrated, "reality" or one left. Either way, the Soviet authorities could not have cared less. Westerners, even the most important, and other dubious categories such as the Chinese and Japanese, were regarded as "useful idiots" – potential hostages who were tolerated for what they might add to Soviet hard currency balances or technical knowledge as well as for the reciprocal access they offered the Kremlin in return.

Once we escaped the dreary Peking Hotel and our predecessors, Jim and Haya Wallace, had departed, our first port of call was the *US News* apartment and office at Leninsky Prospekt 36, some three miles from Red Square on the road out to Vnukovo airport. In many ways we were privileged. For a start there was no militiaman on the front door. For some reason, the magazine had been allocated quarters in a 1950s-built complex reserved for Soviet military veterans and East European diplomats. I never did discover why. Our flat – a large living room, sizeable bedroom, kitchen, two bathrooms and a boxroom – was roomy by Russian standards (in fact it was two apartments knocked into one). And it was snug on even the coldest nights in winter. On the other hand it had its downsides. A tram bustled noisily up Leninsky Prospekt right under our front windows. Dowdy, unmarked trucks came and went daily at the rear of the building, delivering china and glassware in coarsely-made brown wrapping paper and straw to a store called *Dom Farfor* sited underneath the apartment. And right outside our front door a filthy, smelly cast-iron rubbish shute occupied by cockroaches and the odd rat paralleled the lift shaft from top to bottom of the eight-storey building, clanking open and shut noisily every time it was used.

Each summer we endured a weird hiatus at Leninsky Prospekt – six weeks without hot water while the local power station had its boilers overhauled. At the time it was said to be under *remont* – such a commonplace phrase in the Soviet Union that once you heard it you never forgot it. When "real" winter began in November you knew the snow in the large courtyard below was there to stay for the next five months from the sound of metal shovels wielded by elderly *babyushkas* scraping away in doorways and around cars. Summer brought different neighbourhood sights and sounds – bemedalled and grizzled military types sitting on wooden seats under poplar trees in the courtyard reminiscing about the past; squawking ravens; incessant pop music from an apartment balcony by our bedroom; teachers shouting orders at young children in the school opposite as they marched around a tennis court readying themselves for a life of "socialist realism." Then one day early in September autumn would be heralded by a sudden blizzard of falling leaves that signalled the time was fast approaching to retreat indoors.

On the floor above our apartment *US News* had rented a three-room office, painstakingly fitted out by the Wallaces during the preceding three years. One room was given over to a clunky East German telex machine and storage shelves on which were stacked precious non-perishable items like tins of food, paper products and hard-to-buy necessities such as toothpaste, batteries and light bulbs. Another room, next to the front door, was occupied by the mercurial office interpreter. In between was my office – a comfortable, warm refuge and one of the best working environments I had in my journalistic career. Here I could research, interview and write in peace, aided by the eight-hour time difference with my masters in Washington. Maybe someone was watching me or listening to my phone calls? In the Peking Hotel at the start of our assignment we had had the eerie sensation of not being alone. Two decades later Valentina Fedorovna, the no-nonsense manager of the hotel in 1995, confirmed we had not been. "Half the rooms were occupied by the KGB – I'm free to tell you now," she laughed, before adding, "They're still on the sixth and seventh floor. Much better behaved. More modest. More polite." Yet apart from one memorable occasion, when sawdust fell like snow onto our sitting room chairs from a hole bored in the ceiling above, I never felt especially pressured in Moscow. Outside the capital it was another matter.

US News's set-up was typical of most one-person news-gathering bureau in the Soviet capital in the 1970s. Lucy, the temperamental, red-haired interpreter, played multiple roles – translator, fixer and flirt (an important attribute when dealing with Soviet officialdom). By then in her early 40s, she was volatile and easily distracted and had a history of failed relationships. At lunchtime she was forever rushing off to a nearby "polyclinic" for some unspecified health reason – in all likelihood, another hoover-type abortion popular with Russian women at the time. How she worked was a mystery to me, but deliver she mostly did, often earning my gratitude. Moreover she was not acquisitive and, if her chaotic personal life was anything to go by, could not be relied on by the KGB to provide accurate information about the Knights – an inevitable part of the job of every Russian employed by a foreign organisation during the Cold War. In contrast Boris, the driver, was sly and required close attention. He spent much of his time trying to discover who we met when he was not with us, and was always soliciting western goods, especially medicines and jeans, for his ostensibly sickly son Kyril – a shadowy youngster who we never encountered. Competent and reliable behind the wheel, Boris also had a sharp nose for the right bribe (he once acquired an old Moscow street sign for me, from workers removing the unusual hooded nameplate from a condemned building, in return for six bottles of vodka), looked after the office car as though it was his own and seamlessly handled the endless insurance claims (eight in one 12-month period) caused by local *hooliganis* with a penchant for Mercedes parts.

Typically, my week would begin with an hour-long Russian lesson given by a true believer called Galya who lived further up Leninsky Prospekt. I made slow progress, hampered by our mutual suspicion and my lack of opportunity to talk Russian to real Russians. It's surprising, though, how much of this self-satisfied teacher's efforts stuck. Years later, when communism had collapsed, I was to return to Russia several times and find that I could communicate easily in Russian with Russians. How different to the late 1970s when the number of "ordinary" Soviet citizens I got to know well could be counted on one hand. Interviews, briefings and other staged events invariably led nowhere. So did unscheduled encounters on planes and trains, which were often illuminating but never consumated by a second meeting. I suppose I was fortunate; earlier generations of western correspondents were even more isolated. Yet to gaze out of the office window and realise that the people in the courtyard below would never invite you into their kitchen for a cup of *chai* (tea) and a chat could be very dispiriting, especially in the dog days of February and March when the sun rarely shone and winter seemed endless.

Other highlights of my week included the Friday afternoon off-the-record briefing given by the American ambassador to 25 accredited US correspondents (I counted as one since I worked for an American news organisation), and lunchtimes on Saturdays when we were allowed to buy fast foods like hamburgers and french fries (then unknown in Moscow) at the US Embassy snack bar which was run by a cheery Italian called Alfredo. Milk and mail arrived via the embassy – a rare privilege for non-diplomats. Sometimes we visited the better restaurants in Moscow – the Aragvi, Metropol and National to name three – but one meal at each was usually enough. Any concept of quality or user-friendly service had long since been destroyed by the proletarian revolution, and every outing sooner or later became an ordeal – although also another shaft of light on Soviet reality.

More enjoyable leisure diversions included cross-country skiing in winter in the pine and birch woods outside Moscow, picnics in pristine meadows around the capital in summer, horse riding at the Hippodrome (Jean favoured a rough old nag called Gonk), and a weekly game of squash in the evening at the Indian Embassy which possessed the only court in the Soviet capital. Occasionally some of us would make weekend expeditions to major cities in the USSR or historic towns near Moscow, and once we drove south with two friends to Tolstoy's hauntingly evocative home at Yasnaya Polyana near Tula. In between times we entertained foreigners in our flat – from ambassadors to business representatives and journalist colleagues, all eager to pick each other's brains. Lasting friendships were forged across cultures, religions and generations based on a feeling that, regardless of where we came from or what we did, we were all in this together. One winter, when supplies of fruit and vegetables in Moscow were particularly poor, spur-of-the-moment supper parties were held in various foreigners-only compounds around Moscow on the arrival of delicacies like lettuce and cheese and oranges from Helsinki, our lifeline. Any Russians we invited never turned up.

The weather preoccupied us the longer we lived in Moscow. "Winter" was a loose term, but generally it meant a five month stretch from November to April. Our first year was not too bad; snow did not settle on the streets until after the 7th November parade and the thermometer never dipped below -20C. In 1977-78 snow began falling in mid-September and continued to fall for seven months, even hitting the May Day parade in 1978. But it was relatively warm throughout. We made up for this the following winter, our third, when temperatures dipped to -45C on New Year's Eve and locals said the harsh conditions for months on end rivalled the fabled 1941-42 winter. As much as the biting cold, it was the combination of a procession of grey days and our vitamin-deficient diet that got to us. Each winter felt longer than the last. Muscovites (and the Canadians among our ranks) seemed unconcerned and everyday life went on regardless, putting Britain's "leaves-on-the-line" mentality to shame. Streets were cleaned in an orderly way, huge icicles were removed safely from rooftops to protect unsuspecting pedestrians below, trams, buses and cars kept running (Boris used vodka to prevent windscreen water icing up), every manner of warm clothing came out of the cupboard and all over the city balconies were festooned with piles of cabbages as a fall-back against the inevitable day when no vegetables were on sale in the markets.

For Jean it proved to be a very hard transition. Nothing in her upbringing had prepared her for such a wrenching and total change. In our first year she was often bored and fed up, not finding Moscow or the Russians or the Soviet system as interesting as I did and missing her job and a purpose to life (spouses of western reporters in the USSR were not allowed to work in the Soviet economy). After a reporting swing through Eastern Europe in the Spring of 1977, which we made together, she returned to London for the summer, meeting up again with me on holiday in Portugal. On return to Moscow that autumn she had a stroke of luck when the wife of a colleague suggested that she help her in the library of the Anglo-American school up the road from our apartment. It was the break Jean needed, and over the next two years things looked up and she took over the running of the school library entirely in our third year. An assignment in the Soviet Union in those years tended to make or break marriages. We emerged stronger and closer – a real team – and though Jean never wanted to go back to Russia after the incident in Tashkent, nevertheless we owe our assignment in Moscow a lot.

I soon found that being the second *US News* correspondent to base in the Soviet capital had distinct advantages. Jim Wallace had set up a functioning office, imported and installed all the necessary machinery and established a working relationship with UPDK, the Soviet organisation which provided services (anything from translators, drivers and cooks to apartments and offices) to the foreign community. Just as important, he had got the magazine used to the idea that nothing happened quickly in Moscow. Censorship had been abolished on outgoing cables in the early 1960s. But this did not mean it was any faster or easier to file out of the USSR. Arranging an interview took weeks while setting up a trip to a specific city or region open to westerners could take half a year. I would routinely labour away at five, six or seven articles at a time, often taking several months to complete a single piece. I learned to be patient and persistent. While enduring this water torture I would justify my existence by writing short analytical commentaries and scouring the Soviet and western press, and Russian translation and broadcast services, for insights and information. It was painstaking work – more dogged detection than reportorial journalism – but played to the magazine's bias towards long deadlines and relative lack of interest in day-to-day news, and often paid off.

Strange though it sounds 30 years later in an era of instant global communication, *US News* had given me little or no instruction about what it wanted from its costly new toy. All that Marv Stone – by 1976 at the height of his powers as editor – had indicated in a roundabout sort of way was that my focus should be on everyday life in the Soviet Union rather than on high-blown East-West diplomacy, Kremlinology or the burgeoning dissident movement. He wanted me to travel the USSR as much as possible, and he wanted stories which would resonate with middle America – meaning articles that reflected Americans' gut concerns and curiosity about Russia and its worldwide empire. It was a broad mandate made broader by my almost total lack of input from Washington. In three years in Moscow not a single visitor from head office arrived in the Soviet capital. As a result I originated most of the articles I wrote, decided when and where to travel and how best to operate. By far the greatest influence on what I did and how I did it came from friends and colleagues in Moscow – a reflection of the way western journalists, even those competing directly, cooperated out of necessity under Soviet conditions. Two years into the assignment the magazine was sufficiently pleased with my efforts to despatch me on a cross-country promotional speaking tour of the United States and to invite Jean to accompany me. So I must have been doing something right.

None of this should imply that I never heard from Washington. Far from it. Unfortunately the input was mostly misjudged and petty, frequently involving money. For a start I was forbidden to file before 8.35am Washington time – 4.35pm Moscow time. This resulted in a lot of unnecessary and disruptive late-night work. The bean-counters refused to make regular monthly dollar transfers, instead insisting on receiving expense statements first. As these took ten days to reach Washington through the Soviet mail system, which we were obliged to use for outgoing mail, credit cards did not exist, we had no overdraft facilities at the Vneshtorg Bank and a dollar transfer from Washington took five days to reach our account, the bureau was always short of funds. In desperation I kept a store of personal travellers' cheques and hard currency in the office to deal with emergencies. Much the same paper-clip mentality made it difficult to import spare parts for the apartment, service and replace the office car, use an immersion heater in summer, import stationery from Finland or even revarnish the wood floors in the office and apartment each year to neutralise the hoardes of insects which infested our building. This stinginess – symptomatic of an underlying lack of imagination and resources in Washington that eventually would force the sale of the magazine – infuriated us both. It reached a nadir early in 1978 when I was reproached about the number of magazines being distributed free in Moscow (less than a dozen each week, and just about the only public relations tool we had) and told that I could no longer use freelance photographers.

Others suffered similarly, I found, and the only answer was to ignore the sniping from the rear. This was hard enough in normal circumstances, let alone in the pressure cooker conditions prevailing in

Moscow. But it had to be done. Reporting Soviet reality meant making maximum use of any and every reportorial tool, opportunity and contact starting with my "minder," AK Voznikov of the Soviet Foreign Ministry. Alexander Konstantinovich walked a fine line – personally affable, long-suffering in the face of my insistent demands, but at bottom a Soviet official happier saying *nyet* than taking an initiative. Within weeks of our arrival he had invited me to join a press trip going by rail to the huge, Fiat-designed car plant at Tolyatti on the banks of the river Volga 500 miles south of Moscow. My notebook of the visit contains just one interview. This session, with the director of the factory, typically revealed a mass of useless information such as how many workers ate dinner together (27,000) or were women (38%), and nothing at all about labour relations, pollution, production costs and wage differentials. It was a first taste of the underlying cultural and ideological divide, and the deliberate obfuscation, which dogged every formal encounter between a western reporter and a Soviet official. Yet it still represented opportunity – the chance to add colour and life to my first long piece on Soviet reality. With the general theme of the car in the Soviet system, this appeared in *US News* some two months later.

Over the next three years a series of socio-economic pieces about the Soviet Union was published in the magazine in contrast to the more news-driven agenda favoured by our rivals *Time* and *Newsweek*. Traffic conditions, racism, crime, the Soviet legal system, water shortages, nationalism, shopping, alcoholism, housing, vacationing, absenteeism, problems on the railways, shoddy goods, Soviet "elections," Russian humour, the Lenin myth, ID cards, passports, the Russian beat generation, the life of sports stars, female worker heroes, the Bolshoi, air travel, harvests, gambling, inflation and religion were just a few of the many topics that came under the Knight microscope. Read decades later, each leans to the sceptical. All proved sensitive given the pervasive Russian belief that everything was better *u nas* (literally 'with us') and the USSR had nothing to learn from the West. Various reactions followed from Soviet propagandists and apologists including many Letters to the Editor, happily offset by rather more supportive ones from American readers. Weightier pieces on such topics as the development of Siberian oilfields or the future of the ruling elite in the Kremlin or the ailing state of the Soviet economy or the fragile condition of Soviet-American relations usually appeared without any response.

Access to the topmost echelons of the Soviet power pyramid was non-existent. In three years I was invited once to a Kremlin reception when a visiting US Senatorial delegation was in town. Even then the ranking official to put in an appearance was the egregious Boris Ponamarev, a reactionary best known for his dislike of America and Americans, who quite deliberately steered clear of us reporters. Letters requesting interviews with state institutions invariably went unanswered. Almost the only senior figure accessible at all was Georgi Arbatov, head of the USA and Canada Institute. Cautious but articulate, he saw Leonid Brezhnev regularly (or so he implied) and was available to people like me in order to put a human face on the latest Soviet ploy. Not once did I encounter even a junior government minister. On a visit to western Ukraine in late-January 1977 I did meet a Brezhnev protégé by the name of Viktor Dobrik, then party chief in the Lvov region and a member of the Communist Party Central Committee. Dobrik was the prototype of a russified, trustworthy Ukrainian and lasted well into the Gorbachev era, thanks to a reputation for innovative economic management – the reason, of course, we foreign correspondents had been taken to Lvov. In person he revealed a nice line in self-deprecation, but nothing at all about the power struggle then raging in the Ukrainian ruling establishment or the underlying crisis affecting Soviet productivity and industry. But the session with Dobrik was the exception that proved the rule – Soviet officials did not meet with western reporters if they could possibly avoid it.

This was one trip, however, and there were many others, where the advantages of getting out of Moscow and seeing things first hand were demonstrated admirably. At the *Progress* shoe factory, where we were greeted with champagne and caviar at 10.00am, a worker on the production line admitted quietly when her supervisor was looking elsewhere that 25% of the shoes being made on the line were rejected because they had no matching pair. In the *Electron* television plant the manager acknowledged that the Leninist notion of paying workers equally for time on the production line had been abandoned in favour of rewarding individuals according to work they actually did. In three days in the area I got a feel of how Lvov – the most westerly city in the USSR and once part of Poland – had been frogmarched into the Soviet Union by Stalin and his KGB henchmen after the Second World War. I talked to a trade union official, a collective farm manager, a prosecutor, a journalist, a village official, a factory fitter and a woman who farmed her own private plot. None of these interviews was noteworthy in itself. Yet each formed part of a large mosaic known as "Soviet reality" that one day might be of use to me when the right moment arose.

I was to travel nearly 50,000 miles around the Soviet empire on 17 separate trips over the next three years despite 80% of the USSR being "closed" to foreigners. I visited Siberia half a dozen times, journeyed south by train through the dramatic Caucasus mountains to Tbilisi in Georgia, watched Russians relaxing on holiday by the Black Sea at Sochi, touched base in all three mutinous Baltic republics and made that ill-fated journey through Central Asia (see Chapter One) in the last months of my assignment. Mostly I moved about with other western correspondents as a precaution against incidents, either in a largish group of eight or ten or in twos and threes. In Moscow the KGB seemed to leave us alone, but outside the capital we were pursued relentlessly – by teams of agents in Tbilisi, for example, where I sat on a seat in the centre of the hotel lobby watching men being assigned to tail me before trying, and failing, to shake them off in the city's underground train network. In Vilnius the pair following Jean and me got so fed up with their boring lot that I bought them a bottle of wine one evening in the hotel restaurant.

Every expedition outside Moscow had a certain rhythm. Armed with food, toilet paper, bath plug, film and soap as a matter of routine, I would leave Leninsky Prospekt very early in the morning or last thing at night for one of Moscow's three airports. With eleven time zones to work around, such inconveniences have always been the norm for internal travel in Russia. At the airport I would check in at a special desk reserved for foreigners, board the plane at the front after Russian passengers had been herded on at the rear, and disembark immediately after the pilots who always left first. On arrival I would be collected by an obsequious "guide" from Intourist or Novosti (the Soviet news agency) or UPDK and taken to a standard-issue Soviet hotel. The facilities were always much the same and always rudimentary – barely furnished bedrooms, curtains which never fitted, dark pokey cafes dotted around the building selling tea and hard-boiled eggs, near-deserted dining rooms and a glowering *dejurnaya* on each floor checking your every movement. Yet each trip produced its own harvest.

In 1979, to give an example, I set off with seven American

correspondents, one Swede and two translators at 4.00am one freezing
March morning to visit Yakutia in the Soviet Far East. The trip had taken
six months to set up and I decided to keep a diary. After an eight-hour
flight and a stopover in Novosibirsk, we arrived at Yakutsk airport – it
"resembles a refugee camp" – at 11.00pm the same day. Outside it
was -29C. Inside the scruffy Hotel Lena, with its tilting floors and triple-
glazed windows and doors, we were informed by an official from Novosti
that we would not be visiting a diamond mine at Mirny or a gold mine
at Aldan – the supposed purpose of the trip. Instead, we were promised
a visit to huge gas fields at Kyzyl Syr provided we coughed up 650 rubles
an hour (about $1,000 then) to charter a helicopter. In any language this
is known as a stick-up, and the group resolved to resist. Next day, still
feeling on Moscow time, I got up to discover that I had left my precious
bath plug behind. One unenlightening interview followed another, and
that evening the first day of the nine-day trip was pronounced a disaster
by all except me and a colleague who bumped into a Jewish woman in a
street selling sealskin boots, visited her apartment and were told all about
"real" life in the Soviet Far East.

This set a pattern for the rest of this trip and, indeed, for many other
expeditions outside Moscow. Official meetings produced little of interest.
Unofficial encounters were always illuminating. So the more adventurous
of us, and/or the more fluent Russian speakers, constantly tried to escape
the clutches of our minders as we criss-crossed Yakutia. Still refusing to
pay for a helicopter, we flew around on regular commercial flights that
left or arrived at ungodly hours. Everywhere we went the emptiness and
harshness of Siberia in winter was revealed in all its starkness. On a 90-
minute flight from Yakutsk to Chulman we saw no tracks or buildings
at all on the land beneath us. "It is a wilderness but one that conceals a
treasure trove," I reckoned. Later that day we tramped around one of the
largest open-cast coalmines in the world at Nurungri and visited a long
tunnel on the new BAM (Baikal-Amur) railroad in temperatures below
-30C. It was an eye-opener that helped all of us, even the most dim-
witted (there were some), appreciate how the dogged toughness of
Russians can be such an asset.

By Day Five we were back in Yakutsk. First thing that morning we
boarded a helicopter (provided free) to get to Kyzyl Syr. Here our group
was squashed into four rooms in a guesthouse with one toilet and no
bath. At least it was warm; seven weeks into 1979, so we were told, 30

work days had already been lost because of the ferocious winter –
meaning that the temperature outside had dropped below -50C on all
those days. On our arrival in Kyzyl Syr it was a mere -40C which at least
meant that people were working. At a rig in the gasfield we met an
engineer and his youthful team. Were they paid enough to work outside
in these extraordinary conditions, we asked? Half said yes, the other half
remained silent. That afternoon we picnicked on an ice flow covering
the river Vilyuy. Great preparations had been made for us, including
erecting a tent, lighting a fire and catching tasty-looking fish in a net
strung on poles beneath the ice. As the wintry sun sank below the
horizon in early afternoon we toasted our hosts in fiery vodka, ate strips
of raw fish brushed with pepper and washed them down with hot fish
soup. By now almost out on our feet, we then drove six kilometers in
mini-buses along the frozen river back to Kyzyl Syr. Here we met a
"typical" family, the Zaitsevs. The session with them ended at 9.45pm,
after which we sat down to dinner with our hosts. A sticky time followed
which we tried to enliven by telling jokes. The Russians were not
laughing. Eventually one of them responded with a joke of his own –
about Angolans eating an American ambassador in Africa. At 11.00pm
we staggered to bed in our four little rooms.

So it continued for another three days. By Day Seven strains were
beginning to appear in our group – journalists do not all share the same
agenda or behave similarly. Our manners began to fray – never a good
idea with Soviet officials who always expected westerners to be polite
regardless of their rudeness to us. On Day Eight we went further north
and east than any party of US correspondents had ever been – to Ust
Nera, a gold-mining centre reputed to be the coldest permanently
inhabited community on Earth, a two hour flight from Yakutsk. For the
last hour our old prop plane skirted spectacular mountains before
skidding down the icy runway and almost into the terminal building at
Ust Nera. The town itself proved a bit of a disappointment after a
landing like that – grey and forbidding and unworthy of the dramatic
setting at the confluence of two wide rivers surrounded by snow-covered
mountains. Winter here, we were informed, lasted ten months. I went
into a shop and discovered that hunting rifles cost $400 and famous
foreigners (such as the Shah of Iran's brother) came here most years to
stalk deer and haul away the antlers. Truck drivers were the town's lifeline
and we managed to spend our evening with one of them. On the way to

his home we drove along the road to Magadan, an infamous KGB-run settlement built by slave labour in the 1930s. "Even now the name 'Magadan' evokes grim memories for our translator," I recorded.

Back in Moscow I noted in a letter to a friend in the West that Russians, when they wanted, could be a warm, friendly and helpful people – and the further one got from Moscow the more likely one was to discover this. We had been treated so well by our hosts in these remote, hard-to-supply places that it was almost embarrassing. In my diary I concluded: "Yakutia is the true Russian frontier – barely inhabited, resource rich. Man seems puny in such a bleak wilderness. Life in this part of the Soviet Union is never easy and often dull. The winters test everyone, and the summers are too short to make a real difference. There are many pioneering types to be found, but most of those we met in these isolated places were there for the material rewards on offer, which can be considerable. To have experienced Yakutia in winter, even for a few days, is a privilege given to few." A constructive comment on Soviet reality, for once, and one that money could not buy. An upbeat piece on life in Siberia appeared in the magazine three months later, to the chagrin of Anatoly Dobrynin, the Soviet ambassador in Washington and one of the most persistent critics of my "negativity,"when he met an editor from *US News* for a clear-the-air chat later that summer.

A trip of a different kind took place in November 1978, when *US News* unexpectedly asked me to go to Afghanistan to assess whether a Marxist takeover was underway. Unrest had surged across the country since April that year after a corrupt government was overthrown violently and replaced by an already deeply unpopular quasi-communist regime. Kabul, I soon realised, was seething with rumour and uncertainty. The fear in the air was palpable. The wife of the planning minister was on the incoming plane sitting next to me. She whispered in my ear that her husband had fled to Moscow after several provincial governors had had their throats slit. An armed guard thrust his bayonet suspiciously right through my suitcase at the airport. At night a strict curfew was in place; even standing on a balcony at the Intercontinetal Hotel high above the city was forbidden after sunset. On the streets Russians walked around with guards, and heavily armed Afghan soldiers roared about in trucks shouting slogans, waving red flags and scattering all and sundry in their wake. It felt like a very strange "People's Revolution."

I did the usual round of embassy, government and civil society organisations, sought out a local editor who had been recommended, and drove safely to and from Jalalabad through rocky mountain vistas, all the time marvelling at the sights, sounds and smells of one of the world's last true feudal societies. In the streets of Kabul you could still find scribes writing letters for the illiterate, craftsmen making tiles, men being shaved, women covered from head to toe, and men and boys and donkeys pulling huge cartloads of farm produce to market. So unpopular had Russians become (and this was before the full-blown Soviet invasion at the end of 1979) that Americans were being advised by the embassy to announce their nationality in shops to get a better (lower) price. Everything pointed to worse violence ahead.

Goodness knows what it was like behind the scenes, but one day I got an inkling when I was summoned to meet the foreign minister and number two in the regime, a vigorous and scheming individual called Hafizullah Amin. By this stage Amin was plotting to have the new president, Nur Muhammad Taraki, eliminated having already overseen the murder of Taraki's predecessor and his family and many of their colleagues six months before my interview. A small concern did flicker across my mind as I entered the heavily-fortified palace that Amin had seized. But this US-educated (Columbia University) revolutionary was way too smooth to give anything away to the likes of me, denying that a Marxist takeover was contemplated, let alone underway, or that the West was being sidelined or that the socio-economic change his dysfunctional government was championing was unpopular. The problem was that no one, including his Soviet sponsors, trusted him an inch. I waited to the end of our session before introducing the touchy subject of Taraki. Amin never missed a beat. Pointing to an enormous ten-foot portrait of his rival which lay slung horizontal across the top of a fireplace mantel in his office, he remarked sardonically, "I wrote his biography myself. He's a fine man. There's not enough praise of Taraki. We need more." Ten months later Taraki was dead, smothered by a pillow wielded by the commander of the palace guards on Amin's orders. In its wisdom *US News* sat on my article for weeks, turned it into another predictable East-West power struggle piece, cut out all the local colour and removed any reference to the blood-thirsty Hafizullah Amin. I might as well have stayed in Moscow.

Inevitably there were few such high spots like the trip to Afghanistan in these years yet the Soviet story always had a real edge throughout my time in Moscow. Mostly this was due to the steady deterioration in East-West relations during this period. In 1975 the West had finally got the handle it wanted to throw a light legitimately on human rights inside the Soviet empire by agreeing to the Helsinki Accords, which also recognised the postwar division of Europe. To the Kremlin this had seemed a reasonable trade-off – or so the group of ageing and out-of-touch *aparatchiks* at the top believed, assuming they would be able to stonewall the West on human rights. They soon learned otherwise as a persistent and courageous network of unauthorised monitoring groups sprang up inside the Soviet Union, aided and abetted by supporters in the West. Would-be Jewish emigrants, nationalists, artists, intellectuals and religious minorities quickly coalesced into a potent mix of dissent – the first real political opposition inside the USSR since 1917 – which wrong-footed the inept authorities over the next decade until Mikhail Gorbachev altered the terms of reference in Russia forever.

Most western correspondents in Moscow regarded the dissidents, as they became known, as manna from heaven and a symbiotic relationship soon developed. This was epitomised by the unfortunate Bob Toth of the *Los Angeles Times* – a non-Russian speaker with a science background who came to rely on the skills and insights of Anatoly Shcharansky, a young unemployed English-speaking computer programmer refused permission to emigrate to Israel. The close link these two forged was to result in Toth's arrest and interrogation and Shcharansky's trial and imprisonment in 1978, partly on "evidence" derived from Toth's incriminating, signed statement (in Russian) and partly on the word of a KGB *agent provocateur* who penetrated the American Embassy and compromised some of its diplomats. Sadly, it was only the worst of countless confrontational, staged incidents in the 1976-80 period designed to crush the dissidents and cock a snoop at the West.

Editor Stone had implied before I went to Moscow that he was reluctant to devote overmuch space to the dissident story, partly because he judged it of marginal concern to Americans and partly because the competition had already made it their own. So it never became central to my reporting which at least spared me the considerable time and effort involved in close association with people who invariably needed help of some kind or another in return for their insights. There was also always the question of motive. One man, in particular, who insisted on meeting me several times in a car parked on Leninsky Prospekt, aroused my suspicion that he was preparing the ground for a set-up similar to the one which snared a *US News* successor of mine, Nicholas Daniloff, in a KGB trap some years later. Occasionally, though, the human rights angle became too strong to be ignored – as when a battered young man by the name of Igor Gavrilov turned up unannounced in the office one day with a chilling tale of persecution, harassment and ill-treatment over the previous two years which shamed a supposedly civilised people. Gavrilov returned several times and on his last visit described in graphic detail how he had been forced into a psychiatric hospital, drugged and beaten up by the KGB. This story did make it into *US News,* touching off a flurry of congressional interest in Washington and an offer of help from a Russian immigrant who had known Gavrilov in the USSR.

At the time the nuclear scientist Andrei Sakharov and his feisty wife Yelena Bonner bestrode the dissident scene in Moscow like colossi. Sakharov was always a good person to approach for context, despite his habit of falling asleep in the middle of a conversation. Focused and stoic, he was never a natural boat-rocker but someone forced by conscience and experience to speak out. In his presence one felt like a pygmy. Bonner, I found, was better kept at arm's length because of her propensity to interfere. My best dissident source tended to be Alexander Lerner, a father-figure personality in the Jewish refusenik community for nearly two decades. Formerly a scientist who specialised in cybernetics, and therefore was barred from emigrating, Lerner was a kind man with great strength of character, numerous ideas and many contacts. His apartment on Ulyanova Street became a haven for dissidents and people like me, and nothing ever seemed too much trouble for him. He was eventually allowed to go to Israel in 1988.

Lerner was brave, too, making a point of turning up at Anatoly Shcharansky's grotesque parody of a "trial" in June 1978 held in a nondescript courthouse a mile or two from the Kremlin. He was there, he explained, to comfort Shcharansky's elderly mother Ida Milgrom. Only Shcharansky's brother Leonid was allowed into the court to witness the pre-determined proceedings. Twice a day he would emerge to brief some 50 doughty supporters, western diplomats and foreign correspondents like me gathered in the street outside. While this went on, grey-uniformed militiamen and thuggish-looking "volunteers" in civilian clothes glowered at us from behind metal fences a few yards away.

When the harsh sentence was revealed (13 years hard labour), one could feel the shock waves reverberating through the dissident and foreign community in Moscow. At the time we wondered if we were seeing a return to the Stalin show trial era of the late-1930s. It never came to that. Shcharansky remained defiant and unbowed and, after seven tough years in jail (mostly spent in solitary confinement), he was swapped in a Cold War deal in 1986, later becoming a senior politician in Israel and even visiting Moscow in this capacity.

If the Shcharansky trial was a wake-up call to some people, however, they must have been asleep for the previous couple of years. Détente may have been proclaimed from on high by the likes of Henry Kissinger and Jimmy Carter, but on the ground pressure on western, and especially American and British, journalists, diplomats, businessmen and military attaches never ceased and was ratcheted up significantly in the 1976-79 period as the dissident movement took root. Colleagues were picked off relentlessly from the mid-1970s, starting with the determined *AP* reporter George Krimsky who was expelled in early 1977 for getting too close to refuseniks in Moscow. In the following three years two good friends, Craig Whitney of the *New York Times* and Hal Piper of the *Baltimore Sun*, were put on trial and fined for their reporting. Another, David Satter of the *Financial Times*, had his car tyres slashed and camera smashed. Bob Toth was framed and others denied visas, threatened in the street or harrassed over the phone and subject to a variety of ludicrous and false claims by the authorities such as trashing hotel rooms or not paying bills. Life was never dull, and it took a certain sort of defiant, hard-edged bloody-mindedness to shrug off the endless provocations.

It helped that so many colleagues stood out from the usual run of journalists. Many went on to distinguished careers like Whitney, who rose near the top of the *NYT*, Peter Osnos of the *Washington Post* who founded Public Affairs Books, his successor Kevin Klose who became head of National Public Radio, and David Shippler of the *NYT* who won a Pulitzer Prize. Satter, a close friend of ours and a Rhodes Scholar, wrote two fine books on the Soviet system and worked for years at the Hudson Institute. Both my direct competitors, Marsh Clark of *Time* and Fred Coleman of *Newsweek*, were leading newsmagazine practitioners. Marsh moved on to South Africa where he died from cancer, while Fred joined me at *US News* for a short time in the 1990s and wrote a perceptive book about the reasons behind the collapse of the USSR. British journalists, too, had a strong pedigree, especially the ever-youthful Michael Binyon who became diplomatic editor and chief leader writer at *The Times,* the *BBC's* enterprising and resourceful Kevin Ruane and Dick Beeston who went on to represent *The Daily Telegraph* and *The Daily Mail* in Washington.

Much the same quality was evident in the western diplomatic community. The US embassy was home to numerous future ambassadors – mostly young men and women already marked out for higher things. Ted McNamara became ambassador to Colombia and a national security adviser to successive American presidents. The No. 2 in the embassy in our time, Jack Matlock, was US ambassador to the USSR in the dying days of communism and wrote a magisterial account of the Cold War. Dick Miles became a three-time ambassador. It was a similar story in the UK embassy. Two people we saw a lot stand out – John Holmes, who rose to become the highest-ranking UK official in the United Nations hierarchy having been ambassador in France and foreign policy adviser to two prime ministers; and the enigmatic MI6 agent-runner John Scarlett, who later headed the spy agency and became a controversial figure because of intelligence advice given to the Blair government in the run-up to the second Gulf war. Other embassies, such as the Australian, Chinese, Yugoslav and Colombian, had experts in various fields well worth cultivating. For better or worse, many of these specialists became valued sources – better because they had access to as much information as existed, worse because we would all have preferred to rely on first-hand Russian sources if we could.

Ambassadors were usually less informative and less in touch with events on the ground. Three stood out in my time. Robert Ford, the Canadian, had long experience having been in Moscow since 1964, good contacts in the Kremlin going back years and usually read the tea leaves accurately in his dry way. Ned Brennan, the erudite head of the new Irish embassy, and his capable No. 2 Daithi O'Ceallaigh (a future head of the Irish diplomatic service), cornered the market in Kremlinology – an arcane subject akin to palm-reading, but a topic that intrigued me as Brezhnev-era nonentities jostled for position, faltered, collapsed or simply disappeared. Ned paid attention even to the smallest straws in the wind – often little more than a new position for a member of the Politburo on the top of the Lenin mausoleum at official parades, or a public image suddenly removed or a dissonant article in an obscure regional newspaper which he read while standing in the shower each morning. Real dedication!

Towering above them all, though, was the acerbic American representative, Malcolm Toon (see Chapter One). Nothing about Mac Toon was run-of-the-mill. As a young and opinionated diplomat he fell out with George Kennan – by far his senior and the architect of the US Cold War policy of containment. He lived to fight another day, further spats followed with other senior diplomats and yet he ended up a four-time ambassador in the US foreign service despite its tradition of political appointees. Toon had a large ego and was highly status-conscious, above all resenting the privileged insider position enjoyed in Washington by Dobrynin, his opposite number. Utterly clear-headed about the Soviets and their system (which meant he was forever depicted as a "hardliner" which he was not necessarily), he routinely insulted the Kremlin leadership off the record and damned it with faint praise on the record. Yet in retirement he proved to be the soul of discretion – laconic and reticent about his extraordinary career. "A strong man with strong views who led a full life," remarked Bob Toth, his paddle tennis partner, after Toon's death.

It was a privilege to listen to Mac Toon brief US correspondents on the events of the week on most Friday afternoons. He played us like a harp, knowing that his remarks would reach three key audiences one way or the other – the American people, Washington officialdom and the Kremlin. The sessions were strictly off the record but my notebooks contain the verbatim gist of 62 sessions held over three years. They make fascinating reading three decades on as Toon ranges over the diplomatic issues of the day with a focus on SALT negotiations, the Middle East, Soviet-American relations and Russian attitudes to gathering crises in such countries as Iran and Afghanistan, pausing only to deliver barbed comments on the realities of life in the workers' paradise. To suggest that he was sometimes undiplomatic is putting it mildly. It was a real bonus for me to be able to resurrect these briefings in a long article which appeared in the US *Foreign Service Journal* in June 2011 – more than 30 years after the event and long enough on from the episodes being described to upset no one.

Toon had got off on the wrong foot in Moscow in 1977 when he was left hanging in the air and unconfirmed in his position by the incoming

Carter Administration. He made sure we correspondents knew how he felt about this. He survived. On one famous occasion ahead of Secretary of State Cyrus Vance's first visit to Moscow later in 1977, he announced bluntly that the new Administration's first arms control proposals would fail – "this bird won't fly." On another occasion he was asked who he trusted. "Hell," he replied, "I don't trust the British" (he was the son of Scottish immigrants), before spotting me sitting in front of him and adding hastily, "present company excepted." He certainly tested that trust. Time after time he let his contempt for Dobrynin and Kremlin double-dealing show, in particular after the US embassy was subject to an arson attack in 1978 when the KGB tried (unsuccessfully) to gain access to its secure upper floors. Sometimes shooting from the lip, he did get things wrong and was notably cool about the place of human rights in diplomacy. Like just about everyone else, too, he was blindsided by the sudden collapse of the Soviet system, having forecast that Brezhnev's successors would remain in power for a generation. Yet he was a class act – someone who tested the limits of off-the-record briefing to the limit but never, to my knowledge, got burned.

Perhaps it was just as well that Toon was as cordial to correspondents as he was. None of us had diplomatic protection, and most of us needed the US Embassy's support at one time or another. I had only been in the Soviet Union four months when attacks on my work began with a blast on Radio Moscow about the article I wrote on car ownership – "a mixture of truths, half-truths and lies" according to one Igor Dmitriyev. I was, he concluded, "a poorly trained reporter." This characteristic mix of libel, abuse and counter-attack set a pattern that went on even after I left the USSR. More than two dozen increasingly shrill critiques appeared in the Soviet press over the next 30 months, culminating in three withering outbursts in *Pravda* (the official Communist Party organ) in 1978-79, one of them by the leading Soviet propagandist of the day, Yuri Zhukov. Letters to *US News* in Washington cascaded in each week from allegedly "ordinary" Russians who had somehow got hold of the magazine in darkest Siberia, and the epithets used about me grew more and more lurid. A journal called *New Times* charmingly described me as a "boot level" journalist. There were, claimed *Moscow News*, "no limits" to my ability to invent things. "We have a bone to pick with you Mr Knight" added the same paper ominously a couple of months later.

Soon after this blast *Soviet Life,* a glossy magazine distributed free in the USA under a bilateral cultural exchange agreement, devoted an entire article to rebutting a piece I had written on the use and abuse of bonuses in Soviet factories. This led to an official US protest since *Soviet Life* was meant to improve mutual understanding, not muddy the waters by replying to American magazine articles. In February 1979 I joined a very select group of misfits when *Journalist* magazine reviewed the work of western correspondents in the USSR and lumped me in with other well-known "anti-Sovieteers," including Hedrick Smith of the *New York Times* (author of *The Russians*) and Piero Ostellino of *Corriere della Sera* – high praise indeed. When I met Smith years later in a Washington television studio, and told him of our connection, he laughed and shook my hand. Under the Soviet lash we all felt like that; it was almost a badge of honour to be singled out and a sure sign that one was getting something right. "This correspondent dislikes everything," reflected *Pravda* in its final blast in July 1979, which was not the case, but no Russian journalist ever bothered to call me to find out. *Sovietskaya Rossiya* delivered a final kicking three months later, alleging that my reporting was all myths and lies. "You are gone but not forgotten, and as popular as ever," remarked Pepper Martin, laconically, as he passed on this tirade.

As it happened the *Sovietskaya Rossiya* piece was not the last broadside I received. In 1981 an entire 50-page chapter in a polemical book published in Moscow with the catchy title "Are our Moscow reporters giving us the facts about the USSR?" was devoted to my reporting. Written by an American communist and labour union official called Phillip Bonosky, it threw caution to the wind. No doubt hoping that I would sue for libel, Bonosky accused me of every journalistic sin under the sun – forging quotes, distorting photographs, lying, malice and making "wild allegations." An American student visiting the Soviet capital that Spring got hold of a copy of the book and had it forwarded to Marv Stone, along with the perceptive comment "Robin must have bothered the hell out of the Russians for them to feel they had to devote that much space to condemning him." "You're right," Marv replied, "Robin did bother the hell out of the Russians." I am glad to report that we never rose to Bonosky's bait. He continued to spew out virulent Marxist propaganda long after the collapse of the Soviet system – a true believer to the end.

All this seems ridiculous now when the Cold War has become as hard to explain as the Thirty Years War. At the time it was deadly serious and perhaps, with hindsight, I took less notice of what party hacks like Zhukov were writing than I should have done. After all, few western correspondents made it into *Pravda* once let alone three times. Pressure built throughout 1978, evidenced by the withdrawal of invitations to trips, a refusal to arrange interviews, lengthy delays getting routine permissions to drive outside Moscow, enhanced KGB interest when I did escape the capital and all-too-obvious telephone bugging. At least I was spared the 'honey pot' trap, and in November 1978 Voznikov still felt able to do me a personal favour by getting Jean a ticket to the annual 7th November parade in Red Square. He also indicated that he had nothing to do with the Soviet press attacks, once urging me to write letters of complaint to various editors. I complied but, needless to say, no replies were received. I cannot say I was surprised. Seeking the truth was never part of a Soviet journalist's role. This was memorably defined by Lenin in the 1920s as "collective propagandist, collective agitator and, above all, collective organiser." Nothing had changed since then. By the time the bear's jaws snapped tight in Tashkent five months later, I could hardly say it was a surprise. I guess I had been riding for a fall for a long time.

Each of us western correspondents in Moscow in the 1970s developed our own way of operating under these pressures. Many factors came into play – personality, background, language skills, resourcefulness, maturity, one's own interests. What was paramount, I discovered, was one's inner drive allied to strong nerves and patience. My approach to reporting from the Soviet Union was essentially analytical and forensic – to hoard every piece of information I acquired by whatever means for the day when I could use it in some way in an article. Working for a weekly publication with its avowed interest in everyday Soviet life encouraged this approach. It helped, too, that I was rarely second-guessed in Washington, which was unusual for newsmagazines at the time given their rigid formats and propensity to rewrite files from the front line. As for risk-taking, I felt that it was simply an occupational hazard. I knew that the Soviets would hit back once they came to believe, for whatever reason or no reason, that my articles or behaviour offended their "norms" or threatened them in some way. Yet it never occurred to me to back off. The only reason I was in Moscow in the first place was to shed light on the Soviet system for American readers thousands of miles away. Moreover, until Tashkent, I never felt victimized or in physical danger despite all the unpleasant press attacks and KGB attention.

Exactly what I thought of the Soviet Union and its system was never much of a secret either since I interviewed myself several times for articles published in *US News* – an unusual reportorial format, but at least it ensured that I had the last word! As I was leaving I did this one final time. That question-and-answer "interview" was headlined 'What Does Russia Want?' Re-reading it decades later, I would change very little. My main impression of the Soviet system in 1979 was "the enormous contrast between Soviet claims and Soviet reality. There cannot be another people on earth with a greater capacity for self-delusion." The gulf between reality and theory that westerners constantly confront, I continued, "was not one that particularly impacts the Soviet people because of the limits to their freedom." This remains true today even in the freer, post-communist Putin era. So, too, does my conclusion: "My lasting impression of Russia and the Russians is of a country and people that largely have the government they deserve. The whole philosophy of individual freedom and the rule of law as we understand it in the West has simply never taken hold in Russia." Just to underline how much I knew, I added: "That's why . . . communist dictatorship will survive in the USSR for a long time to come."

So my assignment in Moscow drew to an end in the summer of 1979. "Everybody, when they left, took a piece of Russia with them and left a piece of themselves behind," a contemporary of mine in Moscow, Harry Dunphy of the *Associated Press*, once remarked. Jean and I departed with nerves jangling but heads held high. Both of us were dog tired and longing for a break. *US News*, in its wisdom, decided to replace me with a couple in their late-60s who spoke no Russian and were all too evidently running out of steam as they shuffled hesitantly down the platform at Leningradskaya station to meet us one morning in late-June straight off the night train from Leningrad – surely the last American journalists to sail across the Atlantic to an assignment in Russia. Apparently no one else on the staff had wanted to go to Moscow. Those at the top, typically, made no attempt to ask my advice or to look outside the magazine for someone better qualified. To suggest that I was disillusioned by this turn of events would be an understatement; it was "my most depressing experience with *USN&WR*," I wrote in a letter soon after, even worse I felt then, than the lack of support after our incident in Tashkent. Over the next two years the magazine's coverage from the Soviet Union collapsed, and incredulous letters reached me from former colleagues in Moscow asking what was going on. By then it was not my problem. I left behind a reasonable legacy – files and articles, a detailed manual on how to operate in Soviet conditions, some contacts and a working bureau – and if people in charge in Washington wished to squander it, that was their decision. But it was a great waste nevertheless, and it pained me.

The ultimate Soviet response to my time in Moscow came the following year when the Soviet authorities refused to accredit me to cover the 1980 Moscow Olympics, despite an earlier pledge to do so. It was a tiny harbinger of what was to follow once the games ended. With the Brezhnev era imploding, western journalists resumed their front row in the firing line. As late as August 1986 the Daniloff incident shocked everyone. Yet even in Russia the ice age eventually faded, *perestroika* got a grip and attitudes mellowed. Once the Yeltsin era began I was able to return to Moscow for several reporting visits.

My three years in the Soviet Union were not the high point of my journalistic career – that came later, with the collapse of communism and the five-year period from the late-1980s when *US News* was well led, better funded and staffed by some fine journalists. But it was the most memorable assignment I ever had – the one that told me most about myself, the one that had the most journalistic impact, the one that achieved the most for my employer and opened the most doors for me and the one that made us both some friends for life. I left feeling that I had come out ahead of the game. I had arrived in the USSR in 1976 as a relatively callow 33-year-old tyro in the business of foreign reporting. I left as a fully fledged, tried and tested 36-year-old foreign correspondent.

6

African Interlude

*"I can tell you the things that happened as I saw them, and
what the rest were about only Africa knows."*

HERMAN CHARLES BOSMAN

In our last few months in Moscow, while dicing with the KGB, I was
also engaged in protracted arm-wrestling with my masters in America.
They wanted me to move to Washington and become deputy foreign
editor – in every respect a dead end. It seemed a poor reward for three
years' hard slog in the Soviet Union. In any case, I was looking for more
foreign adventures – and life as rewrite man to a second-rate boss did
not fit the bill. I held out and eventually, with bad grace, it was agreed
that I would become Africa Editor and live in Johannesburg – for one
year. After that, I was told, all bets were off.

In the event everything about this particular move proved fractious
and frustrating. To begin with, as I discovered later, Marv Stone had not
intended to allow me any "wiggle room" in his offer, but his newly-minted
foreign editor made a mistake by suggesting an alternative to Washington.
This irritated Stone, who then focused on the minutiae of my move. In
London, en route to Johannesburg, we discovered that the South Africans,
deeply suspicious of anyone who had lived in Moscow, needed weeks to
issue a work permit and also required a complex x-ray to prove we were
not carrying tuberculosis. As a result we reached Johannesburg some days
later than Stone, in his wisdom, had decreed. This led to a tirade about
"reneging" on a non-existent "deal." Hard on the heels of that little upset,
our possessions were delayed by a dockers' strike in the UK and took four
months to make it from Moscow to Johannesburg via Helsinki and Cape
Town. And when we did finally reach South Africa with our bits and
pieces, we found ourselves in the middle of a local property boom that
made it next-to-impossible to unearth suitable furnished accommodation
with the money at our disposal.

US News was absolutely no help – a pattern of blinkered, stingy behaviour that repeated itself in each of our five moves for the magazine around the world. The one-storey house we ended up renting (from a departing *NBC* correspondent) was run-of-the-mill by the upmarket standards of northern Johannesburg – handily located and suitable for use as an office as well as a home, but in poor decorative state with a leaking roof, no heating and no carpets or curtains. We ended up having to furnish the place, take over a part-share of a live-in maid called Violet from a neighbouring correspondent and buy a secondhand car with 35,000km on the clock and no air conditioning. Yet from Day One the micro-managers in Washington decided, on no evidence whatsoever, that we lived "in the lap of luxury."

Fair or not, we felt let down when we finally came to rest at 26 Sturdee Avenue in the suburb of Rosebank, having lived out of three suitcases in eight places for the previous four months. Jean discovered that the South Africans had a cunning way of ensuring that pesky foreign correspondents did not become too entrenched in the country. If she wanted to work locally, I was told, I would have to pay income tax locally. I discovered that my bachelor predecessor had made no attempt to establish a presence or to make contacts, instead preferring to live out of a suitcase in an anonymous high-rise in one of the shadier parts of town. In any case the "bureau" subsisted on a shoestring – which meant no office, no local staff and no transport. To file stories, I was supposed to make use of a colourful character called Fingers van der Merwe who occupied a cubby hole next to the *AP* bureau in downtown Johannesburg. Even in Moscow the magazine had stretched to its own telex machine. Hovering like a black cloud over everything, Washington refused to spell out what it wanted me to do – and Africa is a rather large place in which to get lost.

This tell-tale silence persisted for the rest of my time on the continent. In retrospect *US News* simply "lacked the breadth or depth or assets" (as I put it to a friendly colleague in Washington) to delve beneath the headlines or to cover Africa in any other than a cursory, pro forma way. No attempt was made to think through how best to use a bureau in a place like Johannesburg, and the only consistent story themes of real interest to my far-away editors proved to be a fixation with the possibility of something called a "race war" in South Africa and the East-West superpower struggle for influence in places like Angola, Ethiopia and Mozambique.

For months (once for an entire 16-week stretch) I had no communication with the foreign editor, my nominal boss. It became almost routine for my ideas to be turned down with a curt 'No,' to the extent of refusing me permission in 1980 to fly north to cover crucial elections during Rhodesia's stormy march to black rule. On one occasion I was told to airmail a 200-word analysis for one of the magazine's "telegram" pages – the first time this had ever happened to me in eleven years on the staff. On other occasions I was sent off somewhere "urgently" only to be told when I got there to airmail my piece. Often it felt like working in a vacuum where time was of no consequence – anathema to any normal-thinking journalist. Not surprisingly, output measured by published articles fell sharply from my Moscow peak. In my first six months in Johannesburg I originated just two per cent of the longer stories from the foreign staff that appeared in print – thin gruel indeed after my heady days in the Soviet Union.

Being me, I did not take this fall from grace quietly, and by the end of February 1980 – only five months after reaching Johannesburg – I was at odds with many of the "decision-makers" in Washington. I began "considering my future" and casting around for other employers. No one nibbled. By then, in theory, I was already half way through the one-year assignment, but the following month I was unexpectedly asked to remain in Johannesburg for a second year. Another sacrificial lamb had been found to become deputy foreign editor. So I gambled that a third foreign posting might still be possible, accepted the proposal that I stay put and determined to do my own thing for the rest of my African sojourn.

Work-wise, matters did not improve much and throughout our 27 months in Africa my employers behaved like bears with sore heads, carping over petty things, counting the pennies fanatically and making numerous ill-informed editorial judgement calls. The result was irritation and frustration all round. In truth, there is nothing more morale-sapping to a correspondent thousands of miles from base than to be sent somewhere off the beaten track and then be unable to get the resultant story into print. In my case, writing for a weekly newsmagazine, matters were made worse by US News's penchant for sitting on articles for weeks on end. In consequence even a half productive reporter could soon find himself competing with himself for space – a total waste of time, effort and money, and utterly de-motivating.

On top of this there were purely African factors at work – or not, as the case might be. Almost all flight routes around the continent at that time were north-south, making it difficult to go east-west except via Europe – a very expensive option. Hotels were mostly rudimentary, communications on arrival always complex and unreliable and local interpreters and fixers of wildly varying quality and trustworthiness. In addition, working conditions for reporters based in South Africa were far from straightforward. Flights out of Johannesburg still stopped in Nairobi. But getting visas out of embassies in a country in which one does not reside has never been simple – and basing in Johannesburg just made things worse. Yet the longer I remained in South Africa the more I found that I had to travel simply to get on to the radar in Washington. Inevitably, after about a year, the law of diminishing returns set in and I was reduced to lobbying for marginal stories in out-of-the-way spots like Mauritius and Madagascar which *US News* was never going to buy.

All this suggests that Jean and I came to regret moving to Johannesburg, and it is true that when we left for the last time neither of us was too sorry to go. Yet in little over two years much that was positive and worthwhile happened to us. In the course of a career and a life the irritants we faced then mostly seem like niggles today – hardly worth a mention. I do so now only to provide a context. In effect, I tried to sell an unpopular product to Washington and largely failed. Africa, and an essentially provincial publication like *US News & World Report*, were chalk and cheese. When I moved on in August 1981 the bureau in Johannesburg was closed, no Africa travel budget was set for the following year and no *US News* staffer ever based in Africa again.

At the time, of course, I was not to know any of this. So on arrival in South Africa I set about raising the magazine's profile as quickly as possible on the basis that I would only be around for a year. I had the perfect vehicle – our headline-grabbing exploits in the Soviet Union. South Africa's isolation in 1979 can hardly be exaggerated. Apart from geographical distance, cultural and sporting sanctions were beginning to bite and the apartheid government was whipping up a siege mentality among the entire population. A Marxist plot known as the "total onslaught" was alleged to be threatening civilization in southern Africa. All kinds of civil liberties were being curtailed, and in Pretoria government ministers routinely railed against the West for turning a blind eye to the communist-inspired threat it claimed to be facing, so further heightening the feeling of remoteness.

Mostly, this analysis was self-serving and hysterical– a diversionary tactic dreamt up by the slippery regime led by President PW Botha to justify ever-more repressive policies and its failure to institute meaningful change. Not everyone bought the official line, though, and one of the organisations that did not was the South African Institute of International Affairs (SAIIA) and a contact I had made there called David Willers. David and his wife Joy (who later worked with me in London) were former South African diplomats and skilled networkers. One day, following a story in the *Rand Daily Mail* about our time in the USSR, the phone rang and I was invited to talk to an SAIIA audience on "Russia and Afghanistan." Three hundred people turned up, and so successful did the event prove that I was asked to do a follow-up on the Soviet Union "After Brezhnev." Both lectures were published in pamphlet form and the following year I toured the republic for SAIIA, giving four further lectures on the USSR – "a resounding success," according to its director, the ever-charming and solicitous John Barratt. In all, I gave a dozen public speeches in twelve months before finally shutting up shop. The effort served its purpose, quickly introducing me to a range of South Africans from white, well-heeled women in the Johannesburg suburb of Bryanston who wished to know if the Russians used toilet paper to, somewhat amazingly, the newly-appointed head of South Africa's National Intelligence Service. Only 31 at the time, Niel Barnard was to play a key role later in South Africa as the ground-breaking intermediary between PW Botha and Nelson Mandela. In the early 1980s, though, he was feeling his way – a pragmatic hardliner, if such a beast existed, who had never been to the Soviet bloc, was fixated by the so-called "communist threat" and wanted to learn what he could.

US News was less than enamoured by my speech-making (I made the mistake of sending the foreign editor a copy of my "After Brezhnev" presentation), and I received a pathetic reproach from the executive editor to the effect that he had not given me permission to make public appearances regardless of whether I had been paid (which I had not). This was par for the course. In David Lawrence's day only a decade earlier *US News* staffers had not been allowed to make any public appearance at all. I ignored the strictures and carried on in a prominent role, most notably as chairman of the Foreign Corespondents' Association of Southern Africa (FCASA) in 1980-81. Inevitably, this set me on a collision course with Pretoria. Issues involving the 80 or so foreign reporters based in the republic proved to be endless – access to military briefings and trips, access to official press conferences, attempts at censorship, attempts to manipulate coverage, visa and work permit renewals, police actions in black townships and the behaviour of individual FCASA members being just a few. My FCASA clientele, it is true, were a mixed bag. But their mere presence in South Africa outside the authoritarian apartheid straitjacket was like a permanent red rag to a bull with the authorities.

Time and again we had to resist government efforts to co-opt the FCASA as part of a press self-censorship system. In July 1980 the government denounced foreign journalists as "agitators and inciters of unrest" – a totally baseless charge never supported by any evidence. This touched off an almighty public row and led to me "negotiating" a face-saving compromise with Foreign Minister Pik Botha, who was upset by his colleagues' crude intemperance. "Thick-headed clowns" was one of the kinder FCASA descriptions of the officials who touched off this particular row. As one of my friends, Quentin Peel of the *Financial Times*, put it all too accurately if less colourfully, "Foreign correspondents are seen by the South African authorities as a cross between voyeurs, spies and agent provocateurs." At Parkview, the white-dominated golf club I joined in Johannesburg, this was certainly the prevailing attitude, although a minority did make it clear to me that not everyone went along with the official paranoia.

These harsh and prejudiced attitudes to the media, both domestic and foreign, reflected whites' growing sense of insecurity. The 1972-79 civil war in Rhodesia (in which 34,000 African lives had been lost) had underlined that a fight to the finish over race in South Africa would be disastrous for all sides. Meantime external opinion was hardening, even in the US and UK which were both led by right-of-centre governments. Violence and intimidation were increasing, especially in black townships. Civil liberties of every hue were under strain, including the independence of the court system. And the gulf in race relations was widening appreciably. In 1979 more whites voted with their feet and left South Africa than arrived. An unexpected boom in 1979-80 powered by rising gold prices relieved some of the pressure for a couple of years, but the upturn proved short-lived. The bottom line was that without an educated, skilled black workforce, black trade unions to represent it, black property rights and black inclusion in the political process the country had no hope of a peaceful or prosperous future. Yet in 1979-81 most whites in their silos still believed they could dictate the pace and terms of change and retain their privileged position.

How things looked to a cartoonist in the Johannesburg 'Star' in 1981

If siege politics and sham reform dominated my period in South Africa, brave critics prepared to attack the status quo were easy enough to unearth. My reporter's notebooks are full of revealing quotes, few of which saw the light of day in *US News*. "The whites have to realise they've had it unless they come to terms with us," Bishop Tutu, then in his 40s, informed me in October 1979. Tutu always spoke in such a throwaway style, with a smile on his impish face, that it was easy to miss the edge in his words. The same month Frederick van zyl Slabbert, the telegenic and earnest leader of the opposition Progressive Federal Party, termed the Botha administration an "oligarchy obsessed with total control" to such an extent, he claimed, that it was encouraging black revolution. Eighteen months later he was of the view that "more and more it's a question of keeping the lid on the pot." The editor of Soweto's *Post* newspaper, Percy Qoboza, accused Botha of "playing with reform" and ignoring the real issues of the country – a view surprisingly echoed on the right by the maverick editor of the conservative "*Citizen*" newspaper, Johnny Johnson, who a year later accused Botha of "lacking any vision or sense of what he can do."

One of our closest friends, Benjamin Pogrund, had pioneered white reporting of black affairs in South Africa in the 1960s, and by 1979 was deputy editor of the country's main opposition newspaper the *Rand Daily Mail*. His compassion and optimism shone through "despite a life full of disappointments and betrayals" as I put it once in a *Time* magazine review of his fine memoir *War of Words*. Never a political activist, and always first and last a newspaper reporter, Benji and his wife, the artist Anne Sassoon, introduced us to a wide-ranging liberal milieu at their home in Parktown that otherwise would have taken years to enter. On one occasion the meaning of being "banned" – that pernicious apartheid punishment which forbade named (but untried and unconvicted) individuals from contact with more than one person at a time – was driven home to us when a party held by the Pogrunds was raided by the security police and two of their guests, both banned, escaped through a bathroom window.

On several occasions I talked one-on-one to the "banned" Afrikaner churchman Byers Naude as we strolled around Zoo Lake near our Rosebank home. Naude's speciality was to challenge whites to see life through black eyes – and the laser-like gaze he directed at you as he talked stripped away any equivocation. Helen Suzman, the redoubtable and ever-courteous opposition liberal MP, was another "precious mouthpiece to the world" (in the words of her obituary in *The Economist*). She certainly was! I kept up with her on a regular basis, and on one memorable occasion she took me to lunch in the members' dining room in parliament to the amazement of those sitting near us. Always in command of the facts, and blind to colour and belief, Helen knew her rights and said what she thought. Her counterpart in the black community was Dr Nthato Motlana – an exuberant, perceptive medical practitioner who lived in Soweto, the huge black "township" on the outskirts of Johannesburg. Laughter was never far away in the Motlana clinic, however awful the recent circumstances.

Much of my journalistic fire power was wasted on a futile assault on the bureaucracy instigated by *US News* to secure an on-the-record interview with PW Botha. In its wisdom, the magazine believed that President Reagan's arrival in power in Washington would open doors in South Africa. But the "great crocodile," as Botha was known, mistrusted

Americans and disliked journalists, especially foreign ones. His English, while serviceable, worried him and he hated being challenged in cross examination. British visitors bore a particular cross and were apt to be reminded that his mother had been interned during the Boer War. Only the boldest responded by pointing out that he had been a member of an organisation that supported Nazi Germany in World War II. Botha was also quick to lose his temper. The result was that his aides were reluctant to expose him to reporters. History conceivably will treat PW more kindly than his contemporaries. He did, after all, abolish the hated pass laws, legalise inter-racial marriage, tolerate black trade unions and meet Nelson Mandela – all revolutionary developments in the apartheid context of the day. But such was the polarized tenor of the 1980s in South Africa, and so deep was the mistrust that his iron fist and manipulative approach aroused, that any credit Botha might have gained has never materialised.

In the end it took me seven years to crack this nut (see below), but first I thought it prudent to exploit my FCASA role. I began by arranging an excruciating dinner for the FCASA in Pretoria in late 1980 with the two Bothas and their wives. PW was in feisty form, claiming South Africa was "acting from a position of strength" and berating us journalists for not having sufficient contact with Afrikaners. Pik, just back from Europe and only present because PW ordered it, slept through the meal and then played footsie under the table with the female guests. Two months later we reached out again by agreeing to spend a weekend with our partners in an Afrikaner farming community in Eastern Transvaal on the border with Mozambique. Here cane sugar was king. Our host had a private plane but no books, kept a sub-machine gun in the loo and employed 200 Africans ("serfs" in my notebook) on a 10,000 hectare estate. This must be one of the few recorded instances in journalistic history when 30 or so foreign correspondents dutifully dressed up on a Sunday morning to go to church – in order to hear what the local Dutch Reform minister might say about them from the pulpit (perhaps he said nothing; history does not record the sermon).

As in Russia, a number of contemporaries in South Africa went on to notable careers. Pierre Haski, a young *AFP* reporter, helped to found *Liberation* in Paris. Quentin Peel became the *FT*'s long-serving and respected foreign affairs commentator. John Humphrys of the *BBC* and Mike Nicholson of *ITN* starred on British television and radio. Nick

Ashford, a squash partner of mine, did well at *The Times* before dying prematurely in 1990. Caryl Murphy of the *Washington Post* won a Pulitzer Prize for her reporting in Kuwait in the First Gulf War. Joe Lelyveld of the *New York Times* rose to giddy heights, producing a fine book on South Africa titled *Move Your Shadow* and eventually becoming executive editor of the paper. Jon Kapstein of *Business Week* pursued a successful career in public relations in Brussels. Others, maybe, were less distinguished – the flotsam and jetsam of international journalism who had washed up at the bottom of Africa. To varying degrees, however, all of us faced the same underlying problem. At the time the real story was elsewhere.

In retrospect, the 1979-81 period was a disappointment for almost everyone in South Africa except, no doubt, PW Botha and his friends in the defence establishment who were given a free hand to counter ANC military pin-pricks around the country and in Namibia. As time went by it became clear that Botha lacked the support in the ruling National Party to push through any sort of radical change. Nor, as Johnny Johnson had maintained, did he have the vision. A well-placed Afrikaner source, Ton Vosloo, editor of *Beeld*, once confided to me that PW "had never had a single original idea" in his life. Instead the longer he was in power, the more truculent he became as when he dressed down Herman Nickel, US ambassador to South Africa in 1986 (and a former *Time* magazine staffer) with the vainglorious boast "I'm not going to be buggered about by the likes of you." By the start of the 1980s, 342 restrictive race laws were on the statute book and another 100 parliamentary acts limited press freedom. Together they promoted a head-in-the-sand sense of false security among whites which was reinforced by the short-term economic boom. For their part, blacks inside South Africa were marginalised and divided at this time and, Tutu aside, largely leaderless, rarely risking a direct challenge. Botha, as a result, was able to press on with various divide-and-rule tactics and wasteful, dead-end policies such as the creation of unviable black "homelands."

As a white, it was all too easy to get up in the morning and think that South Africa worked – to ignore the daily charade in parliament, the biased and tendentious reporting in the media and on government-controlled outlets such as the SABC (South African Broadcasting Corporation), the iniquitous pass laws, police suppression of any challenge to white authority, and the all-enveloping red tape of the apartheid system which tied up the simplest matter if you happened to be born black. One day I was brought face to face with this other side of life. We shared a gardener called Ian with Marsh Clark, *Time's* bureau chief in Johannesburg, who lived nearby. Ian came from Rhodesia and lived a split life, returning home once a year. Every time he came back to South Africa he had to renew his work permit. In 1981 permission was refused, and he faced deportation. Marsh and I sallied forth to the bowels of apartheid to vouch for him and ended up at a dank, squalid building in central Johannesburg besieged by blacks in the same position as Ian. Here we entered a Kafkaesque world where no one took responsibility, no one answered your question, no one knew anything and no one wanted to deal with your problem. After several hours moving fruitlessly from one booth to another, it was clear to us that you could get lost in this maze for ever. So we decided to play the only card we had – to inform our faceless tormentors that we were foreign correspondents and all this obstruction was giving us excellent material to write about the reality of apartheid. The threat touched a button, and Ian had his work permit renewed. He was fortunate. At the time tens of thousands of foreign migrant workers were being expelled from South Africa each year, driven in trucks to the Rhodesian or Angolan or Botswanan border and dumped.

Mostly, though, we lived in a white bubble. Initially Jean had to sort out some serious health problems left over from our years in the Soviet Union. Once this was achieved, she took several jobs which circumvented the ban on local employment including working in a charity shop in glitzy Hyde Park that sold items made in Soweto, helping out at an art gallery at Wittwatersrand University and selling clothes to the spoiled white ladies of the northern suburbs at an upmarket dress shop in Rosebank which rewarded her in kind. We entertained and were entertained a lot, often at a high level befitting our curiosity value as refugees from Russia. And I played golf whenever I could and had some unusual and revealing encounters, including a memorable round with the tetchy former British Open champion Bobby Locke – by then a shadow of his old self and prone to embarrassing flashes of temper at the expense of his black caddies.

A few interesting local assignments did trickle in including a highly staged press visit to the Nambia/Angola border just days before the South African Army invaded Angola in June 1980 (we got no inkling of what was to come), and an edited 'Conversation with . . .' the golfer Gary Player. This was held in Player's enormous thatched house surrounded by a riding school and training track. Getting Player, then 45 and on a hectic world schedule, to sit still in a chair was a feat, but once he began talking it was hard to stop him. Later, after we visited Washington on "home" leave early in 1981 (and found the magazine mired in petty politicking and my African coverage damned by faint praise), I was given four pages to describe the varying attitudes to race and the future that coursed through South Africa. Asked to dig out in-depth profiles of individuals from different race groups to tell the story – a belated act of contrition by my editors that resulted in a prize-winning feature – I was delighted to oblige. But this piece truly was the exception. When the country held an important (whites only) election in 1981, my analysis was returned to me for a hasty rewrite and then never used – the one time this happened to me in 30 years in journalism. It reflected, of course, the crippling lack of interest in the politics of South Africa among my editors and, most probably, the American public.

By way of compensation – a huge compensation – we travelled as much as we could, and the unique sights and sounds we met as we moved around are the memories of Africa which remain most vivid decades later. In South Africa we journeyed everywhere, once spending a week in the black homeland of Transkei – "just like Titipu in the Mikado" I wrote – to see if there was any reality behind the claims of black rural development. There wasn't. But we enjoyed the magnificent scenery, the deserted beaches and the memorable spectacle of female porters carrying our heavy suitcases on their heads. One December we drove to Swaziland and spent five rainy days on a mountainside near Mbabane. On other occasions we explored the Garden Route from Cape Town to Port Elizabeth, drove through the Drakensberg mountains and stumbled across gold mining ghost towns in Eastern Transvaal. In Namibia we slid down massive sand dunes and took tea and cakes in a refined German café in Swakopmund. Flying in to Rhodesia, we corkscrewed down to a small landing strip near Victoria Falls to avoid missiles from Zambia, and hiked in the Mtopos hills in eastern Zimbabwe to the breathtaking "World View" where Cecil Rhodes is buried. However traffic-free the road, however hot and tiring the journey, a friendly African face was never far away. Nor, in those days, was white influence. Once, in a remote golf clubhouse in the middle of nowhere in Rhodesia, a middle aged white woman strolled into the bar, sat down and opened a Harrod's carrier bag to show off her latest purchases in London. It seemed quite normal to everyone there but me.

At least Rhodesia/Zimbabwe provided a running story of sorts as the black liberation war wound down, the first multi-racial government was formed and the Mugabe era began in early 1980. I never had much sympathy for Rhodesia's whites – "a miserable bunch" (I wrote once) "stuck in a time warp where the British Empire is intact and the virtues of King and Country go unchallenged." Many, like the stubborn prime minister Ian Smith, fought valiantly for Britain in the Second World War, but by the mid-1970s that period already belonged to history. Whites in Rhodesia never got it. Salisbury began to resemble a down-at-heel Cheltenham, armed patrols accompanied us on a tourist jaunt up the Zambesi, most of the white population ended up spending six months a year on military service, travel outside any town became hazardous in the extreme, and everywhere one went the pitiful sight of African refugees streaming into desolate cardboard slums which sprang up around the major urban centres reminded one of the huge human cost of what was always an unwinnable war.

I interviewed "good old Smithy" twice – on the second occasion because, embarrassingly for his officials, their Japanese-made tape recorder failed to work thanks to the economic sanctions which were making it hard for everyone to acquire spare parts. Though normally dour and humourless, Smith took this particular setback in notable good spirits. Socially awkward, he avoided publicity, but by the time we met in 1979 was desperate for external support. He was also hard to pin down, shrewder than his rough-hewn image might have suggested and courageous – as his lone stand in parliament against the excesses of black rule later underlined. The catastrophe which overtook Zimbabwe under Robert Mugabe's tyrannical government hardly vindicates the 15-year civil war to protect white rule which followed Smith's unilateral declaration of independence. But perhaps it makes it more understandable.

Africa, sadly, offered all too many disaster stories like Zimbabwe for a western correspondent in search of a strong story. As Africa Editor I was supposed to travel or, at a minimum, to make story suggestions involving travel. Invariably they seemed to involve coups, famines, corruption and post-colonial failure and disillusion. Western reporters were forever being attacked by Third World zealots back home for this focus on the negative but, in reality, there was very little else to report. I did once get a story into *US News* about African conservation, but even this had a negative tinge – it was all about species at risk from poaching or land grabs or drought. Upbeat articles were apt to produce a yawn. One such, about Botswana, did run in the magazine eventually in order to justify an overnight trip to Gaborone to acquire a second passport from the UK High Commission there and a means to apply for more than one visa at a time. Mostly, though, Africa was its own worst enemy – shakedowns at airports, sleaze around visas, endless prevarication about appointments, offhand indifference and pointless delay at every turn. Nothing was ever gained by trying to force an issue to a head or throwing one's weight around; it just made things worse. I found that dogged persistence was usually the best tactic, but the gulf of understanding with editors in Washington was unbridgeable. They lived in a world where things worked. I lived in a world of excuses and lethargy.

Three reporting trips in 1980 stand out nevertheless – to Mozambique in its Marxist pre-Commonwealth phase; to Uganda following the overthrow of Idi Amin; and to Liberia soon after the violent coup that brought Master Sergeant Samuel Doe to power. At least it was straightforward to get into Mozambique – one just drove east from Johannesburg and, for all the paper enmity between the apartheid regime in Pretoria and the Marxist Frelimo government in Maputo, at the border one was waved through with a smile. Jean was accompanying me on this occasion to take advantage of a few days relaxation at the famed Polana Hotel in Maputo – one of the classic colonial era hotels of Africa where I had enjoyed a luxurious stay six years earlier as the Portuguese were exiting. Washington had cabled that a story on Mozambique's re-education camps was "urgently" required. That was a first. But from the moment we entered the Polana and sniffed the familiar odour of Aeroflot carbolic soap – a sure sign that Russians were in occupation – things went awry. The (once and future) five-star hotel now had no toilet paper or hot water. Light bulbs were rationed. Room service no longer existed. At breakfast most mornings it was a question of stale rolls, coffee and nothing else. The command economy had taken over.

After some days of hard lobbying of government officials I teamed up with Jay Ross of the *Washington Post* and we were promised a trip to a camp said to be 50 miles north of Maputo. One hot, sunny April morning around 7.00am, wearing a cotton shirt, carrying a water bottle and camera and promising to be back that evening, the two of us set off with a driver and interpreter provided by the Information Ministry. It quickly became apparent that the driver had no idea where he was going and nor did the interpreter. We kept stopping to make navigational inquiries (these were the days before sat navs and mobile phones). After a couple of hours we branched off the highway on to a sandy track that snaked its way through dense plantations of cassava (tapioca). This made it impossible to judge where we were going or how we would get out. Lunchtime came and went and we ploughed on.

Around 4.00pm, having driven 250 miles into the middle of nowhere northwest of Maputo, with the sun going down and our nerves in shreds, we stumbled on Chirumo re-education camp and its 750 internees. There was barely time to take a photo or interview more than a handful of inmates before our guide was insisting that we get back to the coast before nightfall. After a few hurried exchanges we set off, reaching a war-damaged, deserted hotel on a beach where a couple of rooms still had beds and there was food and drink nearby. Back at the Polana, Jean had no money and my credit cards were unusable. The management refused to let her sign for anything and she got more and more anxious as the hours ticked by without word from us. After a miserable night for everyone, we met up next day in the hotel some 30 hours after we left, unwashed and unshaven and at odds with our hosts. We had, however, reached one of the five camps causing waves in Washington. Chirumo turned out to house convicted criminals and resembled a military-style youth training job scheme in the bush rather than a Marxist indocrination centre. We rushed back to Johannesburg and filed our stories. Mine appeared in print three months later, long after Jay had thoroughly debunked the latest African "Red-scare."

The visit to Uganda in August was altogether more alarming. Idi Amin had been removed from power by an invading Tanzanian force some months earlier, but Kampala remained in a terrible mess and the country was ruled by decree by a military commission that would not, or could not, contain growing political violence. Nothing worked, the one hotel in town had degenerated into a cesspit, the atmosphere everywhere was repressive and suspicion of foreigners was endemic. Schools and hospitals had closed and rows of shops, once owned by Asians expelled by Amin, stood abandoned and gutted. A dusk-to-dawn curfew was in place, the noise of shooting regularly disturbed the humid night air and roadblocks manned by wildly excitable armed youths were positioned round every corner.

US News had a stringer in Nairobi called John Worrall and he arranged for me to stay with his son Nick who was freelancing for the *BBC* at the time in Kampala. It was a fortuitous bit of networking – typical, in my experience, of the way journalists in foreign lands tend to look out for each other in dangerous circumstances. Nick possessed one of the two functioning telexes in town. He also had floor space on which to bed down, in a house without furniture or food that he was renting a short way out of the city. Each morning and evening we ran the gauntlet in Nick's Land Rover to and from his office. As a commute, it was hazardous in the extreme. Every intersection or bend in the road seemed to herald a new threat, and when we did make it back in the evening it was to be besieged by locals with new horror stories or urgent pleas for help. Soon after I left Uganda following an edgy week-long visit, Nick decided that enough was enough and pulled out. By then law and order had collapsed totally as had any semblance of central authority. Even shoe shine boys on the street were deserting Kampala; they had no foreign exchange left to buy imported boot polish. My report on the country in October, 1980 – "Uganda Near Bottom And Still Sliding" – pulled no punches, describing in gruesome detail the self-inflicted disintegration of yet another African state.

Uganda, however, proved only a warm-up for my next disaster port-of-call the following month. Earlier in 1980 a particularly bloodthirsty coup had taken place in Liberia, the West African state established by freed American slaves in 1847. The old Americo-Liberian elite was butchered by indigenous Liberians, and a tribal-based regime headed by an illiterate 29-year old sergeant in the previously moribund army proceeded to cosy up to the Soviets, Libyans and Ethiopians. At that point even *US News* sat up and took notice, given that Liberia was still regarded as a "strategic" American asset in the East-West struggle for influence in Africa. However, getting to Monrovia from Johannesburg via Nairobi was an epic in itself and took the best part of a week, with numerous stops in central and west Africa en route. In Togo I remember buying a bottle of beer in the airport transit lounge with a label showing the image of the head of state, one Gnassingbe Eyadema. Another sergeant who seized power in a violent coup, Eyadema lasted from 1967 to his death in 2005. Doe was not to be so fortunate, being murdered in 1990.

Landing at Robertsfield aerodrome and bribing my way through customs, the 35-mile journey into Monrovia, Liberia's capital, was enlivened by the taxi driver attempting to sell me a unique 13-month calendar. Thirteen members of the previous government had been executed by firing squad on a beach in Monrovia, and each month of the 1981 calendar showed one of them slumped against a telegraph pole jammed in the sand having been shot. The extra month, I was told, was for "luck." Delighted that I bought the calendar (it seemed wisest), the driver took me to the common grave into which former President Tolbert's body had been dumped and to the beach on which the executions had taken place. Only then did we head for the hotel. It was a suitably grisly introduction to a shell-shocked society awash with fear, rumour and menacing undercurrents where rats, it was alleged at the time, were eating hospital patients. Rather aptly, it deluged with rain each day I was in the country, adding to the general sense of decay and gloom.

Monrovia proved to be a rundown shambles. The streets were full to overflowing with sewage and garbage and angry young men seeking out the remnants of the *ancien regime*. The two large hotels in town were deserted except for ten members of the revolutionary council staying with me and a dozen other misfits in the Intercontinental. We eyed each other warily over breakfast. The elaborate senate building was gutted. The telephone system barely worked, but in any case no one knew the right number since so many of those listed in the one directory had been killed or had fled the country. Doe was an alarming fiend overshadowing every meeting and discussion – fearfully praised to the skies, rather like Stalin during the purges in Russia in the 1930s, and similarly arbitrary with his favours and hard to read. One Sunday morning his newly-appointed finance minister, Dr Tippoteh, invited me to his ministry for a chat. He opened the door of the building himself, glancing furtively down the street to see if he had been observed. Inside his office, having quickly explained that Liberia was bust, he opened his briefcase and pulled out a sheet of A4 paper on which he had listed his entire worldly assets. "Do you think they're reasonable?" he asked me rather plaintively. They seemed modest enough except, I suggested gently, for the large Rolex watch he was wearing. Doe had demanded that all his civilian officials give a full account of their possessions at a crucial meeting next day – and you just never knew what the Master Sergeant might seize on. Tippoteh, an educated man, must have realised he was skating on thin ice. Soon after, he resigned, citing human rights abuses.

A day or two after this revealing encounter the phone in my hotel room rang – an event in itself – and it was Doe's office summoning me to attend a broadcast to the nation to be made that same day by "Our Redeemer." One did not turn down such invitations, especially as the chance to ask a question or two was dangled. The master sergeant, it was whispered, would be announcing further executions. At the appointed time I arrived at the radio station and found that only one other reporter was there – a down-at-heel Russian from *TASS*, the Soviet news agency. This proved to be the first and last time in my career that, as I saw it at the time, true East-West goodwill prevailed. It helped that I spoke a bit of Russian. Six months later I bumped into my former Russian language teacher, Alexander Fainstein, in Rome on one of his foreign excursions. He recounted how he had been reading a Soviet newspaper in London the month before and had come across an account of this meeting written up by the man from *TASS*. Our encounter, he wrote, had been anything but friendly and I was still the "well-known anti-Soviet slanderer."

Face to face with Doe, things had seemed a little different. The two of us were ordered to sit side by side in the middle of a row of chairs opposite a rectangular table festooned with microphones. Doe swaggered in, wearing his trademark battle fatigues and expensive tinted glasses and armed with a pistol. He glowered across the room, sat down and began speaking off the cuff in a lilting sing-song English that had its roots in the American Deep South 150 years before. At one point he stopped and stared at us. "What are you writing?" he demanded. We stopped writing. The monologue went on, more executions were threatened and then Doe suddenly got up and left us alone and somewhat nonplussed. For once I was glad not to have had the chance to ask a question. Almost none of this drama appeared in the piece *US News* grudgingly ran, after repeated prompts from me, two months later.

So our African interlude proceeded. In December 1980, in measures directed at the foreign staff, Editor Stone slashed our cost-of-living allowance by 80%, closed the Johannesburg bureau from the following September and announced that I would be moving to Rome as

Mediterranean Regional Editor. There was to be no discussion. I was sad that my African posting had proved so unrewarding professionally – "it often seemed more like an extended vacation," I wrote in a letter at the end of 1980, "but even holidays pale after a time." I knew that I had not done full justice to the continent or to its people. Our expeditions far and wide had often been exceptional, the incomparably beautiful and matchless sights and sounds and smells of Africa would remain with me as would the memory of the friendly, if all too often fallible, people I met along the way. But career-wise Africa had proved to be a sideshow and South Africa, in particular, was treading water. In a departing interview with the *Rand Daily Mail,* and a self-interview in *US News,* the more-in-sorrow-than-in-anger verdict I gave was that I had been witness to a missed opportunity in South Africa. By 1981 it was already too late for whites in the republic to determine the pace and scope of change and by then no outside power, and certainly not the United States or Britain, was going to come to their rescue. They were on their own – and tough economic sanctions seemed probable sooner rather than later.

A postcript to my South African experiences came five years later. By then I was back in London and the magazine had been sold, but I still had responsibility for Africa. In 1985 I made a long visit to the republic and again pressed for that elusive on-the-record interview with PW Botha. Nothing came of it then, but the next year the South African embassy in London let me know that a meeting might be possible in April. *US News* was in chaos and no one would take a decision, so I took a chance and flew to Cape Town and waited. Eventually six weeks passed and it became clear that the Botha regime, too, was in turmoil and the rigidities of apartheid were under real pressure. I filled the time by interviewing everyone I could think of in the country to build a snapshot of the period. At the end of April things calmed down, and the interview was set for the following week. At this point *US News* woke up and my latest (and least effectual) foreign editor called with an incredible proposition – I must persuade the South Africans to delay the interview until the end of June when the magazine's new owner, Mortimer B Zuckerman, and his multipurpose sidekick Seweryn Bialer, expected to be in the country "as guests of the government." Having spent seven years getting this far I felt as though I had been stabbed in the back by my own side. I went through the motions, got a suitably dusty response from the Information Ministry and proceeded as though nothing had happened. My time with Botha was then cut from an hour to half an hour, whether in retaliation for Zuckerman's impertinence or not I never found out.

On the day PW was in a cheerful mood and rather defied his taciturn reputation. Right out he wrong-footed me by saying that he had read *US News* and had quoted approvingly from it in a speech the previous weekend. He then changed tack abruptly and alluded to Proverbs 28, verse 2, saying that 3,000 years ago it had diagnosed the right prescription for ruling South Africa in 1986. Louise Gubb, the able photographer who accompanied me to the interview, later called a friend who unearthed the relevant quotation for us heathens – "When a country is in rebellion, it has many rulers, but a man of understanding and knowledge maintains order." What Botha failed to mention was the very next verse – "A ruler who oppresses the poor is like a driving rain that leaves no crops." All reference to Proverbs was cut out of the published version by Botha's aides – one of the occupational hazards of *US News's* authorised Q&A format. The actual interview was run-of-the-mill stuff and made no waves, although it did contain a revealing jab at Mandela to the effect that he preferred to stay in jail rather than negotiate. Visibly in his dotage by then, Botha had trouble moving his hands. He compensated with a relentless stare that dared his interlocutor to disagree, and seemed untroubled by any self-doubt whatsoever, rather like one of his authoritarian predecessors "Oom Paul" Kruger.

Interview over, the South Africans then tried to double-cross us by demanding that *US News* publish the entire unedited text or nothing. After two days' stand-off, and protracted person-to-person negotiations with Louis Nel, the Information Minister, we came to a compromise – eleven of the sixteen questions in the interview survived intact. But we lost an important answer about the possibility of a black president (Botha said it was "theoretically" possible) and several other answers were watered down. Some of this, it's true, reflected an underlying Afrikaner unease with the nuances of the English language. But it also underlined the white minority regime's increasing distance from reality.

Trying to convince me later that PW Botha was really a closet radical, Jack Viviers, his devious and notoriously unreliable spokesman, claimed that the most significant race reform in the world in the 1980s had been the repeal of South Africa's Immorality Act – because a great psychological burden had been removed from the shoulders of a white man forced to share a lift (elevator) with a black person. He also stated with a straight face that Britain had imperialistic designs on South Africa. Viviers was usually accompanied by a shadowy individual from Botha's office who called himself Dr Prinsloo. The day after the Botha interview Prinsloo telephoned and asked if he could meet me alone. A discussion ensued around one point – what should South Africans do in the current circumstances? Needless to say, I advocated talks with the ANC, little knowing that around this precise time Niel Barnard had begun to sound out Mandela on Robben Island.

This drama lay nearly five years down the road as a huge Zulu overseer arrived with a container and a dozen workers to begin our evacuation from Sturdee Avenue in August 1981. We said goodbye to the amazing array of birds and plants in the garden, ate our last breakfast on the terrace in the shadow of a large jacaranda tree and followed the removal van down the road. Before too much longer the house had been razed to make way for an art deco-style office block. South Africa itself proved to have a more enduring impact. I returned many times to report on the end of apartheid and the arrival of black rule. Later Jean and I trooped south for ten years in a row to grab some winter sun in Hout Bay, near Cape Town, play golf and look up old friends. Yet at the time the negatives of living and reporting in what was then an isolated, claustrophic and truly "very strange society" seemed to outweigh the positives by some considerable margin.

7

Midlife Surprises

*"Life is a gamble at terrible odds. If it was a bet,
you wouldn't take it."*

Tom Stoppard

If there is one piece of advice worth passing on from our Italian *intermezzo* it is not to arrive in Rome for the first time in August. *Ferragosto* is the most important holiday in Italy. All the Romans who can leave the city, do so – and head for the coast or the hills. We flew into a humid, stifling oven in mid-August 1981 to discover empty streets, closed shops and shuttered restaurants. Officials were conspicuous by their absence, newspapers half their normal size and the chances of seeing a dentist non-existent. A deceptive calm prevailed, what traffic there was flowed quietly and freely, and even dogs sought out shady nooks under the large plane trees lining the *Lungotevere* and let the world go by.

Perhaps we should have done the same. But, as usual, *US News* was on our backs to find somewhere to live as soon as we touched down. Our possessions were trundling north by sea and we were keen to settle ourselves too. We had barely begun searching for a flat when I was sent off to Madrid, and then to Athens, with Jean in tow. A month after our arrival, and still homeless, we were getting anxious. When a large unfurnished apartment with lizards and geraniums adorning its generous balcony, and elegant black and white marble tiles on its entrance hall floor, came to our attention on Via Nemea, we quickly signed on the dotted line. There were shops nearby and it was only 20 minutes by the orange ATAC 911 bus to the magazine's office in the *centro storico*. It was a big mistake – as we realised within another month when the schools in Vigna Clara reopened, flotillas of scooters driven by hairy teenagers roared by our building four times a day on their way to and from a nearby technical college and traffic screeched round the sharp lefthand turn at the end of our road. Physically, we retreated into a room at the back of the apartment and rarely re-emerged. Mentally, we decided there and then that we would spend as much time as possible getting to know the rest of Italy.

As it turned out, our initial *faux pas* was the making of our years in Rome. Because of it we journeyed the length and breadth of the Italian peninsula and saw and experienced much that otherwise might have passed us by. Because of it, we never settled into a routine in Rome – if such a thing was possible in such a frenetic environment. Because of it, and the nature of the job I had, we enjoyed a taste of life in continental Europe instead of living in an expatriate bubble. Italy was memorable – a constant clash between the emotions. On the one hand, chaos, strikes, drama, inefficiency, red tape, cynicism, frustration. On the other, unrivalled beauty, friendliness, history round every corner, style, breathtaking culture and an epicurean feast of the senses. As a story for *US News* the country barely rated – like poor old Canada, forever taken for granted and dismissed in a paragraph or two by the prevailing American orthodoxy. As an education and an adventure in life, it took some beating.

For a time the practicalities of moving in and getting to know Rome had priority. The apartment contained nothing at all – not even light bulbs or a kitchen stove or a sink. "Unfurnished" in Italy, we learned the hard way, means unfurnished. We bought a few household items, but baulked at cupboards and hung our clothes in cut-out cardboard moving cartons for the next two years. The *US News* office, located in Piazza Augusto Imperatore in a Mussolini-era complex still adorned with *fasces* (sticks and axe) insignia, was owned by the Croatian College in Rome. The lift smelled of camphor and the monks proved to be tough negotiators. Things had slid badly during the seven-year tenure of my ageing predecessor, and it took months to clear out the mounds of old newspapers and old files, re-decorate and reorganise. Almost none of the so-called office "contacts" existed in reality and, once again, it was a question of starting from scratch. I did, though, inherit a pretty young part-time secretary called Miriam Codutti who was relieved to have some real work to do at last. She became my Girl Friday and an invaluable source of local information, contacts and insights. She was also a true Roman. One day I asked her where I could get a pair of shoes repaired. Chracteristically, she replied that she never had shoes repaired and always threw them away when the heels wore down! *Bella figura* (cutting a dash) still mattered in Rome in the early 1980s.

It was Miriam who unearthed a competent and tolerant (of my frequent absences) language teacher – a Canadian married to a university professor – and a keen young wire service reporter called Phil Pullela to act as a stringer. She also opened negotiations with the firm of Italian lawyers downstairs who had designs on our unused office space. Eventually we sub-let two rooms to them and in return got access to their telex machine. One of the lawyers, an engaging cynic, became a regular lunchtime companion, introducing me to a down-at-heel cafe in a cobbled backstreet behind the fruit and vegetable market near the office. The *pasta* was out of this world. Restaurants were still cheap – this was the era before the euro – so we ate out a lot, and in two years I reviewed nearly sixty Rome restaurants in a day-book which I kept.

That said, money was always a problem for us in Italy. Of all the places I was based abroad, Rome was by far the most expensive. To make matters worse, in 1981 *US News* introduced a new cost-of-living allowance system for its correspondents abroad. In South Africa this had led to an 80% drop in the payments to me. In Italy I got nothing at all – the only US-accredited correspondent in Rome in such a position. Even our stringer received $350 a month from impecunious *UPI* to help with the cost of his housing. At *US News* there was also no office car and no budget for interpreters, while a new air conditioner was deemed to be a luxury and even the purchase of local newspapers was scrutinised minutely. Matters got worse after we left Rome to the point where the Trimbles, our youthful successors, had to scrape by like students having been informed by the editor before they left Washington that on no account were they to produce any offspring (they ignored this stricture, with happy results). With hindsight it is obvious that the magazine was living beyond its means and could no longer afford a network of bureaus across Europe. At the time it was not so clear. Every month, however, would bring a new cutback or complaint from Washington – and a fresh protest from me about our situation. Through membership of *L'Associazione della Stampa Estera* (the Foreign Press Association) I did qualify for some discounts, including on rail travel and Italian-made cars. So I bought a blue Fiat 131 and took to the roads. Driving in Rome proved to be a life-and-death matter at which only the most cut-throat thrived – "all you can do to survive is to behave similarly," I noted wryly on one occasion. Before long we were acting like Romans, if not thinking like them. That would have taken a lifetime.

Settling Jean into the rhythm of Italian life was more difficult. Her options were limited. She wanted to travel with me when she could, she had to go back to London for medical treatment from time to time and she spoke little Italian – certainly not enough to work in a local environment. The obvious answer was to worm her way into FAO – the United Nations Food & Agriculture Organisation, headquartered opposite the ruins of the chariot-racing Circus Maximus – as a secretary or typist. This she did, even on one occasion working in the office of the director general. Mostly, though, she got by on short term contracts lasting a month or two. During the 26 months we lived in the Italian capital she must have had a dozen of these mini-contracts amounting to about 15 months' work, much of it involving unsocial hours and a 75-minute commute by bus across the city. Every job she did seemed to be a success. Yet it counted for nothing in the labyrinthine, politicized bureaucracy of this archetypal UN agency. Headed at the time by a Lebanese carpet salesman, FAO resembled a madhouse in which vindictiveness and pettiness were actively encouraged by unaccountable management. Too often to recall, she would come home "bemused and unhappy" as she put it. The alternative was to stay in the apartment, read voraciously and be bored out of her mind, particularly when she was on her own during my many absences.

So Italy was not all milk-and-honey. But we made many unforgetable trips around this timeless, vibrant, stimulating land, behaved like professional tourists, criss-crossed Tuscany and Umbria, Lazio and Marche, visited great cities like Naples, Milan and Venice, went to an opera at *La Scala* free (another *Stampa Estera* perk), attended a glittering Italian National Day reception in the beautiful grounds of the Quirinale Palace (made remarkable by the failure of the 86-year old president, Sandro Pertini, to do up his flies), were summoned to the Vatican one Saturday morning for a stern papal lecture on the responsibilities of journalists, drove the *autostrade* at breakneck speed north and south from Rome, and learned to make the very most of every free weekend and every opportunity. Along the way we made some lasting friends, notably James Buxton of the *Financial Times* and his wife Anna who lived up the road from us in a superior compound. The US ambassador, a homespun lawyer called Maxwell Rabb, took a shine to us and we were invited often to Villa Taverna, his sumptuous residence in the Borghese Gardens, for buffet dinners followed by Hollywood films like "The Verdict" and "Absence of Malice." Rabb tended to stir up conflicting views. My old sparring partner in Moscow, Ambassador Toon, by now retired to the golf courses of North Carolina, caused some controversy by saying that Rabb was not qualified to run a garage let alone an embassy, and I wrote once that he "really ought to be selling soap." Yet the truth was that Rabb's warm, encouraging style was just what the widely-disparaged, despondent Italians needed in the early 1980s rather than stern lectures about their responsibilities – even if they were unable to understand a word he said (Rabb spoke no Italian).

Work was another matter. By the time I left Rome after a couple of years I had compiled a respectable, if not overflowing, portfolio of articles with an Italian flavour, notably two long features on the challenges facing Venice and Naples, an obligatory piece about the fight against the Mafia, in-depth "Conversations with . . ." the author Luigi Barzini (then dying of cancer) and the famous Italian-American conductor Gian Carlo Menotti at his base in Spoleto, as well as a memo which surprisingly made it into print about "The ties that bind," (see Appendix) which was written on the spur of the moment after a haunting visit to the US World War II cemetery at Nettuno, near Anzio. But mostly it was a struggle to interest anyone in Washington about things Italian.

As Jean and I understood, to justify my existence I had to travel – something the magazine, for all its parsimony in other areas, was prepared to fund. There was plenty of scope. On paper I was responsible for covering no less than 41 countries, any one of which might flare overnight into the international spotlight. In-depth, consistent attention was impossible. Instead, in time-honoured newsmagazine style, the trick was to dip in and out of places and situations ahead of events and crises, so providing a reader in far-away Middle America with the all-important "context" on which *US News* based much of its appeal. In my case this meant, overwhelmingly, keeping a weather eye open to trends and events in the Mediterranean region and the neighbouring Middle East. I got off to a fast start in my first ten weeks with the visits to Spain (to preview a royal trip to the US) and Greece (before a general election), followed soon after by a foray to Egypt to cover a military exercise, and it went on like this for the next two years.

Early in 1982 I made a fascinating trip to Morocco, at the time an increasingly high-profile ally of the United States. King Hassan and his entourage had decamped to Paris but the US ambassador, a lonely fellow called Joseph Verner Reed who had once been the Shah of Iran's personal banker, proved unusually cooperative, having me to lunch two days running at his residence and opening a number of doors for me. All too often, this cut-price method of working proved to be the pattern. Lacking contacts and not allowed by the magazine's frugality to hire local "fixers," I was forced to rely on the diplomatic and international community, at least initially. Rarely hanging around anywhere longer than a week, there was never much chance of putting the time in to develop good local contacts. The skill, such as it was, came from absorbing information quickly, sensing the best story angle as soon as possible, taking advantage of any interview on offer, being totally adaptable, adding touches of local colour to the text to show that you had been on the spot, and writing fluently and fast. Not for nothing have foreign correspondents been defined as "an inch deep and a mile wide"!

In June 1982, when Israel invaded southern Lebanon following the assassination of the country's ambassador to the UK, our luckless Mideast correspondent (normally resident in Beirut) was on holiday in London. Only two months earlier I had spent ten touristy days based in Jerusalem holding the fort while he took an earlier break. Jean travelled with me on that occasion and we celebrated our tenth wedding anniversary on top of Masada. Now I was sent back to Israel for an indefinite period, but not before I applied for a Syrian visa in Rome. Lebanon would go uncovered throughout the next dramatic month – an unfortunate fiasco which the magazine managed to conceal. By some miracle our Mideast man reached Israel within a day or two of fighting beginning just as my visa to Syria came through. Back I flew to Rome to collect it, and then off again to Damascus where I remained for the next four weeks, holed up in the fortress-like Sheraton Hotel. It was a wearisome interlude. Over the rest of the year I was to spend half my time criss-crossing the region, almost always chasing after events. *US News* simply lacked the drive, imagination and resources to get enough people in place enough of the time.

While marooned in Syria I watched World Cup soccer on television, did some sightseeing in the searing heat and spent hours each morning trailing round government ministries seeking access to the war front or interviews with high-ranking officials. In such a tightly-controlled and secretive society, other sources were meaningless. Next to nothing materialised. The US embassy proved almost as unhelpful and there is a limit to how often one can quote "men-in-the-street." Then I had a stroke of luck and ran into the UK military attache. He was a mine of useful information. Better still, he invited me to join him for a "picnic" on his daily excursions to the hills above the Bekaa valley. On our arrival at a suitable vantage point he draped a large Union Jack over the roof of his car, opened a bottle of red wine and spent hours peering through binoculars while giving me a running commentary on the tank and air battles raging nearby. It was this expert who advised me to get up early each morning to witness the wreckage of the Syrian armed forces being towed back to base through the darkened, silent streets. No word of the military disaster the Assad regime suffered in this ill-judged war was allowed to reach the Syrian population, but the deception fooled few. As I wandered through a bazaar in Damascus one day, people crowded around me clamouring to know why the Americans were attacking them – the official reason given to cover all setbacks. Reading the pieces I wrote from Syria years later, all I can say is that they contain some well-informed military detail!

My other journalistic preoccupation in Rome was the Vatican in general and Pope John Paul II in particular. No Pope in modern times caught the imagination of the world, or the media, quite like this one. A failed assassination attempt in 1981 before we reached Rome had left John Paul physically weaker, but he remained a charismatic, almost messianic figure whose every saying resonated, above all behind the Iron Curtain. Yet the Vatican's sudden ability to capture and dominate global headlines in no way reflected its cool and arms-length relationship with the world's press. "Covering" the Vatican reminded me greatly of writing about the Kremlin. There was no real access, the official papal spokesman was an obstacle rather than a facilitator, and intuition and speculation (often originating from disenchanted Jesuits who were in Rome to have their wrists slapped) counted for far more than the occasional contact one was permitted with members of the Curia.

One evening I found myself sitting next to the self-righteous papal nuncio to Italy at a dinner party. He proceeded to spend the meal haranguing me about the negative attitude of the press to the "trivial" Vatican Bank scandal then unfolding. Not long after, thanks to a mutual friend, I played golf at the Acquasanta Club with Archbishop Paul Marcinkus, the smug American prelate who headed this peculiar financial institution. Stonewalling for 18 long holes, he arrogantly assumed that a blank refusal to discuss or even acknowledge an issue to the press would make it go away. It was a disastrous miscalculation, born of a complete and willful lack of understanding of how the modern media works. Forced out of the bank soon after, Marcinkus departed with the immortal words, "You can't run the church on Hail Marys." The Vatican then had to find £145 million to clear up the mess he left behind, while the mystery of the death in London in June 1982 of Marcinkus's confidant Roberto Calvi remains unsolved thirty years later.

Most of the time such Vatican shenanigans were of little interest to Washington. John Paul's deeply conservative views on issues like female priests, abortion, contraception and celibacy – Italians dubbed his papacy "the Middle Ages plus television" – sometimes aroused an offkey editorial query usually prompted by some dissident, liberally-minded American prelate informing one of the magazine's US-based reporters that "progressive" change was bound to occur soon. No one covering the Vatican in Rome ever bought into that line. What did interest us all, in contrast, was the Pope's increasingly central involvement in the Cold War, his growing political influence especially in his homeland and how he planned to counter Stalin's mocking query "The Pope? How many divisions has he got?"

By chance, in March 1982 I got a first hand idea of the impact that John Paul was having in Eastern Europe when, out of the blue, I received a visa valid for seven days to go to Poland, then in the icy grip of the post-Solidarity martial law clampdown and largely off limits to international reporters. No one ever explained why I was so favoured. I was no longer the magazine's accredited correspondent in the region, and my record in the USSR was there for all to read. Before anyone could change their mind, I flew into Warsaw and produced one of my best received "country" stories. Even Stone sent a note of congratulation, and the piece ended up being used as a model of how to write for *US News* from abroad – "the ideal mix of interpretation, quotes and on-ground color," or so they said. Maybe it was no coincidence that it is one of the bleakest stories I ever wrote. After a gap of three years away from the communist world I was struck anew by its shabbiness and hopelessness and corrupting cynicism. It was impossible to see communism as a model for anything, anywhere, ever. Economically, the country had run into a cul de sac, utterly dependent on subsidies from Moscow to survive. Politically, there was total stalemate. Nearly forty years after the end of the Second World War rationing was in place in Poland, there were queues for the most basic items, armed soldiers stood on every corner, documents were checked endlessly, telephone calls were openly bugged and even the Poles – one of the most courageous and direct people on earth – thought twice before airing a controversial opinion.

It remained in this stasis fifteen months later when I returned as part of the 60-strong papal press corps covering John Paul's second visit to his homeland. The first, in 1979, by all accounts had been happy and exhilarating. This one in 1983, with martial law in place, the Solidarity movement forced underground and the popular mood weary but unbowed, proved to be much more delicate. Throughout it we reporters sat on the edge of our seats, aware that a single misspoken or misunderstood papal pronouncement might touch off an explosion of unrest or even violence. Yet I never had a more riveting, fascinating eight days on the road. Always moving around Poland by bus ahead of the Pope – he flew by helicopter to ten locations in the eight days – and usually leaving events before him to avoid being hemmed in by the gigantic crowds, trying to interview people on the run, keeping abreast of news developments and having to file en route, proved to be a huge challenge. In the last four days of the trip I got a total of twelve hours sleep and missed most meals, existing on chocolate bars, biscuits and fruit. On one particular day that stands out, I left my base (a student hostel) at 7.00am, got to bed at 3.30am the following morning, was woken up an hour later when my (unknown) companion staggered into the room we were sharing, rose at 6.00am and began another 20 hour day. And I was luckier than most in not having to file daily.

Decades later, it is not the tiredness but the sights and sounds of the huge open air masses which linger in my mind's eye. In Warsaw they used the national soccer stadium. It seated 100,000 people; another 900,000 stood outside. The altar was at the top of the stands so that everyone saw equally. At Katowice they used an old airfield and put a white, 70ft high altar pyramid at the end of the runway. In Wroclaw the press sat in rows in the middle of a horse racing track called the Hippodrome. Honoured guests, such as bishops and choirs, were positioned in the grandstand and John Paul carried out his duties at an altar set up by the finishing post. In Cracow, the Pope's hometown, more than two million people flocked to Blonia, the large park in the centre of the city. It was an unbelievable sight. Yet in intensity it was topped later that same day when John Paul visited Nova Huta, an industrial suburb, to consecrate a newly-built church. Here Solidarity and religious banners unashamedly flew alongside each other as hundreds of thousands of tough-looking, poorly dressed steel workers and their families greeted one of their own and the man they had come to see responded with his most political homily.

US News splashed out and sent a real team to cover this pilgrimage – two reporters and two photographers. We were joined by two interpreters, one officially sanctioned, the other roped in at the last moment when the demands of more than 300 foreign journalists overwhelmed the system. I was lucky. Tomek Kuczborski, a graphic designer and Solidarity activist recently released from jail, turned out to be a gem and led me on a parallel tour of Poland – one of the reasons for my extended working hours. At each stop on the papal route the resourceful Tomek would whisk me off to meet local underground leaders and others of interest, such as Lech Walesa's priest and a leading American cardinal. It was hard to conclude after all this that Solidarity had lost any of its grassroot appeal however harsh the military crackdown. At least three quarters of the applause for John Paul followed his repeated appeals for justice. On every possible occasion the crowds would sing the religious national anthem of Poland ("We want God") with hands upraised in the V for Victory sign which had become Solidarity's symbol. The Pope never missed a trick, got the balance of his message right and ceaselessly repeated his demand for reconciliation and dialogue. Even Poland's buttoned-up and rather sinister dictator, General Jaruzelski, was moved to respond, arranging a meeting with John Paul at the last moment which eventually led to an easing of martial law.

This proved to be my first and last trip with a Pope; one might as well go out on a high! In any case nothing was ever likely to beat this journey for colour, drama, interest and global attention. After it was over, the magazine complimented us on our efforts and we went our separate ways. About five years later I met Tomek again on another reporting visit to Poland, and he confessed that Solidarity had used his role with us as we travelled to convey messages to various of its leaders holed up around the country. Everyone, of course, was using everyone else; I certainly

22 *Benji Pogrund supporting the liberation struggle at the Nederburg wine auctions in 1980.* 23 *On a South African Defence Force's visit to the Namibia-Angola border in 1980.*

24 On a reporting trip to Israel with Jean – in Bethlehem, Easter 1982. **25** On a tough assignment in Venice on a cold March day in 1982.

26 The USN&WR team with Pope John Paul II in Poland June, 1983 – (ltr) Stew Powell, RK, Steve Larsen, Linda Creighton, Tomas Kuzcborski. 27 The bloated USN&WR team at the 1985 Reagan-Gorbachev Geneva summit – Hank Trewhitt second left, Nick Daniloff fourth right, David Gergen third right.

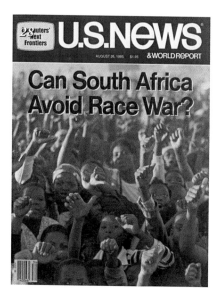

29

30

Previous page: **28** *A South African cover story in US News 26.8.85.* **29** *With photographer Louise Gubb at Ibnet Camp, Ethiopia, in 1985. The baby is dying of starvation and dehydration.* **30** *3, Chiswick Wharf in the snow.*

Above: **31** *Interviewing Erich Honecker of East Germany, December 12th, 1986.* **32** *The PW Botha interview in Cape Town in 1986.*

33 *Albania 1987 - Jeannie in Shkoder.* **34** *Interviewing Borislaw Geremek in Warsaw – my favourite reportorial image of myself.* **35** *Mort Zuckerman with Margaret Thatcher.* **36** *Interviewing President Lech Walesa with Kris Bobinski in 1991.*

37 *Three USN&WR Moscow bureau chiefs together in the office in 1991 (RK, Doug Stanglin, Jeff Trimble).* **38** *The war correspondent in central Bosnia January 1993.* **39** *Under the gun – with Bosnian Serb snipers on the Pale-Sarajevo road in 1993.*

*40 In my local pub behind the office in Picaddily, London, in the early 1990s.
41 At Ambassador Ray Seitz's retirement party with Dan Pedersen & Ray
Moseley.*

benefited, as did the magazine. I returned to a hot and sultry Rome ready to drop. The Pope went off to Castel Gandolfo in the Alban Hills to recover.

It was around this time that a good contact in the British embassy, a youngish bachelor whom I had befriended and lunched with on several occasions, was fingered as an MI6 agent by a rogue officer. A certain gap opened up in our relationship, and we met less frequently. Years later, by which time I was back in London, this same individual popped up again with a startling proposition – would I use any contacts I had inside the South African embassy to compile reports on various individuals there of interest to MI6? I turned him down flat, but was left wondering why anyone in Britain's secret service could ever have hatched such a crazy scheme unless they were desperate for this information. Journalists and spies have always had a murky relationship, often fishing in much the same waters but pursuing fundamentally different aims. Sharing gossip and analysis and opinions with them over a convivial lunch is one thing, working for them quite another.

By early October we had begun to wind down to our departure from Italy with family visits, a recreational trip to the lakes and mountains in the north of the country and a second holiday soon after in the "heel" of Italy which was somewhat disrupted by a lack of electricity in our little villa caused by a mafia-style theft of miles of copper wire from the local grid as we arrived. Then our successors, Jeff and Gretchen Trimble aged 25 and 24 respectively, flew into Rome to take over. At 40, I suddenly felt middle-aged. Italy had been a landmark – unforgettable in itself as much as for anything I achieved professionally. In truth it was always going to be another way stop. Within a year of arriving in Rome, the pressure to move to Washington had resumed, and late in 1982 a deal was agreed. I was to spend two years in the United States from October 1983, and then return to London as the magazine's senior foreign correspondent with "worldwide responsibilities." While in Washington, officially on a "management training course" since I did not have the all-important US green card, I would spend time in various departments of the magazine and Jean would be free to join an international organisation if she could find a job. It was a good offer and this time, we felt, the only alternative was to resign from *US News* and go back to England and start again. Somehow, after 15 years with this idiosyncratic publication, working all over the place for it in so many different circumstances, it seemed a better option to examine close up the reason both for my good fortune and my frequent bewilderment – not to mention irritation and frustration.

Outwardly, at least, *US News* seemed to be going through an expansionist, confident phase. In May 1983 Jean and I had been invited to take part in the magazine's 50th anniversary celebrations. At a grand dinner in the Washington Sheraton Hotel, a Marine band played at full blast followed by dancing to an even noisier Glenn Miller-type ensemble. The Board gazed down on us peons from a high table, for all the world resembling the Politburo presiding in the Kremlin. Later, Vice President Bush laid the cornerstone of a new purpose-built headquarters – part of a $200 million joint venture development with a firm called Boston Properties which also included a couple of hotels on a three and a half acre site owned by the magazine in Washington's West End. Stimulated by this venture, the company's stock, which each of us as employee shareholders owned according to length of service, tripled in value to $470 a share in 1982. A killing had also been made earlier that year by selling off a holding in a start-up computer print technology company. New, younger journalists were being recruited and there had even been extra investment in foreign coverage in the shape of a new bureau in Singapore.

As I was soon to discover, much of this "progress" was illusory. In reality, *US News* was running out of money. In 1982 it made a small loss and had to close its book division. That year, too, it made no contributions to the profit-sharing plan on which many staff counted. The tripling in the value of the stock, and the endemic lack of cash in the company – even in a good year no more than $2 million was ever left in the kitty after all obligations were met – meant that it was unable to buy out shareholders as they retired. Circulation and advertising revenue were stagnating. And in a cut-throat business the stubborn refusal to move the magazine with the times was beginning to make it conspicuous for all the wrong reasons. The chairman of the board, a ponderous chap by the name of John Sweet who had spent too long in the shadow of the magazine's domineering founder, had even given his deadening opinion (in a supposedly upbeat memo to staff in the run-up to the 50th anniversary events) that "fancy writing" had no part to play at *US News*. He went on to boast how the magazine had resisted all efforts to change it or make it more broad-based or "entertaining." Sweet was not a journalist. He was taking his cue from Marv Stone who, having attracted new writing and reporting talent in the late 1970s, then spent much of his time trying to rein it in and mould it to an outdated format.

Many of the people whom I encountered back in Washington left a lot to be desired. In 1970, when I joined the international staff at the age of 27, I was 15 years younger than almost everyone else. On becoming editor in 1976, Stone realised that not much had changed and something drastic had to be done to rejuvenate the domestic staff. His instinct as an old wire service man, surrounded by other wire service types at the top, was to raid *AP* and *UPI,* the two leading American news agencies. So he did. It was a mistake which was to prove fatal when *US News* was sold a few years later. In a short space of time more than twenty new writers and reporters arrived, overwhelmingly from *UPI* which was already in terminal decline. Writing and thinking in weekly terms proved to be completely alien to most of these men (there were a few women too) who previously had been judged professionally by how fast and accurately they filed, not how well they wrote or how expert they were at interpretation or analysis. Much time and effort was wasted trying to adjust the newcomers to the magazine mindset. Many never made it yet hung around, becoming "new" dead wood. Later Stone recognised his error and cast his net wider, but the damage had been done and another nail driven into the Lawrence-era product.

By 1983 I must have made half a dozen "home leave" visits of a couple of weeks at a time to 2300 N Street since 1968, but I soon realised that working there full time was quite another matter. Close up, *US News* came across as a relic of a bygone era – paternalistic, hierarchical, rigid, inward-looking and fatally stuck in its ways. The paternalism translated into jobs for life and perks like an in-house doctor, help with school fees, free parking, a subsidised cafeteria and even free turkeys at Thanksgiving. It was all kindly meant – and utterly inimical to the sort of hard-edged competitiveness that the magazine needed to embrace if it was to survive. Outsiders were almost never hired at senior level. Promotion invariably was from within, seniority was valued far more than talent and new blood and new approaches were mistrusted. The format was so inflexible that editors kept piles of back issues in their offices to search for story ideas. Finding one, they would rip it out and send it upwards with a note attached "This is an evergreen . . . time to revisit."

Nowhere was this paralysis more apparent than in the area *US News* regarded as its life blood – the 'News You Can Use' section. Basically set up to cover consumer issues, it took up large chunks of valuable space and churned out the most amazing piffle. Sample question-and-answer interviews in 1982 (with the text always cleared pre-publication by the interviewee) included 'Why Some People are Always Late' with a psychologist, 'How to Stop Wasting Time' with a management consultant, 'Why You Get Angry' with a psychiatrist, and a showstopper repeated with mind-numbing regularity summer after summer 'How to Guard Against Insect Stings.' To add insult to injury, and a further obstacle to resourcefulness, unless an idea had appeared in print somewhere else (most probably in the *New York Times* or *Washington Post*), any story proposal would inevitably be greeted with morale-sapping suspicion and delay. Initiative, in other words, seemed to carry deeply negative connotations.

Paradoxically, despite 15 years working on the magazine, I appreciated all too little of this when we set off optimistically for Washington early in October 1983. On arrival, our first shock was to be assigned to stay in a down-at-heel duplex suite complete with soiled mattress and filthy bathroom located alongside a busy freeway – the magazine's unsubtle way of announcing that I was no longer living "on the fat of the land" as a foreign correspondent and was henceforth to be treated as a foot soldier. Another row ensued. We ended up renting an unfurnished two-room apartment in a genteel condominium near the Kennedy Centre and George Washington University. Here the only issue we ran into concerned a bird table we wished to attach to our window sill. For the rest it was peaceful and well run – and after Rome, bliss. Jean soon found congenial work at the World Bank, we were able to join a local medical health scheme, the magazine coughed up the rent for our furniture, and both of us were able to do the unthinkable in America and walk to work. At weekends we hired a car if we needed one.

By the time I began my assignment in Washington, however, it had been whittled down from two years to 18 months for reasons unconnected to us. Time, therefore, was short and soon I was fully engaged, finding it tolerably satisfying to put faces to names, to be involved a bit in decision-making and to get to grips for the first time with video display terminals, the precursors of today's desktop computers. Rather unexpectedly, a productive period followed. Over the next 15 months I churned out four Cover stories (all about the USSR to the irritation of Nick Daniloff, the Moscow bureau chief at the time, who generally took a softer line than I did) and three lead articles, including one previewing the 1984 G-7 economic summit in London. Two long features tackled purely American topics – an in-depth examination of the workings of the US Information Agency headed by a piano-playing friend of Ronald Reagan's called Charles Wick; and a lengthy feature on the 'American Dream' which allowed us both to travel to San Antonio and Denver.

In those years Americans felt newly self-confident. "The Gipper," as President Reagan was known from one of his film star roles, had an unrivalled ability to project sunny optimism even after an assassination attempt in 1981. He was lucky too – the economy revived on his watch. Inflation began to abate and the underlying American can-do mentality, so different from British gloom-and-doom, started to kick in. Meantime the shadow of the Vietnam War at last began to lift, and the superpower confrontation tilted decisively America's way as the era of stagnation in the Soviet Union turned into the era of paralysis. Reading my 'American Dream' piece thirty years later at a time of deepening pessimism and bitterness in the US over just about everything, the contrast is stark. Then aspirational hope was alive and kicking among all sections of this huge, diverse land. Hispanics and blacks alike felt there was a future. The middle class felt sure its children would do better than it had. A core belief in upward mobility and opportunity and abundant resources remained the *leitmotif* of the American character and, regardless of the facts or foreigners' irritation with the concept, American exceptionalism was alive and well. No other country on earth, so the popular mantra went, offered more to its citizens or delivered more.

As an outsider it was sometimes tricky to counteract this cockiness without causing offence. After all, in the minds of many of our hosts Jean and I came from a has-been continent and a fading country. Americans' innate good manners and generous hospitality, and our reluctance to provoke an argument with our hosts, meant that confrontation was normally avoided. The best antidote, I found, was just to get on with the job. Many weeks it was hard going as I was deputed to distil dreary bureau reports into another of the magazine's out-of-date staples – "round-ups" from all corners of the globe which purported to give an informed overview on topics such as "world trouble spots" or "world leaders to watch." A spell on the magazine's White House team, led by a generous and well-connected Texan called John Mashek, proved a welcome respite and resulted in a two-page piece headlined 'Fortress in a Fishbowl' which gave a distinctly British perspective on how power was exercised in Washington. Later I was assigned to follow the Reagan and Mondale campaigns in the 1984 presidential election, travelling with both for a few days and observing politics American-style close-up. The razzmatazz was engrossing, the content non-existent, and by the time I caught up with him in early autumn Walter Mondale gave every sign of knowing that he was well beaten. The editors again indulged me with space to compare and contrast US and British elections. In between times I made apearances on several leading current affairs television shows like *'Washington Week in Review'* and the *'McLaughlin Report'* and twice appeared on a challenging early morning radio call-in programme run by C-Span, where my role for a couple of hours was to answer live any question from any part of America about any world issue. Life was anything but monotonous or repetitive.

At weekends we often hired a car and explored Washington or further afield including New York, the beautiful Blue Ridge mountains in Virginia and Williamsburg. One longer break was spent in Charleston and Savannah, another in Colorado. After six months I had to leave the US for a brief visit to Canada to renew my entry visa. Joe Fromm, comfortably ensconced in the No. 3 slot on the top of the masthead, entertained us, as did many others. Thanksgiving, that most American of holidays, was spent one year discovering the delights of grits (coarsely ground corn) and other southern foods with friends who lived in a glass-and-timber house in a wood in Maryland. The natural generosity of Americans, we decided, is never to be under-estimated. At work, too, I was flattered to be invited occasionally by Marv Stone to join his inner circle for dinner on Thursday nights (when much of the magazine went to press) at Le Jardin, his favourite watering hole on 19th Street. It was here, I discovered, that most key decisions were made, to the intense annoyance of those who were not invited. Newspapers and magazines never have been democracies! Time passed quickly. Christmas 1983 was spent happily with our old Moscow friends the Beestons. A couple of weeks earlier the magazine had moved into its gleaming new headquarters building at 2400 N Street, just across the road from its old home. We took the chance of the upheaval to take possession of a much-needed bookcase and carry it down N Street to our apartment one Saturday morning.

Behind the scenes, though, the company was being torn apart by debate at the top about its future, yet until the spring of 1984 I had no real inkling. The problems facing *US News* had come to a head in the autumn of 1983 when an unnamed bidder offered $100 million for the company – far more than the appraised value of the stock which was then $425 a share. Not a word of this offer leaked out, and when we moved to our new building in December the occasion was described by the publisher, a born salesman called Bill Dunn, as "one more sign of this magazine's growth and vitality." Yet even as Dunn gave his rosey prognosis, the board was instructing a Wall Street investment bank to seek bidders. Fourteen came forward and a chain of events began which ended the following June with the sale of the company to an ambitious New York real estate developer called Mortimer B Zuckerman for $176 million, or an eye-watering $2,842 a share. Given that *Newsweek* and *Business Week* were sold two decades later for $1 each, the extraordinary price *US News* achieved can only be considered one of the business coups of the late twentieth century. It remains the highest price paid in the US for an employee-owned company. Overnight, a dozen staffers joined the ranks of dollar millionaires. Even the recently retired, long-serving company chauffeur became a wealthy man; he used his windfall to benefit his church.

Zuckerman kicked off his era with a bromide: "We recognise that the soul of the magazine is its straightforward, no-nonsense, issues-oriented approach. That will not change," he told the staff in mid-October 1984. That was the last time he felt it necessary to utter any reassuring words in public. What happened next on the editorial side of the magazine is a sorry tale that will be covered in a later chapter. In my case an unsettled phase began which was to last for five years until the husband-and-wife team of Mike Ruby and Mimi McLouglin took over as co-editors in late-1989. In business terms, the sale of *US News* caused equally lasting reverberations. A group of 220 retirees launched a class-action suit against the company's former directors and appraisers, claiming the stock had been deliberately under-valued in the past and demanding $100 million in compensation. Although they lost on all counts, it took four long years for two-thirds of the money from the sale to be paid out to current employee shareholders like myself – by which time the majority had lost their jobs in the upheaval that followed the Zuckerman takeover.

This cataclysm caught up with me early on. The plan had been to return to London in 1985 as the magazine's chief foreign correspondent. Now, I was told by Stone, all bets were off since Zuckerman had imposed a veto on all staff promotions and transfers. In addition, all appointments had to be sanctioned by the new owner's editorial sidekick, one Harold Evans, the redoubtable former editor of *The Times* and *Sunday Times* in Britain. Having been abruptly sacked in 1982 by Rupert Murdoch, Harry had decamped to America to begin a new life. Somewhere along the line he hooked up with Zuckerman (a Faustian pact if ever there was one) and became his "editorial adviser" – an anomalous position that meant everything and nothing. Around September he arrived unheralded at 2400 N Street. Stone, who viewed Evans with infinite suspicion, assigned him a small inside office next to a broom cupboard and tried to ignore his presence. This hubris backfired spectacularly and Stone resigned early in 1985. Evans, on the other hand, hung around for years, rewriting Zuckerman's pretentious editorials, playing a central role in the scheming and manoeuvering around the selection of editors (there were to be six in the next dozen years), levering in favourites from earlier incarnations and always being on hand to whisper in the owner's receptive ear – a classic example of power without responsibility, unfortunately.

Mostly, all this lay down the line. One day in the autumn of 1984 I wandered into Harry's gloomy closet and introduced myself. We were the only Brits in the building and from the outset I got on well with him. Ever upbeat, an inspiring leader and excellent writer and editor, he was also prone to over-enthusiasm, over-spending and over-selling. At *US News* he polarised opinion from Day One. Ostensibly his task was to formulate an "editorial plan" for Zuckerman – a wide-ranging brief which allowed him to roam the corridors and ask any question he liked. Always curious, and not easily hoodwinked, he set about his task with gusto. I was required to write a lengthy memo about the magazine's foreign coverage. It was not very complimentary. All of us were asked to explain what we did. Harry soon concluded that *US News* was ripe for a total makeover of the sort he had master-minded at all his editorships in the UK. The challenge he faced was that anything he proposed to Stone or the *ancien regime* was dismissed as unsuitable for a weekly American newsmagazine or irrelevant in the American context or simply impractical or too costly.

Harry needed allies and set about finding them to help launch a revolution. In the shake-up that followed, few of the old staff had a future and within three years more than 80 per cent had gone. Many of the senior types brought this on themselves, rarely venturing out of their 7th floor offices, talking only to each other and being largely unknown in the wider world. I survived, thanks in part to the rapport I struck up early with Evans but also because, unlike too many others, I was simply not wedded to the stodgy *US News* "way." Like Harry, I felt that to flourish the magazine had to adjust to the more questioning times, attract a younger audience, improve its writing and cover a broader range of topics while not upsetting its middle America constituency overmuch. To achieve this it had to attract a new generation of better-quality, better-educated editors, reporters and designers. It was, therefore, with some relief that I learned from Stone in November that my move back to London at the end of the year had been agreed. Somehow I had passed Harry's talent threshold test – a mysterious process which he never defined but which relied heavily, I reckoned, on experience and Lancastrian common sense. I was to become "Senior European Editor" – the title held all those years before by my mentor Joe Fromm.

8

The Collapse of Communism

"Marxism has been the greatest fantasy of our century."
LESZEK KOLAKOWSKI, THE POLISH PHILOSOPHER
WRITING IN 1978

No one who I had contact with, professionally or personally, ever predicted the imminent collapse of communism. When it happened in Central and Eastern Europe towards the end of the 1980s, I was as surprised, and hesitant, as everyone else in the West. The Soviets, surely, would intervene? But they did not, and the grass root revolution rolled on, finally reaching the Kremlin itself in the early 1990s and consigning a disastrous, murderous and venal era to the dustbin of history. It was my fantastic good fortune to have a ringside seat in this momentous transformation, and also to have editors behind me who understood the significance of what was taking place.

Over ten amazingly eventful years as European editor of *US News* I made some fifty visits to practically every country involved in the transition. I talked to presidents and paupers, revolutionaries and time-servers, young and old, was present on several historic occasions, covered the wars in the Balkans and graduated to writing bristling opinion columns in the magazine lambasting the West for its mealy-mouthed response to a variety of challenges thrown up by the "new" Europe. It was a very heady time to be a fly on the wall – by turns magical and uplifting, but also on occasion depressing and discouraging. One of my colleagues in the stalls, John Lloyd of the *Financial Times*, once confessed that he had included a chunk of Schiller's 'Ode to Joy' poem in something he wrote about the retreat of communism – and his editor allowed it to appear. Most of us roving wordsmiths from the western democracies felt much the same. The times were like that. It was as though a huge, crippling load had suddenly been lifted from Europe's aching shoulders.

Perhaps it is a fair criticism that we all became too caught up in the exuberant mood of the times and were insufficiently sceptical. Yet to make that kind of sober judgement decades later, with the knowledge of the disappointments and setbacks which later overtook countries like Russia and Romania, is to ignore what the Iron Curtain meant in real life over four decades – and what communism had mutated to in Europe by the early 1980s. Whatever optimism once underpinned the system had long since withered. In its place was a rusting ideology enduring only through force, corruption and hypocrisy which was practising the exact opposite of what it preached. Everyday life in the Soviet empire had become utterly pointless and cynical. Signs of decline, like derelict factories and neglected infrastructure and backward technology, were everywhere to be seen – if you wanted to. The coercive power of the state – barbed-wire death strips on "friendly" borders, informers in every workplace, castrated courts, suffocating censorship, single candidate "elections" to name a few things – fatally corroded civil society. A political class, whose only rationale by this stage was to maintain its privileges, squatted on top of this putrid carcass, preventing all meaningful change and all accountability. By the late-1980s virtually every country in the Soviet bloc was bankrupt and resembled a giant Ponzi scheme, kept afloat mostly by self-serving western bankers. In the end, all it took to bring the whole system crashing down was the rash decisions of one man, Mikhail Gorbachev. The paradox, of course, is that Gorbachev believed then and for ever after that the communist system could have been reformed.

So why did the events of the late-1980s and early-1990s take virtually everyone by such surprise? With hindsight, several factors spring to mind. I would argue that we were all too impressed by Soviet power and the ruthless way it had been deployed, in 1956 and 1968, to crush dissent in Eastern Europe. We under-estimated the impact that the failed intervention by Soviet forces in Afghanistan had had on confidence in the Kremlin. Time had taken its toll on Soviet willpower, and so had the "era of stagnation." We assumed too much – that the regimes in Eastern Europe could fend for themselves if the Russians ever cut them loose, that East Europeans (apart from the Poles) had no stomach for a fight, that idealism was dead. We never had access to the bottom line on the Soviet empire – the real scale of the debts, the true cost of the repeated failure to introduce market-based reforms, the technological deficit with the West and the full extent of the inertia at every layer in the system. Day to day we were kept strictly at arms' length, rarely (even at ambassadorial level) being able to judge first hand how mediocre the coterie in charge truly were. The imposition of martial law in Poland in the early 1980s – in retrospect, the dying spasm of this rotting corpse – also reminded everyone, including dissidents, that it remained dangerous to assume rational behaviour on the part of those in charge. In the final analysis who could say which regime would decide to fight it out? The truth was that no one knew. So we all hedged our bets.

Initially, we seemed to be in for an interesting ride but nothing more when Gorbachev became leader of the Communist Party of the Soviet Union in the spring of 1985. Even as late as mid-1988 *US News* felt comfortable running a no-change piece I reported from Czechoslovakia under the mocking headline 'Forever winter in Prague.' But by March the following year the ice was truly melting. From then on too much happened too quickly across the Soviet bloc for one correspondent to witness it all. At the scene, the essence of the situation was that one never quite knew what would happen next – a welcoming handshake or a threatening shakedown followed by summary expulsion. With the exception of Romania, and the Balkan wars where I got into various scrapes, none of the reporting was particularly dangerous. Yet until a regime actually collapsed there was always an element of cloak-and-dagger about gathering information, meeting opposition activists and moving around.

For the first and last time in *US News's* history local stringers came into their own, and when I was not travelling myself much of my time in London was spent coordinating their vivid, and sometimes courageous, reporting. Working for a weekly publication could be a drawback. Events frequently overtook us, most notably when the Berlin Wall was breached late on the evening of November 9, 1989, after much of the magazine had gone to press. On the other hand, we were always freer to look beyond tomorrow's headline and rarely had to chase the news story of the day. It helped enormously to have visited most of the countries involved in this upheaval in calmer times and, for once, to have a few trusted contacts on the ground. My first visits to Poland, Czechoslovakia and Hungary had been more than a decade earlier in 1977 when we were based in Moscow – after the rigors of life in the USSR, a sort of light relief assignment which enabled us to stay in hotels where the hot water worked and people answered the telephone. Even so there were blank spaces on my personal map of the region, notably the Balkans and East Germany. Before the curtain went up on the main event in 1989 I was able to fill in two of these gaps in the most unexpected ways.

The first opportunity came towards the end of 1986. The magazine's Bonn bureau had been chasing the leader of the East German regime, Erich Honecker, for an on-the-record interview for two years without success. Exactly why, was never clear to me – Honecker was hardly of world-shattering significance. Out of the blue, his officials contacted the bureau and announced that a date late in the year had been set for the meeting. But there was a catch. The bureau chief in West Germany was not acceptable; someone more "important" was required. Life being what it was then in Washington – editors and foreign editors were coming and going with dizzying frequency following the sale of the magazine two years earlier – I seemed to be the only possibility.

So it was that on a freezing December night I found myself at Checkpoint Charlie, preparing to enter the unknown on the other side of the infamous Wall for the first time since I was a boy of 13 when my parents had taken me to see the Soviet war memorial in East Berlin while we were on a leave break from our home in Luneberg. A quick glance at my passport, and I was through the nondescript container cabins which served as the Allied border post. After that, there was an intimidating advance alone through no-man's land until one reached the bulky East German encampment fifty yards away. On arriving at the booth, I was looked up and down so many times by the guard that I began to wonder if he thought I wanted to immigrate. East German sovereignty asserted, I was allowed through. In my halting German I asked a guard if there was a taxi stand nearby. 'Nein.' There was nothing for it but to walk, and shortly after I was struggling along a traffic-free, dimly lit street lined by shabby, dirty buildings at 10.00pm on a Sunday night, lugging a suitcase and typewriter. No one was to be seen, I had no idea where I was and the road seemed to go on and on without intersections or nameplates. As luck would have it a man appeared from nowhere – maybe he was my tail – and I explained as best I could that I was looking for a particular hotel. He pointed the way and left me to it.

Interviewing Honecker seemed a breeze after such a bizarre arrival in the German Democratic Republic, as East Germany was known officially. We met in the stark headquarters of the State Council. Then aged 74 and in power since 1972, Honecker turned out to be a classic *apparatchik* – entirely average in clothes, appearance, intellect, style and veracity. He did smile and shake my hand at the start of our meeting but thereafter assumed a cool, low-key tone and an unbending demeanour. Nothing of any interest was said in the interview which focused entirely on international affairs and was cringingly predictable. Everything, he assured me, was "going well" in the workers' paradise. Gorbachev once referred to him as an "arsehole" after also being subjected to such drivel. Our meeting made the front page of the party newspaper *Neues Deutschland* next morning, and ran over a page in the magazine, but I wasn't the only person at *US News* who wondered what on earth the East Germans were seeking from such a sterile exchange – probably more brownie points with the Kremlin.

Encouraged by *US News's* cooperation, another visa was forthcoming the following year, this time to cover an East German election. Having observed several such "votes" in the Soviet Union I was not, perhaps, the best choice to report such a farce. Still, the name of the game was access which we had been granted – although on their terms. A busy programme was arranged, and as my name was on the visa it was my job to go through with it. My notebook is full of material gathered from apparently frank exchanges with mildly critical party officials, tame Jewish community leaders, conformist evangelical church pastors, loyal local journalists and trusty government ministers. By this point the Lutherans were assuming an opposition role but were still of "several minds" as a helpful American diplomat called Imre Lapping put it. This was a good example of how one honest briefing in a controlled society can undermine all the guff served up by one's hosts. The church, Lapping told me, wanted to be "a mature partner with the state" but was being pushed by events – especially the issue of emigration – into leading what opposition existed. The state, for its part, wished to avoid discussion with the church and everyone else including the Kremlin. So out of touch had the Honecker regime become by this point – it was July 1988, more than three years after Gorbachev replaced Chernenko – that only the week before my visit it had issued a justification of the Molotov-Ribbentrop pact of 1939. "There's no real dissident activity in the GDR," Lapping remarked rather bleakly as I left him. "But it's true that the more people they expel, the more come forward to replace those who have gone."

When the Berlin Wall came down sixteen months later I was in London. As soon as I could I flew into Berlin and went straight to Kurfürstendamm, the main shopping street in West Berlin. The pavements that Sunday evening were packed ten deep with 'Ossis' (East Germans) gawping in shop windows and car showrooms. 'Wessies' (West Germans) drove by cheering them and waving flags. At the Wall the mood was joyful, incredulous, amazed, exuberant, happy. Wall "peckers" were hard at work chipping small bits of concrete off the graffiti-sprayed structure as souvenirs. Long-haired youths with guitars serenaded the huge crowd milling around. People hugged each other, and complete strangers came up and began animated conversations regardless of language. It was an exhilarating, intoxicating mix. The next day, in true German style, most of the Ossis returned to work. Within months many were unemployed.

If the GDR proved to be a house of cards, hermit Albania was one big confidence trick. Journalists and Americans and other ne'er-do-wells had been banned from the isolated Balkan country since 1950, but in the mid-1970s one or two tour groups from western Europe began to be allowed in. Then, in the 1980s, the British government gave up its requirement to state one's occupation in a passport. In 1987 I suggested to my editors that Jean and I join a group organised by Regent Travel, a small UK tour operator specialising in travel to unusual destinations. If asked, I would be a property developer in honour of the magazine's owner. Jean would be a photographer (she took 300 images, not one of which was used by the magazine). All was agreed, and in late-April over the Easter weekend we set off on what turned out to be a memorable eight-day trip. *US News* gave it one page.

Albania has had a chequered history, as we were informed almost as soon as we strolled through disinfectant at the Yugoslav border and had the latest western magazines and our recommended guide book confiscated. At the time of our visit Enver Hoxha, a Stalinist who led Albania for four decades, had been dead for a couple of years. Behind the scenes a power struggle was underway between his widow and his successor. To obscure this unfortunate development, the Hoxha "cult of personality" was being intensified – a life beyond the grave episode rivalled only, in my experience, by a very similar event in Azerbaijan in

2003 after the death of President Heydar Aliyev. Even in our antiseptic, controlled environment in Tirana, where it was difficult to ask a question let alone get an answer, no one could doubt who had the upper hand. Hoxha's huge, glowering visage was everywhere – on billboards and buildings, trucks and kiosks and even hillsides. It became a game in our bus to spot the next thing named after Hoxha – a dam, a school, a university, a port, a tractor plant, a library, an exhibition. You name it. At one museum we visited the great man actually came alive, sitting on a rug smoking a cigarette and talking to a 103-year old peasant dressed in traditional Muslim attire. Only Hoxha's tomb was relatively modest – at least, by Lenin's Red Square standards.

Exploring Albania through an organised tour, steered by a guide and shepherded by an "interpreter," proved to be rather like doing a jigsaw puzzle in the dark. Day by day little bits could be fitted in here and there. But large gaps would remain. The immediate impression was one of acute poverty and paranoia. This remained true wherever we went – oxen ploughing the fields, apartment blocks without running water, meat rationed, people living cheek-by-jowl with poultry and sheep, a total lack of private cars offset by a plethora of military trucks, uniformed troops at every street corner and thousands upon thousands of mushroom-like concrete pill boxes all over the place inspired by Hoxha a decade earlier in a fit of acute xenophobia. In most town centres a bust of Stalin held pole position, buttressed by ubiquitous slogans on banners and walls urging the long-suffering citizenry to greater "vigilance." Yet by Day Eight in Shkodër I had succeeded in persuading our guide into increasingly frank indiscretions, Jean was making friends with schoolgirls anxious to know if she could tell them anything about Duran Duran (Princess Diana's favourite band) and we had all been impressed by the innate friendliness of the people we met in this Alice-in-Wonderland country.

One day we were taken to the 'Albania Today' exhibition in Tirana where the guide treated us to a world-class barrage of uncheckable facts and figures. Tobacco production in 1986, she told us, was four and a half times greater than in 1950, mineral output was six times up on that in 1938 while the number of tourist beds in the country had grown 15 times since 1950 – when there were probably none. Throughout the communist era such statistics were advanced as "proof" of progress. It seemed churlish to point out that everything on display looked at least two generations behind the times. The factories we visited left the same impression – decrepit, idle, disorganised, obsolete. Even so, as in East Germany, I departed from another communist-led state little realising that the whole edifice would implode within five years. "It seems most unlikely, short of a world war, that the present system will collapse of its own accord," I wrote in my notebook. "The Army and security organs appear far too well entrenched, there is no reason for outside military intervention and neighbouring Yugoslavia and Greece are unlikely to interfere directly. Moreover, the great bulk of the population has reason to thank the PLA (Party of Labour of Albania) for the material gains made in the last forty years, and at least two-thirds of the population is too young to know any other system." How little I understood!

Albania did eventually choose democracy in 1992, but its evolution has continued to be unpredictable. Moreover, its profound isolation at the end of the 1980s ensured that it remained a sideshow from the main event then underway in the "real" Soviet bloc. This certainly cannot be said of Czechoslovakia, in some ways witness to the purest revolution in the communist world, and the one that the "chattering classes" in the West adopted as their own once a liberal-minded and valiant playwright called Vaclav Havel became president. Over the course of numerous visits during the key years from 1988-93 I must have talked to almost everyone who was to become anyone in post-communist Czechoslovakia. This is less impressive than it sounds. The dissident community in the country was small, and never more than a few hundred until revolution took hold, and it had little direct impact on national life. Nothing like the Solidarity mass movement in Poland took root, and passivity was so ingrained following the 1968 Soviet invasion that I was once informed by a frustrated Prague intellectual that "Czechs feel it's better to be like grass. People walk over grass. It bends. It recovers."

Knowing this, I found the before-and-after contrasts in Prague fascinating. Before, people (with honourable exceptions) spoke in code language and riddles and kept their heads down. A future President of the Czech Republic, Vaclav Klaus, once surreptitiously showed me a photo album with pictures of himself in Chicago with Milton Friedman, the high priest of free markets. The idea seemed to be to emphasise his maverick credentials. To term Klaus a dissident, though, would be to stretch the definition to breaking point. At the economics institute in which he worked, he was always sharp and acute in describing the status quo in quasi-critical, quotable language – "what the (communist) leadership is afraid of is becoming Bolivia" is typical – but always unattributably and off the record, even days before the Velvet Revolution. The result was that he was widely regarded as a compromiser, for all his later transformation into a staunch defender of Czech national interests. Perhaps not surprisingly, when Klaus did eventually become president he would rarely be interviewed by journalists who had met him in his humbler incarnation.

Another contact who stirred up mixed emotions was Jan Kavan of the Palach Press – an exile in London since the purge which followed the Prague Spring in 1968. Often the first port of call for western reporters en route to Czechoslovakia, he helped to open doors and arrange meetings in Prague but always played his cards close to his chest and rarely, if ever, gave out political opinions. It may just have been a matter of prudence and personal security, but his self-contained, rather furtive mien aroused suspicion – and that was dangerous in such a fissile context. On returning to Prague in 1989 he ended up being accused (falsely) of collaboration with the Czechoslovak secret service. Later, in 1998, he became foreign minister. Rather more to my liking were Jiri Dienstbier, Pavel Bratinka, Jan Canorgorsky and Peter Uhl – quite a quartet when one looks back. Dienstbier was a brave, genial, idealistic, urbane polyglot with a big grey moustache and a morbid sense of humour. A former radio journalist, he was one of the original Charter '77 signatories. Like Bratinka and Uhl, he spent the best part of two decades employed as a stoker. He put a brave face on it and claimed that it allowed him time to think. In 1989 he became foreign minister and earned worldwide fame when he used bolt-cutters to chop symbolic holes in the barbed wire of the Iron Curtain. Bratinka, a physicist whose dissent grew out of his Christian faith, was adept at describing the effects of "soft persecution." He became a government minister in 1996 and was one of the first Chartists to distance himself from Havel. Canogorsky, a leader in the underground church in Slovakia, represented Slovaks in the Charter movement. He went on to be prime minister of Slovakia. Uhl, who claimed to be a Trotskyist but had trouble defining the term, specialised in head-on provocations and paid the price by serving more than eight years in solitary confinement. He could ramble on for hours. After 1989 he ran the Czech Press Agency.

I talked with Havel only once. In 1988 Dienstbier set up a meeting in Havel's apartment but when I arrived two burly secret policemen barred the way. I retreated and telephoned. Without a moment's hesitation Havel said he would meet me in half an hour at a pub in Prague's Old Town. He was there when I arrived. In the circumstances it was impossible to conduct a proper interview, but it was possible to form some impressions. Stocky and edgy, he seemed happiest discussing ideas. At the time his core belief revolved around the notion of living as normally as possible in an abnormal society. He had spelled out what he meant a decade earlier in an essay titled *The Power of the Powerless* in which he argued that the critical thing in a dictatorship is to live the truth – all else is compromise. As he put it: "If the main pillar of the system is living a lie, it is not surprising the fundamental threat to it is living the truth." This Havel tried to do in his own life every day in every way. Inspirational and imaginative, he naturally became the fulcrum around which all else moved in the Chartists' world and then in the Czech Republic.

The price Czechs and Slovaks paid for their long ice age was easily overlooked in the 1990s as democracy washed warmly over Prague and star-struck tourists flocked in from western Europe and America. On one occasion, though, I was on the receiving end of an emotional confession from a victim of the system. Cestimir Suchy had once been foreign editor of Radio Prague and an avowed communist. "Until 1968 I always wanted people to like me," he admitted to me one afternoon. "Then, during the Prague Spring, an ugly sophism sprang up in the party along the lines that it was better to be wrong with the party than right outside it. I'd had enough. I knew I'd be expelled, but I was too old to make any more compromises. So I spoke up. I decided my fate myself." Soon after, aged 47, he was out of the party and out of a job. He spent the next 22 years washing windows. "The isolation from my past was the toughest part – that, and the theft of my brain and my life." Suchy was to receive a second chance in 1990 when, aged 69, he was elected Dean of the School of Journalism at Charles University. The last time I saw him he remarked, wistfully but accurately, "I never expected to live in a free country. It's amazing to be here now. Too much of my life was spent following a false star." The sheer waste of hundreds of thousands of lives like Suchy's in the decades after the Prague Spring is what gave Czechoslovakia's revolution its distinct timbre and hue. It took years for Czechs to shake off the fear of a communist revival.

Next door, in Hungary, communism was cast off more easily, yet the past – in this case the violent 1956 uprising and subsequent harsh crackdown – also dominated the present well into the 1990s. When I visited Hungary in 1977 I had found it very buttoned-up. Conversations were stilted and had an elliptical quality, and even buying a piece of china quite legally in a second hand shop involved tortuous negotiation. A decade on, when I next returned, it felt like the most relaxed place in the entire Soviet bloc. There was real diversity of opinion, more decision-making autonomy for everyone from farmers to factory managers, pollsters openly testing the public mood, an irreverent tabloid newspaper called *Reform* stirring things up each week and a growing black economy. And nobody seemed scared of talking politics to foreigners – "the lid has been removed" as an official put it. In reality, this easy-going mood was misleading. Dissent on the Polish scale was non-existent, except perhaps on the issue of a new dam proposed for the Danube. The country was heavily in debt. Many people, possibly a majority, held down two or three jobs to make ends meet. Housing was in very short supply. And the ruling Communist Party had no intention of moving aside, fearful that it would be held to account for its duplicity in 1956 when it had acquiesced in the Soviet invasion and cooperated in the execution of its leader Imre Nagy.

To get a sense of what was happening in this crucial 1988-92 period one had to unearth nonconformist members of the Hungarian establishment – party members, academics or officials – and outsiders with attitude like writers, artists and journalists and young people untainted by 1956. In this I was greatly helped by *US News's* engaging stringer Mihaly Batki. One individual whom I got to know well thanks to Batki, and profiled in *US News,* was Imre Pozsgay, a former confidant of Mikhail Gorbachev. Pozsgay had fallen out with the regime in 1980 but staged a comeback and, by the late-1980s, was the leading reformist inside the party machine. Ebullient, fat and calculating, he was a populist who took risks – among the first in the country to dare to redefine 1956, and the individual most responsible for opening Hungary's border with Austria (including to East Germans) in the summer of 1989. His ultimate intentions were never clear, but in 1992 over a long lunch he confessed to me that "what I was able to do, I did. I'm only sorry for my naivety (in 1989, when he was outmanoeuvred for the presidency). I would have been a stabilising factor. Now I'm a critic."

A less subjective interpretation is that as early as 1990 it was doubtful if anyone with Pozsgay's tainted past could have done much to guide change in Hungary in more orderly, and less nationalistic, directions. The problem was that no one agreed on objectives or the correct pace of change, and very few people understood the meaning of democratic values. The learned minister of justice, Kalman Kulcsar, who always made time for me even while devising a new constitution (and once produced the memorable quote "We must hurry, cautiously,"), had long been shunted aside. Another useful contact, Gabor Damzsky, had become mayor of Budapest and was complaining that his new life was "like a madhouse. You have to make deals every day. We make politics out of everything." Peter Toke's *Reform* tabloid had peaked. Above all, the country's historic mistrust of politicians and parliament dating back to the Austro-Hungarian empire was again colouring national life. Gaspar Miklos Tamas, a philosopher then dabbling in real-time politics, once informed me that the underlying problem was Hungarians' "distorted idea of the role of the state. People don't see the state as a neutral entity but a movement to do things – especially to do down opposition and anyone who dissents. People believe in clientism and want to join in." Many did.

Wide ranging conversations like this were part and parcel of newsmagazine reporting from the disintegrating Soviet bloc. One moment earnest young political neophytes would lay out fantastic scenarios based on a rich idealism which never existed. Another moment party hacks would grasp at straws as they contemplated the onrushing tsunami of change. In between, voices of reason found it very hard to be heard. The sheer pace of change was often bewildering as well as exhilarating. "Events produce their own logic. We're going down a road no one has ever travelled," a Hungarian diplomat called Viktor Polgar remarked resignedly to me in February 1989. "Nobody today is the same person he was a year ago."

At the time this was certainly not true in neighbouring Romania although I had to take that on trust. Visas for journalists to enter Nicolae Ceausescu's utopia had always been complicated to obtain and, as revolution swept across Europe in 1989, they became impossible. The dictator's vanity, however, was his Achilles' heel. Late in the year the Romanian communist party was due to hold one of its five yearly congresses to re-elect the "Giant of the Carpathians," as Ceausescu liked to be known (in reality he was small and nondescript). Foreign reporters were welcome – to witness first hand the rock-solid unanimity prevailing in this oasis of proletarian progress. The downside was the inordinate length of Ceausescu's speeches. The upside was that it might be possible to report the price Romania was paying for this raving megalomaniac's 24 years in power – including food and energy rationing, forced weekend working, mandatory gynaecological testing and a total lack of accountability. It was an opportunity not to be missed, and in mid-November I arrived in rundown, half-lit Bucharest.

It would be quite untrue to claim that I foresaw Ceausescu's violent death only five weeks later. At the time he seemed only too fully in control as he ground out a six-hour rant devoted to the need for greater class struggle. Leering patronisingly over a lectern as he spoke, he orchestrated more than 30 standing ovations for himself from the 3,300 cowed delegates who rose on his say-so like puppets on a string to chant his name over and over. It was an awful throwback to the worst sycophantic days of Stalinism – and a direct snub to Mikhail Gorbachev who had just urged Ceausescu to change his stripes if he wanted to survive. I was not too impressed either, but found it hard to imagine how Romania might follow the path pioneered by Hungary and Czechoslovakia. At least my report ended accurately: "Change will come only after the dictator is dead and buried." With that I flew back to London.

One of *US News's* many quirks was its year-end double issue. This meant that when revolution did break out in Romania in late-December we were well and truly stymied. One of our liveliest young freelancers, Peter Green, hurried to Timisoara as the uprising took hold and spent a scary Christmas Day hiding under stairs in the city centre as the all-pervasive security forces went on the rampage. It was not until the first week in January that we were able to report the 11-day civil war and the carnage involved. Fortunately we made up for the delay by immediately adopting, and retaining, a highly sceptical view of the Romanian "revolution." I returned in April 1990 to cover the first real elections in the country in 53 years. The highlight was a couple of days spent in the company of Petre Roman, "a smooth, 43-year old engineer with film star looks and a communist past" who was heading an interim government in cahoots with the neo-communist National Salvation Front. Roman came from the privileged *nomenklatura* class and had been educated in

France. I quickly realised how murky life in post-Ceausescu Romania had become when Roman and his entourage (me included) were mobbed by a large crowd of women in the Transylvanian town of Sibiu, scene of some of the worst fighting only four months earlier. Flowers and kisses poured down on us and no one seemed to care that this overnight champion of democracy and free speech had once had close ties with the Ceausescus (he dated their daughter Zoia). Romania had been so corrupted and debased by its brand of autocratic communism that its transformation was always going to be ambivalent, slow and tortuous. Years later, in 2006, I had an unexpected chance to see how it was faring when *The BP Magazine* asked me to write a feature on five kindergartens in the country which the company's retail employees in Europe were supporting. The appalling life stories of many of the young orphan children, all rescued from the streets since 1990 – some allegedly retrieved from cages where they had been kept like animals – made it all too clear that a high price was still being paid for freedom.

Poland was fundamentally different from Romania – more economically advanced, more cultured, more pluralistic by temperament, more important strategically. For over a decade from August 1980, when a demonstration erupted in a Gdansk shipyard and an unknown electrician called Lech Walesa climbed on a crane and called for a strike, so taking the first step to the formation of an independent trade union, Poland led the way in Eastern Europe in terms of challenge and threat to the status quo. I visited the country repeatedly from then until 1995 and came to know and admire its spirited, all-or-nothing people who have been so traduced by history and geography.

It helped that the cast of characters on the Polish stage over the next 15 years provided such a rich play list for in-and-out foreign reporters like me. Even at the worst times, someone was always prepared to say what they thought, regardless of the consequences. Everyone I knew in Solidarity was locked up under martial law. The movement was weakened, but the individuals concerned were hardened by the experience and ever after understood that nothing was to be gained by giving an inch – a tough lesson for the fellow travellers (of whom there were some) to swallow. During the Round Table period in 1989 the temptation to waver was considerable as the communists offered one tasty morsel after another to a mass movement that had lost most of its grass root strength. Yet the one concession that really mattered – the end of one-party communist rule – remained elusive. Each fudge only boosted Solidarity's determination, until the historic moment in June 1989 when the communists were humiliated in the first free elections ever held in the Soviet empire. Walesa was amazed by the rout, which became public on the same day as the Tiananmen Square massacre in Beijing, and worried that Solidarity might have won too big and provoked the Soviets once too often. Yet again Poland surprised the world. After much behind-the-scenes arm-wrestling, a compromise was reached ,and it was agreed that General Jaruzelski should be retained as president to reassure Moscow. Within a couple of months he had caved in and agreed that Solidarity should form a government.

The next few years were a roller coaster for Poland as Solidarity predictably split, old underground colleagues fell out, the economy was privatised, the Catholic Church reluctantly yielded its central role and pluralistic reforms slowly took root. For an American newsmagazine it was a running story made in heaven containing, as it did, clear strategic, political, ethical and free market elements. Disaster always seemed just round the next corner, the personalities at the centre of this revolution were high octane and usually accessible and the magazine's editors and readers quickly grasped that what happened in Poland was central to most else in the Soviet bloc. When I touched down at Warsaw's rickety airport for the umpteenth time, drove to my usual base at the Intercontinental Hotel near the Tomb of the Unknown Warrior, set off once more in an aging, smoke-belching taxi for another round of interviews, passed on messages, answered anonymous phone calls late at night, made appointments to meet in out-of-the-way spots and even smuggled a manuscript out of the country (for the *BBC's* Kevin Ruane who had written a hard-hitting biography of a murdered priest called Jerzy Popieluszko) it felt as though one was playing a role, albeit very minor, in a real life contemporary drama.

Covering the story basically required strong nerves, stamina and good local contacts. While based in Moscow in the late-1970s I had persuaded Kristoph Bobinski, then freelancing in Warsaw for the *Financial Times* and *Washington Post,* to string (for a pittance) for *US News* as well. The son of a Polish émigré who reached Britain during the Second World War, Kris had grown up in the UK and moved to Poland after university. In the late-1980s his wife Lena Kolarska-Bobinska became one of Poland's leading opinion pollsters. For more years than I care to recall the two of them provided contacts, knowledge, sensible advice, deep understanding and a friendly welcome. When, in 1994, I managed to interview (by then) President Walesa, Kris came along to the presidential palace to interpret – and later to debunk all Walesa's blustering verbosity. *US News* was fortunate to have such a resource in place when martial law was imposed in December 1981 and Poland closed down to the outside world for many months. Sadly, but typically, it never rewarded the Bobinskis accordingly.

My memories of those years are hard to distil. Mostly they revolve around personalities and endless discussions about the nature of democracy, the pros and cons of compromise and the morality of revenge. In the post-communist era Poles started debating the peaceful end to communist rule, with some revisionists denouncing the 1989 "Round Table" negotiations between Solidarity and the government as "high treason." It was a characteristic squabble. Poles' unfortunate history has made them wary of abstract concepts and innately mistrustful of compromise. They are also argumentative. The moment they were free to debate openly after forty years' suppression, they jumped at the chance and by 1993 there were 29 parties in parliament (67 had contested the previous election). I must have spent days discussing the nature of Poles and Poland over the years with Bronislaw Geremek, the wily, pipe-smoking mediaevalist (later foreign minister) who acted for a time as Walesa's intellectual prop. On one occasion, as the country lurched into another post-communist crisis, he told me that "it was rather easy to get freedom and not so hard to build the first stage of a market economy. The problem is our political psychology. We are in a political desert in this country. There is a Manichean divide between the rulers, whoever they are, and the ruled." Geremek, a communist until the 1968 Soviet invasion of Czechoslovakia, would go on musing in these sorts of abstract terms for hours. For him, the Solidarity movement had offered Poles "a chance to think." I doubt they felt that in the Gdansk shipyard.

Walesa, when I did meet with him in the Belvedere Palace, came across as pragmatic, in love with his bluff, "commonsense man" brand, bustling ("let's get down to work" he began the interview), direct, temperamentally frustrated by his lack of real power and a stubborn battler to the end. In 1995 I trailed him around Poland for the best part of ten days as he fought a vain rearguard action to retain the presidency. The three-page profile I wrote was later syndicated around the world –

a tribute less to my skills than to Walesa's enduring appeal even at his nadir. The contrast to his nemesis, Aleksander Kwaśniewski, was total. Kwaśniewski smoothly transformed himself from a young communist party official to an articulate, free-market, NATO-supporting consensus-builder without missing a blink, and lasted ten years as president of Poland to 2005. I interviewed him several times and had lunch with him once one-on-one – an occasion made memorable by his lawyer wife calling repeatedly with details of a new property deal she was arranging, and his constant checking of the latest stock market prices in the new Warsaw bourse (then housed, most aptly, in the former communist party central committee building). Walesa, in contrast, always remained at heart the shipyard electrician from Gdansk – an old dog unable to learn new tricks in a rapidly changing society. He paid a high price for his obduracy. Put him in front of a live audience, as I saw once in the dank Silesian town of Turow when he was faced by rows of disgruntled miners, and he was brilliant – a witty, coarse, off-the-cuff spellbinder who liked to be confrontational in debate to the point of recklessness. A man-of-the-people if ever there was one, but someone overtaken by the very upheaval he had inspired.

Other larger-than-life characters often flitted across my Polish stage. Adam Michnik – according to Havel, "the intellectual conscience of the Polish nation" – time and again offered sharp, liberal insights. His polar opposites, the nationalistic Kaczynski twins, Lech and Jaroslaw, as early as 1990 were delighting in the split in Solidarity they were plotting and keen to go on the record with a foreign reporter urging a vengeful purge of the old communist elite. Their innate combativeness upset more sensitive souls like the Solidarity spokesman (and later defence minister) Janusz Onyszkiewicz – an essentially decent man who never tried to puff up Solidarity when it was down and so won the respect of many people like me. In Jerzy Urban, the lethal, dwarf-like propagandist employed by Jaruzelski, he had a worthy opponent. Urban was certainly the only Soviet bloc spokesman I ever encountered who happily conceded that the communists had screwed up every chance of party-led reform and were no longer trustworthy. In contrast, Mieczyslaw Rakowski, Poland's last communist prime minister, was usually depicted as a sociable "realist" by his western interlocutors. On the couple of occasions we sat down together, he struck me as a cynical spin doctor-type rather similar to a model patented later in Britain.

One way or another, to my mind, we owe a huge debt to Poland and the Poles. Poland led the way as communism imploded by setting the tone of discussion with its discredited rulers, defining the parameters of change and accepting reluctantly that some compromise was inevitable if violence was to be averted. Without Solidarity and Walesa's ceaseless pressure, Jaruzelski might conceivably have got away with his chimera of "a socialist parliamentary democracy." As it was he failed, and all of the Soviet empire took advantage in the following years. Without the fatal hesitancy displayed by the aging Soviet leadership in the early 1980s, Solidarity might never have taken root. But it did. From then on the movement was central to the democratic revolution everywhere.

Still, without the help, active and passive, of Mikhail Gorbachev not even the Poles at their most determined and united would have been able to roll back the Iron Curtain alone. For a decade after leaving the Soviet Union in 1979 I was *persona non grata* in Moscow, visas being refused to cover the Moscow Olympics in 1980 and on several other occasions after 1984. Then, in the summer of 1989, with unprecedented labour unrest breaking out all over the USSR, ethnic riots in some of the republics and a communist party purge in full swing, the authorities unexpectedly relented and I was allowed to spend two frenetic weeks in the *US News* Moscow bureau in July as a visiting "fireman" bolstering the magazine's reporting. It was to be the first of half a dozen such visits back to my old haunts over the next seven years. Jean remained resolutely in London; nothing could tempt her to give Russia a second chance.

By 1989 Russian society was beginning to awake from its long coma. Substantive signs of change were few and far between and *perestroika* was stuck in first gear. Yet the country was visibly thawing out as *glasnost* began to take effect. "We returned Russia to the world and the world to Russia," was how Gorbachev put it in 2011. Debates about civil society were beginning. Travel abroad was easier and contacts more varied. Freedom of speech and freedom of the press was starting to mean something; even the official Soviet media was covering the labour unrest which was not just about wages but also about the continuing lack of basics in the shops like soap and toothpaste and underwear. Press conferences were scheduled, and officials actually tried to answer questions. Religious belief was reviving and churches reopening. There was less predictability to everyday life. The Memorial Group, set up under Andrei Sakharov's patronage to preserve and explain the Gulag (labour camp regime), dates from 1989. Everyone, indeed, seemed keener to speak out – not just miners in Siberia but also nationalists in the Baltic republics, angry communists, disillusioned war veterans, low wage earners and even (as I discovered one day) zoo keepers in Moscow scandalised that the animals in their charge were no longer being fed regularly. On the sidelines Boris Yeltsin was warning that "revolution" was likely within two years if conditions did not improve. By then Gorbachev must have known that economic reform would make or break him.

On this visit, however, my main focus turned out to be the rising tide of nationalism sweeping through the Soviet empire. As part of the reporting for an article that took in everywhere from Hungary to Kazakhstan, I visited Moldavia (now Moldova) in July and arrived in Kishinev (now Chişinău) in the middle of a highly charged demonstration. Brezhnev-era reactionaries were still in charge here and showing no interest in listening to the protestors. It was this visit that gave me the first of many crash courses in European history that we in the West had forgotten, or overlooked. It also emphasised just how alive numerous simmering resentments in eastern and central Europe really were – something which always caused raised eyebrows back in the Land of the Free when I insisted on including references to Ivan the Terrible or King Zog or Vlad the Impaler in pieces I wrote. The idea that history somehow "ended" with the collapse of communism, first propounded in a Californian think-tank around this time, was always tosh. In the streets of Kishinev that Sunday afternoon, as illicit red, yellow and blue Moldovan mini-flags were handed out covertly, young and old lined up to tell me how their language had been marginalised by Moscow since 1944 and Russian and Ukrainian workers moved in to change the population balance. "Does the world know about our situation?" I was asked time and again. The answer, sadly, was No. Back in the near-deserted Intourist Hotel a barman gave me some heartfelt insights into everyday existence in this neglected backwater. On the surface his life was comfortable – a happy marriage, two young children, a good job, money, a car. But he had already waited seven years for a small two-room apartment, and had another five to go at least. So he rented and was forced to move each year. "A party boss whose son is getting married can make a single telephone call and get three rooms straight away," he claimed bitterly. His only aim was to emigrate – something hundreds of thousands of Moldovans did in the next two decades.

In 1990 I was back in Moscow twice, initially in April for a re-run of the previous summer as defiant Lithuanians and Estonians challenged the Kremlin head on. By then Gorbachev was openly concerned and resorting to ever wilder threats to try to roll back the clock, keep the USSR intact and resuscitate the moribund economy. At the end of June I returned ahead of a momentous CPSU (Communist Party of the Soviet Union) congress. It seemed almost unbelievable to write the lead sentence which appeared in the magazine at the start of July: "Almost 72 years after Lenin imposed one-party rule on the Soviet Union, the Communist Party is disintegrating." Gorbachev, a well-placed source told me, was "making bad misjudgements, getting the mood wrong, exaggerating his own influence and unnecessarily upsetting people. He's not going to last much longer at this rate." The American ambassador, Jack Matlock (a friend from our Moscow years) talked about the "desperation" of hardliners as the power of the party seeped away, and wondered aloud if Gorbachev had used up his nine lives. Dyed-in-the-wool party members candidly discussed the chances of a party split or a coup or even civil war. I had to pinch myself several times when spokesmen for the Politburo, the Central Committee and Democratic Platform (an opposition group inside the CPSU) gave me one-on-one briefings ahead of the congress and uniformly predicted trouble. It felt almost like real democracy.

A year later I missed the August 1991 coup, being preoccupied at the time by the start of the Balkan wars. A couple of months earlier, however, I had been in Moscow to cover the first free presidential elections in Russian history. They were a lacklustre affair reflecting widespread voter apathy despite the unique circumstances. Boris Yeltsin's triumph offered some hope, but even then his erratic behaviour was causing concern. On a campaign stop in Tula which the magazine covered, he managed to skip several meetings, upset his audiences, infuriate embarrassed local officials and vanish into a wood for "a rest" (probably a drink). The following week I was asked to write up the results of an opinion poll that *US News* had, rather surprisingly, commissioned across Russia months earlier. The findings were headline-grabbing at the time. Xenophobia was alive and well but so, surprisingly, was the desire for deeper and faster economic reform.

Three months on, as part of several pieces in *US News* with an 'End of Empire' theme, I was despatched to far-away Kazakhstan. All was chaos and flux here as I was revealingly shown one morning when I attended an editorial meeting in Alma Ata at the local communist party newspaper offices. It became apparent that no one had a clue what to report, what to select from the "official" news service offerings from Moscow or what to omit. All day-to-day "guidance" from the centre had dried up. A strike was going on in the remote coalmining community of Karaganda, 600 miles north of Alma Ata, so I flew there to see what was happening. The labour unrest, and the tough-minded young miners behind it, was interesting but it was Karaganda itself which fascinated me. The city was less than sixty years old but, in true Soviet style, "the whole place seems to have been put together by incompetents," I noted, observing crumbling buildings, rutted roads and hot water pipes lagged with old newspapers.

Karaganda had a chilling history and it was, as one inhabitant put it, "a city of harsh memories" – much of it had been built by Gulag labour. Many nationalities, it turned out, had been deported here forcibly during the Stalin purges in the 1930s. A local grouping called 'Memory' reckoned there were nearly 500 survivors of the 46 camps in the area who still lived around Karaganda. One of them, an elderly, wiry man called Heino Rautiainen, took me to a place called Dolinka where one camp was still acting as a prison, and showed me a cemetery in which friends were buried. His incredible story remains with me to this day – the son of an idealistic father who emigrated to the US from Finland in the 1930s, failed to settle, moved to the USSR in 1933, was arrested as a spy in 1938, sentenced to ten years in jail and shot soon after. His young son, my informant, had been born in the US, moved to the Soviet Union with his father, was arrested in 1941 for having been born abroad and having a foreign name and given an eight-year jail term. On release he was barred from moving to the US or Finland. Heino's childhood memories were of peanut butter and popcorn. In his early 20s he played a clarinet in a Soviet prison camp orchestra formed for the benefit of a General Sokolov who wished to mark the end of the war in Europe with a dance. In his old age, sad memories were all he had left. Above all, Heino wanted the world to know what had happened to him. *US News* generally had little time for such human interest stories. The piece I wrote about this unhappy, marooned man never appeared in print.

In the years following I went back to Russia often, both for *US News* and BP. Nothing matched the reportorial window which opened for a brief, tantalising moment in the early 1990s as the Soviet Union disintegrated. For the first, and maybe the last, time in their troubled history Russians and captive peoples throughout their empire discussed issues relatively openly and largely without the corrosive xenophobia and prickly nationalism which came to epitomise the Putin era. The cost of the country's abrupt transformation was often appalling. In Tyumen in March 1992 I saw old men and women standing outside City Hall in sub-zero temperatures selling pathetic possessions – combs, buttons, a shoelace, two socks – just to survive. "They have nothing else to sell, nowhere else to go and no safety net to save them," I wrote. Some sort of reaction against headlong privatisation, and the "democratic" system championing it, was inevitable; no country on Earth could have navigated such a brutal transition without some back-tracking. A six-week spell in Moscow for *US News* in the summer of 1996 coincided with other difficulties as infighting in the Yeltsin administration intensified and the ferocious war in Chechnya worsened. The Russian financial crisis of 1998 and the destruction of individual savings were still to come. One way or another it simply became harder and harder to persuade Russians that their long-term interests lay in embracing European laws, values and systems. Instead they retreated east to the superficial, and short term, attractions of authoritarian Asia.

This tremendously rich journalistic diet of revolution and turmoil as communism fell apart had a final vicious twist for me when Yugoslavia began to implode in mid-1991 after Slovenia declared independence. At the time, the consensus view in the West was that the Serbs' determination to carve a Greater Serbia out of the ruins of Yugoslavia lay at the root of the several Balkan wars which followed. Put in the context of the rabid nationalism which erupted throughout much of the old communist world once the iron grip of the system began to ease, this can only be part of the explanation. As I discovered time and again on the scene, in practice there was little to choose between Serb, Croat, Bosnian or Kosovan chauvinism. Over four years from 1991-95 more than 100,000 people were killed in these dead-end, sordid and self-defeating conflicts and some two million people driven from their homes.

My memories of this period are a mixture of frustration, anger, shame, boredom and farce. This was a conflict with no heroism. One day I was present in Sarajevo when elderly Serbs were exchanged for similarly aged Bosnian Muslims after both groups of old men had been held for six months by the other side in squalid conditions. The scenes of grief, and the stories these men quietly recounted, would have shocked the most hardened reporter. Later I used the episode as my contribution to a book compiled by western reporters about the four year siege of Sarajevo which was published to raise funds for victims of the war. For the first and last time in my career I was as much a war reporter as a foreign correspondent. The magazine even bought me blue body armour. Once, above Sarajevo, a Bosnian sniper took a pot shot at me as I was interviewing Serb snipers; the bullets hit a rock behind where we were standing and ricocheted along the road near us. Then they told me that a French television journalist had been killed at the same place by a sniper the month before. During the entire Second World War 54 accredited journalists were killed in allied ranks – about the same number as died in the infinitely smaller and less intense Balkan wars. The high toll was no coincidence. By the 1990s, with warfare increasingly dominated by gangs of heavily-armed thugs, fewer and fewer belligerents would accept the non-combatant status of journalists.

One of my first memories of these conflicts is from Croatia in 1992. At a portakabin camp outside Zagreb I talked to well-to-do Croat refugees who had fled from the Serb-held province of Vojvodina – educated types with university degrees, and televisions and skis strapped to their cars. War makes no class distinctions. Soon after I accompanied a nine-truck UN convoy taking supplies to a refugee camp near Banja Luka deep in Serb-held territory. We travelled for hours at a cautious 50 kph, never straying a yard from the defined route for fear of being attacked. The drivers, brave volunteers from the UK and Denmark, may have been used to the freezing fog, icy roads and hostile checkpoints manned by trigger-happy and surly Serbs, but even they went silent at the extreme devastation we saw along this route. Quite what the nervous, freezing Jordanian and Nepalese troops in their summer uniforms, whom we also encountered as we drove along, were meant to be doing here, only the UN far away in New York could explain.

In Bosnia, particularly, one never felt safe. On one occasion in Mostar I inspected the ruined shell of the Roman Catholic cathedral patronised by the Croats and soon after walked across the famous bridge in the centre of the town into Muslim-held territory – only to be attacked by wildly firing Croats who had just been talking to me. To get from Split (the nearest functioning airport to Bosnia-Herzegovina) to Sarajevo involved a hazardous drive across rough, icy mountain passes and along narrow ledges to avoid the worst of the roadblocks. One never knew what was around the next bend. Usually it was a good idea to travel with UN forces or other reporters, but not always. Just choosing the wrong nationality interpreter could be dangerous. Once my Croatian interpreter, Erica, and I got stuck in freezing conditions for 18 hours near Kiseljak while a UN convoy negotiated its way through a roadblock. When it finally got going, we were deliberately left behind. We eventually arrived in the divided town of Travnik at 3:00am where my generous hosts, a Croatian schoolteacher called Ivo Curak and his wife, treated me to a lesson in 14th century Balkan history, a cup of tea and a much-prized orange before we retired to our sleeping bags on the floor.

Reporting this war threw up other challenges. On one occasion, travelling overnight to Belgrade from Budapest by train in 1992 (sanctions had closed Serbian airspace) I was robbed of my passport and cash (credit cards were useless because of the sanctions) at knifepoint. A kindly front desk manager at the Intercontinental Hotel called Rados Lekic paid my taxi fare and lent me some money until I was able to take a minibus back to Budapest and collect funds there. On another occasion, en route by bus on a seven hour journey to Pale, the ski resort "capital" of the Bosnian Serb "republic," I was saved from arrest at a roadblock only by the intervention of a colonel in the regular Yugoslav army who vouched for me. We had been sitting next to each other in the bus discussing the war. Afterwards I wondered why he had stuck his neck out until it occurred to me that he had been explaining (he was a communications expert) how the Bosnian Serb military logistical system worked. Clearly, he was worried I might incriminate him.

It was after this epic bus ride in January 1993 that I interviewed the entire civilian Bosnian Serb leadership – Radovan Karadzic, Momčilo Krajišnik and Biljana Plavšić – across a small table in a freezing ski chalet. It was somewhat daunting. Karadzic had a definite purpose in mind – to send a defiant message to Washington. Krajišnik, with his distracting single bushy eyebrow, played the hard man. Plavšić, a Fulbright Scholar and Sarajevo academic, resembled Rosa Klebb in *From Russia With Love*. Her fanaticism was staggering even by comparison with that of her colleagues. All three ended up being charged with war crimes in The

Hague. Karadzic, always preening himself, came across as glib, insisting that communism in Yugoslavia was to blame for what was happening. "It put everything under the carpet. For 45 years we lived an illusion. It was inevitable when Yugoslavia collapsed that there would be an explosion. We are different, very different," he argued. Without batting an eyelid he denied all knowledge of Serb war crimes and Serb ethnic cleansing, and revealed that he had urged President Clinton to reconsider US policy and align it with Woodrow Wilson's views on the right of small nations to self-determination. Karadzic's gall was always world class but he consistently had trouble with the truth. A failed poet and a failed psychiatrist, everything he said was shaped to the needs of the moment – someone, like Ian Smith before him in Rhodesia, incapable of understanding the damage his pliant extremism was having on his own people.

On another occasion I was holed up in the Belgrade Intercontinental Hotel in 1993 for six long weeks waiting for NATO to attack the city. Each Friday Washington told me that the following week would be the one. It never was, until the Western powers finally lost patience and bombed Belgrade six years later. Most days I called in at the grubby press club in the centre of the city to exchange dollars for huge piles of rapidly devaluing dinars. So bad had hyperinflation in Serbia become by then that the Intercontinental was insisting on being paid daily, in cash. There was nothing for it but to convey the loot back to the hotel in large plastic bags – just like the wheelbarrows used to carry money around in the Weimar Republic in the early 1920s. Then, out of the blue, one Saturday morning I was granted an audience with Slobodan Milosevic. The leading perpetrator behind the myth of Serb victimhood, he managed to leave the Serbs worse off after every war he instigated. Yet nothing stopped him. In person he came across as thoughtful and shrewd, and my forty minutes with him stretched to an hour and a half. All the cunning ruthlessness Milosevic displayed in his daily decision-making was well hidden from sight. Instead I was treated to another Balkan history lesson and a display of sweet reason that ended with him asking me to return one day for another conversation. My questions can't have been tough enough. This interview joined a lengthening list of meetings with the main Balkan protagonists that was never reflected in the magazine.

I was not without a platform however. Some of the best pieces I wrote for *US News* arose out of the conflicts in Bosnia. One, in particular, 'Hostages to a brutal past' about the underlying situation in February 1993, won several awards. Encouraged by John Walcott, the canniest foreign editor I worked with, I began to contribute by-lined opinion columns. Years later, one stands out. Headed "A test the West is failing" (see Appendix), it appeared in late-January 1993 and laid into everyone – the UN, the European Union, the US and NATO – for a collective failure of will in the Balkans. "The crisis in Bosnia . . . is a test not only of the West's values but also its credibility as democracy's champion," I argued two years before the Srebrenica massacre of 8,000 Bosnian Muslims. The column stirred up a storm of protest from furious Serb and Croat émigré groups in the United States and Canada. One angry reader tore out the offending page and returned it *US News* with incoherent comments scribbled in green ink in the margins. It reached me eventually, and was framed by Jean and hung on a wall to remind me that sometimes a journalist does have real impact. The worldwide yearning for truth about contentious events in the past, such as the Srebrenica massacre or the 1968 Prague Spring, provoked another column in the magazine – my last as it turned out – three years later. This, too, resonated with readers but in a more restrained way.

The collapse of communism in the Soviet bloc and outlying satraps like Yugoslavia and Albania was the most historic and inspirational event in my 30-year career as a journalist, even more so than the end of apartheid which had fewer global ramifications. The political and material difficulties which have followed were, to my mind, inevitable. There was simply no easy, smooth or fair way of ending such a bigoted, totalitarian system that in some cases had endured for four generations and everywhere had corrupted entire societies and peoples from top to bottom. What has mattered far more, to me at least, is the liberation of the spirit, the chance given to individuals to realise their potential and the prospect of revival and rebirth in so many debased institutions and activities. To put a bottom line value on such a once-in-a-century upheaval is to miss the point entirely. Communism, as an ideology, had been a snare and a delusion from its genesis in a totally different age, but it took more than 150 years to demonstrate this beyond argument. For all its many flaws and abuses and failures the only political system that truly offers hope and a future is democracy.

9

A House Built on Shifting Sand

*"The truest characters of ignorance are vanity
and pride and arrogance."*

SAMUEL BUTLER

Years after they ceased to work for *US News & World Report* some ex-staffers were having an email exchange about life and times at the magazine in the 1980s and 1990s. One of them, a blunt sort of character from Dixie called Lew Lord – always a great one for the pithy phrase and the usable rewrite on a tight deadline – summed up his quarter century's employment like this: "I showed up every day for the same reason rednecks go to NASCAR races – to watch the wrecks."

That about sums up much of the 1985-96 period for me too. Apart from a halcyon interlude from 1989-93, when the stars coalesced in a great running story (the collapse of communism), an able and inclusive foreign editor and rare stability at the top, my twelve years as Senior European Editor were a constant struggle – against self-defeating budget cuts, intruders on my turf, sycophants, schemers and frauds. Right from the outset turmoil proved to be the *modus operandi* of the court of King Mort. No one could be sure from one day to the next who was up, who was down, what was in, what was out. Editors and well known writers came and went in a dizzying procession, on several occasions before I met or even talked to them. Rewrite types piled on top of each other in promiscuous profusion. The future of the foreign bureaus was a running sore that lasted more than a decade until the bottom liners, led by a wisecracking philistine from Brooklyn, won the argument and closed the lot.

The magazine seemed to be doing well for a time in the early-1990s only to fall back in the mid-1990s and end up holed below the waterline. It never recovered. An abiding lack of vision and consistency made everything worse – morale, quality, focus, effort. Much of the time it was better to laugh (if you could) than cry at the antics of those nominally in charge as they sought to justify their salaries and titles, and it certainly helped to be at arms' length from the daily absurdities perpetrated in the name of progress. In truth, Zuckerman and his allies in the acquisition of *US News* at no time defined their aims and objectives convincingly. Instead, right from the day Marv Stone bowed out in tired exasperation in early 1985, it became a matter of dog eats dog – a sort of crazed game of musical chairs in which the last one left holding the parcel when the music stopped was the one forced to tell Mort that the ship was heading for the rocks. The sad thing was how rarely this occurred.

Almost before the ink was dry on the takeover, Zuckerman's rosy words of reassurance to the staff in October 1984 were undermined by his actions. In short order he closed the company pension fund, siphoned off the surplus, sold the new *US News* building to a Japanese pension fund, cancelled severance payments to most employees and cut in half the insurance on correspondents travelling abroad. For the next three years the masthead was churned mercilessly until, by 1988, no more than thirty of the two hundred or so people Mort inherited still worked for him. Loyal older readers were described in staff meetings as a liability, out of step with the "more contemporary flavour" of the "new" magazine. Similarly cast aside without much of a backward glance were the last vestiges of the solid, unflashy institution founded by David Lawrence 50 or so years before – assets like the excellent library, an in-house nurse, the cafeteria and the gym. As another emailer – this one part of the post-1984 intake – put it long after the event: "What I still resent is that the guy who had the money to buy the place didn't love it and care about it even as much as we cynics did."

The downward slide began immediately Stone left. In quick succession he was replaced as Editor by Shelby Coffey (1985-86), David Gergen (1986-88) and Roger Rosenblatt (1988-89). None of them had edited a magazine or managed a staff of any size. Coffey, the recommendation of Harry Evans, came in hungry for success but also from left field – the Style section of the *Washington Post*. He claimed (perhaps tongue in cheek) that editing *US News* was "one of the great journalistic opportunities of the decade." That was before he dealt on a daily basis with Zuckerman who, by this stage, had named himself "Editor-in-Chief" and revealed that he wanted heads to roll. By way of a retreating defence Coffey, who favoured a more evolutionary approach, quoted Chinese poetry, avoided making decisions and refused to take offence. The passive tactics failed, and he left abruptly to pursue a stellar career elsewhere in American journalism.

Gergen was a more calculating character. He was not a journalist, and never pretended to be one. As a magazine editor he was hopeless, forever getting involved in the production process at the wrong moment or being nowhere to be found when most needed. Yet he was also open-minded and happy to debate issues and prepared to delegate. A former and future communications director in the White House, he worked with four US Presidents and was the epitome of a Washington "insider." Much of his time at the top of *US News* was given over to outside activities, such as speech-making and television appearances, and he never took root. Some of David's staff decisions were quixotic in the extreme, with the result that layers of editors piled up unchecked – eleven, by one count – between the original writer and a published story. I met him for the first time at the Reagan-Gorbachev summit in Geneva in 1985 where we were two of no less than a dozen people sent by the magazine to cover the meeting – about three times more than necessary. The recently appointed foreign editor, Hank Trewhitt, the hapless leader of this malfunctioning "team," lost his passport and wasted his time in Switzerland acquiring another one. The rest of us were left to twiddle our thumbs. Recently-recruited members of the magazine's staff used the chance to bad-mouth old timers. I cornered Gergen and spent hours trying to educate him to the realities of the weekly newsmagazine cycle. An anguished call from Washington on the Friday afternoon inquired where our files were. Trewhitt, it turned out, had planned to write everything himself and had made no alternative preparations. Somehow we survived this fiasco at the cost of a late closure, but it was not a good omen.

After a couple of years in the hot seat Gergen moved aside "to develop my own voice." In his place Zuckerman chose a polished and fluent writer on American social trends from *Time* magazine called Roger Rosenblatt, who lived in New York and also had never run anything. Like Coffey, he claimed to be over the moon at being named editor – "I feel like I've just inherited a fortune." Friendly and charming, Rosenblatt was just the sort of "smart" journalist Mort lusted after – at a distance. As soon as the marriage was consummated, the pair began to quarrel over new hires, story concepts, structures and budgets – "two people coming from entirely different perspectives on the profession and life" as Rosenblatt later put it with some deftness. As a manager he never stood a chance. He was also unfortunate in his timing, arriving in mid-1988 as the first company-wide cutbacks of the post-takeover era were being driven through. Fifteen months after he blew in, he walked out citing "personal reasons" following one disagreement too many with Mort, who then added to the confusion by paying him a gushing tribute which left everyone mystified.

Used to the somnolent stability at the top of the old magazine, this turmoil left me somewhat disoriented thousands of miles away in London. The largesse being lavished on new staffers in Washington passed the foreign bureaus by entirely. Our budgets were pared to the bone in 1985-87 regardless of realities like contractual rent hikes, and no provision was made year after year to upgrade our technology. Story suggestions went unanswered, pieces that were filed had quotations and analysis inserted by unknown persons, newcomers challenged assignments they disliked and the sense of drift and lack of unifying purpose – the essence of a newsmagazine – was palpable. Several people in Europe were fired. Others left voluntarily. No one abroad, including me, knew what to do or what was going on. By mid-1986 I had had enough and felt that I had to kick-start my career elsewhere before it stalled for good.

The opportunity of a change came by pure chance. Through a mutual friend I met Charles Wilson, then editor of *The Times* of London. He was looking for a new foreign editor and, after a cursory lunch (he was an abrasive Glaswegian not given to dallying over the bread rolls), I was made an offer in July which I accepted. Gergen was only mildly taken aback and wished me well. Then doubts began to set in. One day I visited Fortress Wapping, where *The Times* was produced, and was disconcerted to discover that the foreign editor had no back up and no office and was expected as a matter of routine to work 13-14 hour days single-handedly running a team of 25 correspondents and stringers all over the world – on top of the daily two and a half hour commute I faced on the underground to and from work. Soon after *The Times's* senior foreign correspondent, Robert Fisk, came to lunch carrying a large satchel. Based in the Middle East and well known for his ferocious dedication to the job, Fisk wished to probe my views on the Arab-Israeli conflict before "anointing" me. Prior to our lunch he sat in our little garden ignoring me and frenetically burrowing through a mountain of office mail, all the while throwing away letters from lunatics (of whom there seemed to be many). During the meal he began talking, and it emerged that he was being paid half as much again as Wilson was offering me – and I was taking a substantial pay cut by leaving *US News*. We parted on civil terms, just. Wilson, meanwhile, made it clear that he felt he was taking a chance with me since I had never worked in daily journalism; I was to be, he said, "on probation." Given his reputation for hiring and firing, the implication was clear. When I learned from a confidant in Washington that Gergen would be delighted to have me back, I changed my mind – to Wilson's undying fury (I met him again a few years later and he cut me dead). Generously, David gave me a pay rise and confirmed my position in London for another two years. Soon after, Zuckerman wrote to express his "genuine pleasure" at my change of heart. "It means so much to the magazine and to me."

I had been very fortunate and realised there would be a price to be paid. The bill fell due the following summer after more disarray in the foreign staff as the wretched Trewhitt screwed up repeatedly and Zuckerman, who always regarded the magazine's foreign component as the icing on his cake, grew more and more exasperated. One evening in late May the phone rang, and Gergen was on the other end. The Trewhitt mess could continue no longer, he said. Would I come to Washington for four months to help clear it up while a search for a new foreign editor proceeded? He made it clear that I was not in the frame for the position on a permanent basis; Zuckerman, he said, was chasing Joe Joffe, a well-known German columnist and opinion page editor at *Süddeutsche Zeitung*. The pair had met recently at a conference and Mort was smitten. Jean was going through a bad patch with her health, and we were supposed to be going on a long holiday to aid her recovery, but we realised I had no choice. So off I flew to Washington a week later for what turned out to be an extraordinary roller coaster of a ride.

Nothing had quite prepared me for the chaos reigning at 2400 N Street. My objective, Gergen had said, was "to restore the morale of the foreign staff, to get it to pull together and to provide leadership." All in four months. On arrival I was given a day to get back up to speed on the magazine's complex computer-based editing and design system. Then it was heads down as the gruelling weekly production cycle began anew.

Right away I discovered a vacuum in which no decisions were being taken, no stories were in the pipeline, no ideas were coming in and none of the senior editors around me was prepared to stick his hand up until Zuckerman had pronounced. Sometimes he obliged, other times he did not. All those working on the foreign side in Washington seemed unhappy and demoralised. Trewhitt took his demotion hard and disappeared for days, while one of the senior writers – an old friend and potentially a key ally – made it clear he thought that he should be stepping in, not me, and effectively went on strike. I behaved true to type, waded in feet first, took decisions, followed the foreign news like a hawk, sent out clear assignments promptly and generally gave the impression of knowing what I was doing. Americans, I realised, preferred it that way; any hint of doubt or hesitation was taken as weakness and might be exploited. Within a few weeks I felt on top of the job. Joffe had been "paraded like a taunt in front of me," I wrote to Jean at the time, but I refused to let that situation get me down. After a month or so he sensibly declined Zuckerman's offer.

The biggest challenge was the editor-in-chief. Second-guessing was Mort's second name. Some of his input was helpful, but mostly it was a daily struggle to avoid getting drawn into arguments with him over his latest pet theory, of which there were many. One day he made me sit in his office while he tore apart a fellow real estate developer down the phone with a ferocious outburst of threats and gutter language. I concluded that the idea was to overawe me, but in reality the display left me feeling embarrassed, for him. Still, that was nothing compared to the trials and tribulations we faced every week over *Depth*, a shady Israeli news service that Mort had subscribed to earlier in 1987 convinced that it offered exclusive material. By the time I got to Washington *Depth* was deeply embedded and its input was popping up like a virus everywhere in the magazine. What had begun as a purely Mideast-focused operation had spread far and wide to take in every corner of the globe, including the US. None of its information was sourced, its key individual answered only to Zuckerman and the claims it made were getting wilder and wilder. By July the situation was spinning out of control, threatening *US News's* reputation. Something had to be done if disaster was to be averted. With Gergen's connivance, a reporter was detached from his normal beat covering the State Department and instructed to do nothing else except check out *Depth* stories. This often took weeks, so in the meantime excuses had to be found to mollify Zuckerman. At a rough estimate eight out of ten of *Depth's* claims proved too unreliable to be printed; in particular, I remember one about an alleged Iranian suicide bomber who was supposed to have been strapped to an underwater torpedo that, *Depth* claimed, had been fired at a named US Navy vessel in the Persian Gulf. As far as we could ascertain, no such incident had ever taken place. Mort, of course, leant the other way. Another tug-of-war ensued.

After four months of this sort of Alice-in-Wonderland pressure week after week, it was a relief to learn in October that a new foreign editor had been found and that I could return home. Emily MacFarquhar was to survive a year – a former foreign affairs specialist at *The Economist* in London who had moved to Harvard when her husband was appointed to a senior post at the university. Not everyone got on with Emily who could be semantic and humourless and disputatious, but I warmed to her from the outset. In return, she improved my writing, moving it decisively away from the old formulaic *US News* style towards a more discursive technique which served me well later in my career. Before I left, Gergen took me out to lunch by way of thanks and later paid me a handsome tribute at a staff meeting. "Robin did a superb job. I really do think that, and am very grateful to him as are a lot of others here." My *Times* debt had been repaid with interest.

Zuckerman was not so easily satisfied. On a personal level he took a lot of getting to know and, despite having far more dealings with him than most people at my level, on a wide range of issues and projects, I'm not sure I ever cracked his veneer. His conflicting personalities did not make for relaxed company at the best of times even if he had not been the owner and editor-in-chief of the magazine. Just when you thought you were making progress, he would pull back and go into reverse gear. Slight of build, with a noticeable lisp and geekish manner, he could appear unimpressive and detached. Yet he needed watching. His mood would switch in the blink of an eye – generous and tight-fisted, bullying and accommodating, arrogant and insecure, offhand and capricious and smart all in the same conversation. His political convictions swayed this way and that, and he seemed to have few long term friends. When he wanted to, or when he had a captive audience, Mort could be witty and amusing, and he had a huge stock of jokes and anecdotes always primed for deployment. His attitude towards journalists was complex. He wanted to be one, at least at the topmost level, and admired those with a high profile or some academic reputation. On the other hand, he was dismissive of the foot soldiers without whom his publications would never have appeared, and repetitively critical of journalists' business knowledge and their "limited world view."

Robin Knight is a versatile and experienced correspondent with a sharp news sense, sound judgment and a broad knowledge of international politics. It is a measure of respect for Robin's wide-ranging talents that, as US News contracts its foreign operations, he has been put in charge of a broad swathe of territory including northern and eastern Europe and all of Africa. He has done distinguished reporting from all these areas.

As foreign editor of US News over the past year, I worked closely with Robin and found him a fount of ideas. He never takes no for an answer, either from reluctant interviewees or from obtuse editors, and the magazine is invariably better for his battering. He widened the parochial horizons of the Washington office and alerted us to not-yet-news in Nato, the European community, southern Africa. He is extremely good at seeing the connections between disparate events and drawing together the strands of national politics into big thematic pieces. He has a transatlantic perspective, with a good understanding of political interests and news demands in Europe and the United States.

In a world of competitive egos, Robin is a team player, highly supportive of his own bureau and always ready to provide insightful input for stories written elsewhere. As my immediate predecessor, he was particularly helpful in guiding me, a newcomer, through the technical and human obstacle courses at US News. He is a valued colleague and would be an asset to any news organisation.

Emily MacFarquhar
Foreign Editor, US News (Oct '87-Nov '88)
378 Broadway
Cambridge MA 02139   617 547 8166

After navigating this minefield for more than a decade I came to the conclusion that Mort really had little understanding of what a reporter does or what motivates someone to become a journalist. To him, journalism seemed to be all about showing off – meeting world leaders, acting as a high level go-between, pontificating on an instantly-forgotten television talk show or editorialising in a column. The idea that there is as much truth to be found by talking to the homeless or to protestors at a demonstration or to a barman in a hotel would simply never occur to him. All kinds of speculative reasons floated around 2400 N Street in the 1980s about why he had bought *US News*. Some thought it a calling card to gain entry into Washington's political *milieu* – and he certainly made no secret of his desire to be taken seriously as a current affairs commentator. Others reckoned he had simply outgrown the property world even if he never entirely lost his love of a deal. Still others saw it as a down payment on the road to higher recognition – a seat in the US Senate, maybe, or an ambassadorship. Since he had been born and brought up in Canada the grandson of a rabbi, just about the only thing anyone could be certain of, as his media holdings expanded in the 1980s and 1990s, was that Mort Zuckerman could not run for president of the United States.

To me, Mort was the perennial outsider who wanted to be accepted by the society he had embraced and saw the media as the best vehicle to achieve this. His flaws were all too apparent, but on several occasions he went out of his way to be kind to Jean and me. Once I helped him to organise and pay for a cancer operation in London for the daughter of a Russian official whom he had met briefly in Moscow. His numerous female companions rarely bad-mouthed him even after relationships ended. For three years after he purchased *US News* he sanctioned real increases in spending on infrastructure and redesigns. If the stakes were high enough – for example, when he came to London at the end of 1988 to interview Margaret Thatcher – he would listen to advice. On that occasion I laid on a pre-interview dinner party of a dozen people who knew Thatcher well. Their unanimous counsel was that he should never interrupt her, or try to debate with her (as he had done, disastrously, months earlier when meeting a nonplussed President Mitterrand in Paris). Mort did as suggested – and was then let down by Rosenblatt in Washington, who failed to give the interview the space it deserved.

Time and again, though, the other Mort – scheming, sharp tongued, aggressive, litigious, dismissive, restless – got in the way of acceptance. "Everything is complicated with him" a mutual friend once told me. "His basic approach always is to conclude the deal first, start negotiating afterwards." That was exactly how he proceeded at the magazine from 1985 onwards. The only word to describe his impact at *US News* in the five years immediately after he bought the magazine is "disruptive." Four editors came and went. Around eight out of ten of the staff he inherited left – part of a deliberate culling of "inadequate" employees who did not meet his undefined "new" standards. Big names made futile cameo appearances; Mort was forever getting schoolboy crushes on so-called media stars. Magazine structures were ripped up, rebuilt and dug up again. Every attempt to settle on an agreed philosophy for the "new" *US News* failed. Zuckerman often had good ideas, but he undermined them by meddling and by blurring the lines between journalism and advocacy. His volcanic temper, which was liable to erupt on the slightest pretext (and, to be fair, subside equally quickly), ensured that few would stand up to him. Equally, many of the staff, both old and new, initially deployed a form of foot-dragging passive resistance in the hope that he would lose interest in what they were doing. He never did, proving tenacious in pursuit of all his whims regardless of the effect on morale and commitment.

I met Mort for the first time in London in October 1985 when I received a brusque and unsettling lecture on what was wrong with the magazine, how he was going to put it right and who was going to lose their jobs in 1986. He had arrived in town with his latest Svengali in tow, ignored the bureau and then complained bitterly when appointments made from New York failed to materialise. At that time he was assuming that any interview he did would appear as of right in his magazine. The following year his antics almost capsized an interview in South Africa which we had chased for seven years. Another time I spent a week in Warsaw trying to smooth over relations with the Poles after he failed to turn up for an interview with General Jaruzelski. When I resigned in 1986 I finally registered on his radar; he hated losing people (unless he fired them) almost as much as he enjoyed chasing them. Then, after I changed my mind, he was all good cheer and, until the final denouement in 1995-96, could not have been more supportive. I paid a price, of course, often having to arrange hotels, cars and clandestine meetings for him and to act as a kind of undercover agent sussing out potential employees and media purchases in Britain. One of my prime targets, Martin Dunn, then editor of a Rupert Murdoch paper in London, stayed with Mort for years after I contacted him, and went on to twice edit Zuckerman's New York tabloid *The Daily News*.

History may be kinder to Mort than his contemporaries have been. He did make a lot of people rich at the old *US News*, bankrolled a failing if worthwhile product for years and became a billionaire thanks to his real estate flair. Along the way he did enter the public policy arena and become the sounding board of presidents and prime ministers.

Sometimes he even triumphed. Bliss, for Zuckerman, surely was the moment in November 1991 when Mikhail Gorbachev gave *US News* an interview and began it by quoting back to him some of his critical, anti-Soviet editorials. Yet he was fated always to be the *arriviste* – the outsider from Canada, mistrusted by many and actively disliked by others. This lack of acceptance puzzled him. "What I did is what America is all about," he told an interviewer once rather plaintively. Like most people who had much contact with him, in the end I was let down and he was nowhere to be seen when he was most needed. Loyalty to those around him was an alien concept; you were useful to Mort while it suited him. But I had a good ride and it was, mostly, fun while it lasted. He knew that. Life, for Zuckerman, was always a deal – a black-and-white trade-off – and he had long since fulfilled his part of any bargain with me.

Before this final parting of the ways *US News* enjoyed what, in retrospect, was a golden interlude of relative calm and adult, focused leadership – the Mike Ruby/Mimi McLoughlin co-editorship which lasted from October 1989 to September 1996. Their ascendancy came about by chance. When Rosenblatt jumped ship – the fourth editor to depart abruptly in five years – the derision among the American media *cognoscenti* verged on the embarrassing. Even Zuckerman sensed that the *US News* brand was under threat from this constant editorial merry-go-round. The Rubys, who had been back-stopping Gergen and Rosenblatt, offered a popular and viable in-house option, and Mort was sufficiently off-balance to agree to it. Professionally, their relationship with Zuckerman was often tempestuous; I recall Mike's quip (advice he received from a savvy friend before taking the job): "The main thing you and Mimi have to do when you go into Mort's office is to make sure you're well apart so that he can't get you with the same burst." What price this contrasting couple – he reserved, Jewish and reluctant to confront; she feisty, Protestant and technically proficient – paid for the unusual arrangement only they can say. It must have been high as both felt it their duty to try to shield the staff as much as possible from Zuckerman's tirades and interference. From my point of view the key factor was that the set-up worked, providing the certainty and stability that had been so badly lacking. Even so, it took time to steady the ship and turn it into the wind. But within a couple of years the magazine was clearly moving ahead with morale, circulation, advertising, awards and visibility all up markedly on the pre-sale period, and *Time* and *Newsweek* suddenly paying attention to this upstart. So began what was, I felt even at the time, the outstanding period in *US News's* uneven history.

Most of my dealings were with Mike. He handled economic, business and international affairs while Mimi took the rest. For sometime after he arrived from *Newsweek* in 1986, he treated me with suspicion – a holdover from the *ancien regime* which his previous employer had not rated. Things began to improve when Gergen summoned me to Washington. At that stage Jean had had four serious operations in the previous four years. It turned out that Mimi, too, had gone through a similar challenge. The ice broke, and for most of the years to come we worked well together. Mike loved conceptualizing newsmagazines, tweaking designs and rummaging around for new ways of doing things. He liked "risk-taking" in writing; only by taking risks, he felt, would any improvement be achieved. Whether he was a good judge of character is open to discussion. Over time he relied too much on people with axes to grind who misled him, as I was to discover to my cost in 1994-5. After nearly seven years at the helm the constant battles with Zuckerman over budgets and bureaus and stories wore Mike down, and perhaps he took his eye off the ball. When the owner called one day in September 1996 while the Rubys were on vacation to fire the pair, Mike said later that he was half-expecting it. Such a long stint in such a high-wire job spoke for itself and it was fitting that his peremptory ejection from *US News* did not finish Mike professionally. He went on to have a rewarding career first on a well-respected paper in Milwaukee and later as a biographer and editor.

Ruby's view on the proper role of editors on newsmagazines struck a chord with me. Editors existed, he maintained, solely to make writers and reporters "look better." Late in 1988 he had been instrumental in hiring John Walcott from *The Wall Street Journal* to replace Emily MacFarquhar. John turned out to be by far the best foreign editor I worked with – cheerful, friendly, inclusive, supportive and constructive. No one would call him a great sub-editor; he much preferred to have correspondents write to space and do any rewriting themselves. It helped, of course, that his period in charge coincided with a stellar phase for foreign stories which engaged not only the owner and senior editors in Washington but also the magazine's core "middle America" readership. But John knew how to exploit this situation, banging the magazine drum, raising the collective profile of the foreign staff and giving some of us our heads. Never once, to my recollection, did he disagree with a story line that I advocated from the scene. Given the game-changing events of this period, that is amazing in itself in view of weekly magazines' in-built tendency to use the extra time they have compared to daily publications to procrastinate. I flourished under this grown-up management, and received a series of "herograms" from Mike and John. One from John that I particularly treasured arrived after a long spell in Bosnia in the miserable winter of 1992-93. It contained the sort of words that all foreign correspondents operating in tough circumstances surely crave – "insightful, revealing, informative, memorable and thoroughly depressing."

During this halcyon period imagination, as much as events or budgets, defined our parameters. My long association with NATO produced three timely 'Conversations with . . .' the SACEUR (Supreme Allied Commander Europe) of the day, the cerebral General John Galvin. On one of these occasions Galvin, a noted military historian, escorted me in the afternoon on a detailed tour of the Waterloo battlefield near his residence. It was fascinating to hear a modern commander dissect Wellington's and Napoleon's combat tactics. In 1988 the magazine closed its bureau in Bonn and asked me to cover West Germany from London – another high profile assignment given what was happening then in Europe. Margaret Thatcher was a banker for all US publications throughout the 1980s, punching way above her weight and I often took advantage of this. Her fall in 1990 produced a flurry of articles on the state of Britain. Another memorable 'Conversation with . . .' involved Oleg Gordievsky, the KGB defector. After much back-and-forth with his London publishers to establish my credentials, we met finally in 1991 in a dingy back room off St Martin's Lane in central London for a *tour d'horizon* just as communism was collapsing which made it abundantly clear that the KGB had not gone away. Gordievsky was in disguise, and his ill-fitting wig and false moustache proved constant distractions as we talked in a cubby hole surrounded by musty piles of old books.

One thing I was not during the Ruby/Walcott era was idle. As the new team got into its stride we began to hire young freelancers to string for the magazine around Europe. I was given the job of "managing" them. In London Leslie Viney, Jonathan Ames and Jennifer Fisher backstopped me capably, making it possible to travel as much as I did without worrying overmuch about coverage back at base. John Marks in

Berlin and Peter Green in Prague, both keen and enthusiastic, were endlessly imaginative in their suggestions and happy to be guided in their reporting and writing. John trained on, joining the magazine's international staff and opening a bureau in reunified Berlin after the Wall came down. A sensitive soul in love with words (he wrote several novels later in life), he never found the rough-and-tumble of Zuckerman's magazine entirely to his liking, but before he moved into the world of television he did a lot of outstanding work. Peter was more resilient but also more flaky, ingenuous and unpredictable. When he did surface with a file, it was often terrific – colourful, sharp and immediately useable. For some years after 1989 he stagnated in the Czech Republic, always promising the definitive English-language biography of Vaclav Havel. It never appeared, and he moved back to New York and a desk job with Bloomberg. Others called in from time to time from Warsaw, Budapest, Stockholm, Helsinki, Rome and Madrid – a far cry from my earlier years when freelancers were viewed with suspicion by the magazine and rarely used in any capacity. On top of this it also became part of my job to massage Zuckerman's trophy columnists in England including the well-known military historian John Keegan and the former editor of *The Times* Simon Jenkins, both of whom, unfortunately, had no compunction about covering the same ground that I did.

Life as one of the magazine's senior editors in this period, in fact, had numerous compensations. Zuckerman came and went through London – eight times in 1989 – and was beginning to calm down and place more faith in his staff. His visits always had impact and raised the magazine's profile. As a collective, we seemed to be on top of the job for once, rather than running behind the curve, and this was reflected in the twenty journalism awards won by the magazine in the US in 1991 alone. By 1993 circulation was ten per cent up on 1984 (*Time* was 10 per cent down), newsstand sales had risen by one-third, the median age of the readership had fallen three years to 41.6, advertising sales growth was outstripping *Time* and *Newsweek* and *US News* was alleged (by the co-editors, not Zuckerman) to be turning a profit. Calls started to be returned. Access at a high level became easier to arrange. I was elected a committee member of the FPA (Foreign Press Association) in London and the AACL (Association of American Correspondents in London), and repeatedly turned down efforts to make me president of the AACL on the grounds that I was not an American. Would-be journalists dropped by asking for advice so often that, for a couple of academic years in the late-1980s, I got up early and lectured international graduate students attending media training courses at City University.

Out of the blue I was asked by a New York literary agent to write a book with Richard Goldstone, then chief prosecutor at the United Nations War Crimes Tribunal in The Hague. In the event nothing came of this project and Goldstone later returned to South Africa and wrote his own book. But it was flattering to be asked. One summer I was sent to bicycle around Copenhagen for a week to see if the Danes had the answer to urban gridlock. My answer was yes – provided a city was flat. The various commemorations marking 50 years after D-Day and the end of the Second World War in 1994-95 offered rich pickings of the 'state of Europe' variety, and I duly cashed in. Around this time I also spent ten absorbing days in the UK National Archives at Kew researching a long report ordered up by Zuckerman about rumoured British links to Raoul Wallenberg, the Swedish diplomat who disappeared in Hungary in 1945. This was published as part of an "investigative exclusive" of the type Mort fixated on.

At home, too, the early 1990s rolled out deceptively smoothly. On our return to London we had settled back into our "working man's cottage" in Paxton Road for six months before moving a short distance away to a new neo-Georgian terraced house overlooking the river Thames. It was to be a happy change of scenery. Over the next quarter century Chiswick Wharf proved to be a fine base for me, a secure and welcoming retreat for Jean and a good investment. On summer days, when planes thundered overhead on their approach to Heathrow, we did wonder if we had made the right choice. Then we would look out of our first-floor windows. To one side geese and swans and ducks and cormorants would be flying by, and energetic rowers and sailors and pleasure craft would be doing their own thing on the muddy brown waters of the Thames just twenty yards away. On the other side of the house, oaks and cherry trees surrounded the old Chiswick parish church of St Nicholas. Sometimes flocks of birds would swarm down on the golden-coloured weather vane on top of the building's 13th century tower. In summer the smell of new mown grass in the adjacent churchyard would waft in through our open windows. All this near to a famous brewery, and just six miles from Hyde Park Corner. We made the right decision.

Two US ambassadors in London became good friends and we visited their residence in Regent's Park on many social occasions. The first, the suave and urbane career diplomat Ray Seitz, did me a special favour in 1994 by signing off his glittering diplomatic career with an on-the-record interview that made clear his distaste for the workings of the Clinton Administration – an almost unprecedented public snub by a retiring ambassador which Mike Ruby, for once, mishandled. A small portion of the interview was published one week and created so many waves in Washington and London that the whole text had to be printed in the following week's issue – the only time this ever occurred in *US News's* history to my knowledge.

Seitz's successor, Admiral William Crowe, a former chairman of the US joint chiefs of staff, did me the signal honour of agreeing to be guest of honour on Founder's Day at Pangbourne College in 1995 (I had been elected a governor of the school the year before). On the day Crowe, inspired by the sight of the Stars and Stripes flag flying over the College parade ground, rows of smart teenage cadets in naval uniform awaiting his inspection and the college band playing American marching tunes and the US national anthem with considerable aplomb, rose to the occasion with an inspiring speech he had written himself on the theme of optimism about the future. His press attaché, an old friend from *Newsweek* called Bud Korengold, who had advised against the visit, was suitably contrite.

At the end of that year Crowe repaid the invitation by asking Jean and me to an early evening reception at Winfield House to meet Bill Clinton. In the receiving line I asked the president about his well-publicised attempts to learn to hit golf shots under the wind on the lawn at the back of the White House. He responded with a lengthy description of his swing and a demonstration of his new grip! At least it made a change from the mock-profound exchanges on geopolitics going on up and down the line. Later that night I was one of two US-accredited correspondents invited to a post-dinner reception hosted by Prime Minister John Major for Clinton at 10 Downing Street. The occasion was memorable, not least for the spectacle of Tony and Cherie Blair standing in the centre of one of the upstairs reception rooms "sizing up the curtains" as the political editor of *The Sunday Times* amusingly put it. I was standing in a corner talking to David Trimble, the leader of the Ulster Unionist Party, when Major came bounding over and hissed 'You cut me off at the knees this morning, David!" A heated discussion ensued right under my nose as Trimble defended himself vigorously, having earlier that day criticised the thin-skinned prime minister on BBC radio for some alleged double-dealing. Happy times!

In Confirmation

In honour of
The President of the United States of America
and Mrs Clinton

The Prime Minister
and Mrs John Major
request the honour of the company of

Mr Robin Knight

at a Reception at 10 Downing Street, Whitehall
on Wednesday, 29th November 1995 from 9.30 p.m. to 11.00 p.m.

Enquiries to:
The Secretary (Invitations),
10 Downing Street, Whitehall,
London SW1A 2AA

Dress: Black Tie

The weekly briefings at Downing Street given to American correspondents in London in this period were a particular pleasure. When I returned to the UK they were being conducted by Bernard Ingham, a career civil servant whom Margaret Thatcher plucked from a backwater. Ingham, a large, ruddy-faced, no-nonsense Yorkshireman with bushy eyebrows and red hair, was by far the best No. 10 spokesman I had dealings with – straight, fair and to the point. One knew that he reflected Thatcher's views and could trust his judgement, and he was always good company. Some in the British lobby complained that he was bullying and manipulative but this never arose with the less fevered American lobby which, by and large, liked his direct style even at times of US/UK disagreement.

Ingham was succeeded in 1990 by Gus O'Donnell – cool and rational where Ingham sometimes could be emotional and pumped up. A fast-rising civil servant who went on to become Cabinet Secretary, the likeable O'Donnell tried to be understanding and emollient with journalists, but had the misfortune to represent someone who was damned by faint praise whatever he did. Four years later he moved on and was replaced by Christopher Meyer, a smooth-talking career diplomat who sported red socks and loafers and proved to be surprisingly brash. Chris eventually became UK ambassador in the United States and, in retirement, acted as head of the UK Press Complaints Commission. He had run the Foreign Office press department and the British Embassy in Bonn so I knew him. His time in Downing Street illustrated an enduring truth about all spokesman roles – if the boss is in trouble, for whatever reason, the best tactic is to say and do as little as possible. Everything else is a waste of time and effort. Major, who I once saw kicking a television screen in frustration outside the old briefing room in Downing Street (a lunchtime news item had infuriated him), never could conceal his sensitivity to adverse press comment. True, he was on the receiving end of more than his fair share as his party and government bickered over Europe and fell apart. But he made matters worse for himself by insisting on reading the newspapers each day, highlighting furiously as he went. Calming such a fraught situation was impossible, and Meyer left for Washington after the 1997 general election with a sense of relief.

None of the press secretaries, it is true, ever expressed much interest in *US News* or its coverage of British affairs, which maybe was just as well. By this stage in the post-war world American press coverage of British affairs had shrunk and become distinctly patchy, regardless of the high quality of correspondent still being sent to London. As it turned out, the Thatcher and Major premierships were full of internationally newsworthy episodes which underlined Britain's changing place in the world and the changing nature of British society. The magazine often gave me my head, and my rather ambivalent view of the lasting impact of Thatcher's self-help "revolution" would seep into print. In 1989 I tried to educate Americans to the changing nature of the British class "system." This produced a shoal of critical letters from incredulous readers. When Thatcher was knifed by her own party, I tried to explain the pent-up emotions behind the coup. Again, our readers were unconvinced. Five years later, just before he was promoted, John Walcott bestowed a final column on me to try to describe to Americans why economists should beat a path to North Shields in northeast England where four times as many men as women were registered as unemployed.

Even in these productive and worthwhile years, however, the long-term auguries for foreign coverage in *US News* were disturbing. In 1988 two members of the international staff based in London were fired on cost grounds. One of them, John Harvey-Lee, had selflessly backed up the magazine's correspondents and photographers worldwide for 25 years. He left with no compensation. Two bureaus in Europe were also closed that year. A couple of years later cost-of-living allowances for the foreign staff were abolished followed, shortly after, by the removal of tax equalisation payments. Pay above a certain level was frozen in 1990; I never had another rise. The following year I was instructed to find cheaper quarters and moved the office from a spacious suite the magazine had occupied over New Bond Street since the mid-1950s to two tiny rooms high above Piccadilly. Routine "home leave" visits were postponed on cost grounds and bureau budgets, especially travel, salami-sliced year by year. While the foreign news continued to flow my way, I shrugged my shoulders. But when a memo from Walcott arrived in 1993 announcing that the pages in the magazine devoted to foreign news were to be cut by one-third, alarm bells started ringing. They became louder in 1994 when a 34-page "reassessment" of *US News*, overseen by the Rubys, contained not a single reference to foreign coverage.

Walcott was promoted that year and, with the advantage of hindsight, from then on it was only a matter of time before I was shown the door. The so-called chief of correspondents gave up calling and devoted his energies to undermining me, eventually succeeding in alienating Ruby until Mike realised what was happening. In the summer of 1995 matters came to a head when Zuckerman decreed that one of the three remaining bureaus in Europe had to close. Ruby, for whatever reason (I never found out why) chose London to go, and Paris (which had been closed once and reopened) and Berlin to stay. My nemesis arrived in London in July at a day's notice and handed me a take-it-or-leave it ultimatum – the bureau was to shut at the start of October. I could either leave the magazine then, without compensation, or become one of three diplomatic correspondents in Washington. The "offer" was a calculated insult designed to force me out but over the next nine weeks, aided and abetted by a shell-shocked Jeff Trimble (Walcott's replacement), Ruby and Zuckerman were talked round to accept my "cut price" counter-offer – to work at home on a shoestring bureau budget of $1,000 a month. The chief of correspondents was left with egg on his face and a bitter determination to get even, while I was left upset and disillusioned at being so thoroughly denigrated after the best part of three successful decades with the magazine.

Throughout this period Jean remained the most loyal and steadfast supporter anyone could want. For much of the time after we returned to the UK her health had been an ongoing worry. She battled on, and in the late1980s resumed her administrative career at the Independent Broadcasting Authority (later the Independent Television Commission). In 1987 she was appointed the organisation's social secretary – an all-consuming and stressful job that involved long hours, countless "productions" from scratch and little support or thanks. Her great attention to detail came to her rescue, enabling her to remain on top of what turned out to be a very demanding position as the ITC contracted and then found itself absorbed into another regulatory agency called Ofcom. Successive director generals owed her a considerable debt for keeping the show on the road regardless. Some, but not all, acknowledged it. When the boom lowered on the *US News* bureau in London in 1995, she said instantly that she would move to Washington with me if that was what I wanted to do. For the umpteenth time in our relationship, the tougher the going got, the closer we became – a wonderfully reassuring anchor to have in such turbulent seas.

All the same, the bureau move to Chiswick Wharf one rainy autumn day in October 1995 proved traumatic. Three loyal, hard-working local employees lost their jobs overnight, with minimal notice and no compensation. Our house at Chiswick Wharf in no way was set up to operate an office. Assignments dried up in the second half of 1995, and travel all but ceased. Communication with Washington became non-existent except from Jeff Trimble, who remained staunch to the very end. If this was death by a thousand cuts, as it was, it proved to be painful. Early in 1996 we decided to convert our loft into a proper office. Construction began in March. Five months after shutting the door of the Piccadilly bureau for the last time, and nine weeks after the loft conversion began, I moved into my eighth *US News* work space in mid-May. The arrangements were to last for precisely four months.

10

Reversal of Fortune

"Life is just one damned thing after another."

ELBERT HUBBARD

The telephone rang at about 5.30 in the afternoon. It was James Fallows, the new editor of the magazine, who had taken over from the Rubys while we were away on holiday in Portugal. On returning to work that Monday, the first thing I had done was to sit down and write him a welcoming note. I had never met Fallows, and knew him only vaguely from a book he had written the previous year which attacked journalists in America who earned fees from making public appearances on behalf of special interest groups. That hardly applied to me. In nearly 30 years at *US News & World Report* I had earned barely $1,000 from freelancing.

Answering the call, my immediate reaction when Fallows introduced himself was to congratulate him on his appointment. Hardly had the friendly words left my lips when the blow fell. "For reasons of resources I am phasing out the bureau in London and shifting the money to coverage of China, East Asia and Mexico," this hitherto unknown voice intoned. "You will receive an ample financial package." Fallows went on to say that he "admired and respected" my work and knew what I had done to save the bureau in 1995-96.

At this point the penny dropped. "Resources" meant nothing more than my salary given the penurious conditions now surrounding *US News's* London bureau. Operational costs were down to $12,000 a year, travel had all but ceased, all the local staff had gone, I was working from home and I had taken an 18% pay cut in the past two years. "Resources" was a euphemism. The more I pressed Fallows, the more he floundered. It sounded as though a decision had been taken to pull out of Europe altogether and instead to rely on freelancers. Closing a bureau that had been ever-present for decades sent out an obvious distress signal; *US News & World Report* had been represented in London since 1946 through thick and thin. I was the eighth bureau chief. It meant nothing. No other job was offered. I was not allowed even to freelance for the magazine; someone else had already been given the British string. After five minutes Fallows hung up, promising to call back. He never did – just one of numerous duplicitous actions at my expense over the next few months.

Fallows was my seventh editor at *USN&WR,* and although the previous two years had been difficult I had no real reason to believe that he would be the last. A job in Washington had always seemed to be my ultimate fall-back position. Moreover, my star was shining again after the partial eclipse of 1995. Prior to our holiday I had spent nearly two months in Moscow standing in for the bureau chief – a very lively interlude which ended with generous words of praise from Mike Ruby. This was the period when the Russians' first ill-judged intervention in Chechnya came home to roost. Week after week I had produced well-received pieces and had enjoyed this particular return to old haunts and the prominence given to the story in the magazine. I would have done so even more had I known it was to be my swan-song after 28 years on the road as a foreign correspondent.

That said, and although I hated being "let go" and had hoped to remain with *US News* until I was 60 in 2003, by 1996 much of the gilt had worn off being the European Editor of an impecunious American publication. The endless pressures of the last two years involved in fending off cost-cutters in Washington had become increasingly irksome. So had salary cuts, cheap air tickets and sniping from the rear. It's no coincidence that my most successful spell at *US News* coincided with John Walcott's 1989-94 period as foreign editor. He respected me, I respected him. If money needed to be spent, he found it. His successor Jeff Trimble, one of my closest friends on the magazine but 15 years younger than me and new to his job, never stood a chance. The amount of space devoted to foreign coverage shrank, Zuckerman began to demean his staff again, there was constant niggling over assignments, turf wars broke out as travel was cut back and Jeff had no choice but to take it on the chin and hope to live to fight another day.

I never did get the opportunity to argue the toss in person. I had last gone on "home leave" as long ago as the spring of 1991. A visit due in 1994 had been postponed repeatedly on cost grounds, so it was more than five years since I had touched bases in person with colleagues in

Washington. Inevitably my relationships with other staffers grew more distant, old friends moved on and newcomers lined up to bid for the "plums" they believed were available for picking in Europe should the status quo be overthrown. By the time I was kicked out I must have been a shadowy figure ripe for plucking by the frustrated young Turks – "Jim's altar boys" as they became known – who flocked to the Fallows' banner. Nor did I ever get the chance to outline to Fallows, or to anyone else in Washington, a sustainable strategy for foreign coverage in *US News*. If I had, my concept – based on two regional editors in Europe and Asia, supported by stringers and a couple of Washington-based fire-fighters – would have been affordable and quite different, both to the status quo and to the neither-one-thing-nor-the-other model subsequently adopted.

To this day I am not entirely sure why my particular head was on the block. No other staffer based abroad, or reporter at my level in the US, was sacked in Fallows' initial purge. All kinds of explanations were floated at various times. Some made more sense than others, but none was conclusive and none was authorised and I was never given an "official" justification. Even the "resources" cliché begged the question since it would be at least 18 months before savings showed through on the books given the eventual terms of my redundancy package. Trying to justify himself at the time, Fallows criticised the magazine's foreign coverage for its "lack of context . . . (and) its relentless over-emphasis on the process of politics" – meaningless jargon that underlined how little he knew about foreign reportage in an American national weekly magazine. Those in the know kept their mouths shut out of concern, maybe, that I would sue for unfair dismissal. Whatever the reason, by making an example of me, at the same time as removing all the senior editing echelon in Washington, Fallows ensured that he led a demoralised, divided staff throughout his tenure. Morale collapsed, sycophancy reigned and any sense of collective identity and achievement – the essence of newsmagazines – disappeared. Twenty two months later he had departed with his tail between his legs.

Initially, following Fallows' call, I spent more time dealing with the past than looking to the future. Supportive calls and messages flooded in, including many from friends in Washington who took a risk to make their feelings felt. Most sounded shocked; I simply was not central enough, or so it had seemed, to warrant such brutal treatment. Joe Joffe told me that had I been based in Germany I would have been eligible for a seven-figure payout related to my length of service. Many callers, like Walcott and the deputy editor Peter Bernstein (both fired), made the point that I should look ahead and move on. Yet it was incredibly difficult to do this when poignant messages kept arriving like the one left on our answering machine by Mel Elfin, one of the leading news magazine practitioners of the post-war era. "To say I was appalled is an understatement. No one has done a better job than you for the magazine. This is no longer a shake-up. It's a massacre. It's stirring me up personally . . . If I've gained anything from my ten years at *US News* it is the ephemeral nature of one's employment – and also an appreciation of your skills and talent. I'm dreadfully saddened by this event."

Eventually the hubbub died down, and the caravan moved on as it was bound to do, but not before I had a final run-in with the execrable Fallows. At the end of February 1997 a writer from *Vanity Fair* magazine called. He was preparing a profile of King James, as he had become known, and wanted to check why I had been dismissed. In the course of the conversation he let slip that Zuckerman, Fallows and others in Washington were claiming that I had been fired because I had refused to move to Moscow and/or because I had used company funds to convert the loft in my house into an office. I was sufficiently angry at this slander, based on prejudice and deliberately planted malicious gossip, to write to Fallows and threaten legal action. The claim was never published, and a couple of months later Fallows sent me a note distancing himself from the allegations.

After Fallows left *US News*, I was to learn more about the background to his initial actions. Sometime in the summer of 1996 Zuckerman concluded that the magazine was drifting and needed freshening up. As the owner, this was his prerogative. He approached Fallows, a well-known American columnist, but someone with no management experience, who at the time was working alone at home crafting prudish sermons for a syndicated column. Fallows proceeded to spend six weeks scheming behind the Rubys' back with a coterie of disaffected younger members of the staff, drawing up a hit list of those to be fired, selecting replacements, fine-tuning pet policies and crafting a "new" editorial approach that essentially eschewed the news of the week. One of his promotions, rather typically, was an opinionated contrarian whom he selected to be foreign editor despite that individual never having worked outside the US – according to the Fallows management "philosophy," just the sort of undervalued talent that needed encouragement. It proved to be a disaster. Other appointments were equally misguided, setting a truly horrendous pattern for the next two years from which the magazine never recovered. Self-righteous and self-important, Fallows was the first and last moralist to edit *US News & World Report* and the worst "catch" Mort Zuckerman landed from his relentless trawling of the opinion-forming salons of Washington and New York.

In public Zuckerman supported his new man at first, telling *The Wall Street Journal* in early October that the quick staff changes were "all to the good." Privately, he was less sanguine. Harry Evans vacationed in London that autumn and invited me one evening to the house he was renting in Primrose Hill. Over a drink in the garden he confessed that Mort felt he had lost control, allowing Fallows to interpret his "freshening up" directive too liberally. Seven months after the coup, Zuckerman telephoned out of the blue one Sunday morning in mid-April and spent half an hour explaining his behaviour and distancing himself from his appointee. Eventually he asked my opinion of the changes that had taken place. I was delighted to oblige and gave a blunt assessment of Fallows' ruinous stewardship. In reply he admitted it had been "completely debilitating to have 25% of the staff leaving," said straight out that Fallows was "ruining my magazine" and asked me to put my views in writing, which I did.

Mort and I had always had a cordial relationship. He had been complimentary several times in personal letters to me, lent us his home in Georgetown and been happy to be entertained by Jean and me in London, even over breakfast. Perhaps this call was a guilty reflection of all that. Yet his refusal to intervene when a knife was thrust in my back reflected an underlying moral fuzziness, as well as his core view that journalists were guns for hire to be disposed of when fashions changed. I never heard from him again despite a promise he made during the call to host a farewell dinner for me. However, in July 1998 an excerpt from the memo I had written him at his request appeared in print in an article in the *Washington Post* following King James's own acrimonious dismissal. Fallows sniffily swatted my views aside as those of "an aggrieved party." At least by then he knew what that meant. By 2005 only ten journalists on the magazine in 1996 still worked there. Two years later *US News* declined to biweekly status. At the end of 2010 it ceased regular print publication. The magazine gave Jean and me enviable opportunities all over the world in the first 24 years of our marriage. Neither of us ever forgot that. But the abrupt and unreasonable way that I was forced out left a lasting legacy of regret and disillusion.

All this lay well in the future. My immediate challenge, following the Fallows call, was to exit *US News* on the best terms possible. Characteristically, the company's first move was to try to get me to resign. I refused, and eventually a form of words was agreed that made it clear that my departure was involuntary. In the light of others' experiences I was well treated, receiving a severance package equivalent to three months notice, ten months pay on top of that, a tax equalisation payment covering the whole of 1996, vacation pay owing and rent for the office covering the last four months of 1996. Had they offered me a job in Washington and I had turned it down, I could have left with nothing. The employment lawyer I hired in London (paid for by the magazine) described the eventual settlement as "decent."

Nevertheless, facts were facts and they were not too palatable. The bureau had been closed, I had been fired and there would be no monthly pay cheque from the start of 1997. At the age of 53 I was singularly ill-prepared to branch out into the big wide world. I offered no exceptional skills or unique contacts. Even in media terms my experience was narrow. For 28 years I had worked for a little-known (in Europe) outfit. I had never acquired a green card so I could not move to the US to look for a new job there. In the Britain of the mid-1990s my age was all against me; by 1995 nearly 40% of people aged 54-60 were unemployed, retired or had left the workforce. And I knew already that market conditions were against me. In the summer of 1995, following the first attempt to close the London bureau, I had spent three months job-hunting. That effort produced not a single interview, let alone an offer. Even so, I under-estimated the challenge ahead which may have been just as well. Nothing I ever did in my working life proved harder than starting anew in my mid-50s.

For the three months until the end of 1996 an air of unreality enveloped me. I continued to behave like a foreign correspondent, going to meetings and briefings and even filing a story or two. As ever the magazine arrived each week. I used my expense account to meet contacts over lunch, stock up stationery supplies and make full use of the office computer and telephone. My last day of 10,319 on the *US News & World Report* masthead was December 31, 1996 – by a long chalk the most melancholy of the lot. By chance Jeff and Gretchen Trimble were with us in the morning, having flown in the day before from Ireland where they had spent the Christmas holiday. Once they left, nothing happened. The phone never rang and no one called to say goodbye or to formally close a bureau that had existed in London for so long. I woke up on New Year's Day 1997 unemployed for the first time since the summer of 1968.

In retrospect it was the end of a career as well as the end of a job. Bit by bit over the next four months I shook off *US News* and began a struggle to reinvent myself. I realised that I had to plan for the long haul, but the reality turned out rather worse. By the time I finally got the job offer that I accepted, nine months and eleven days had passed since the Fallows call. In that period I made 265 "approaches" (letters and replies to advertisements) to possible employers and wrote 130 "broadcast" letters to targeted firms and individuals. My telephone, postage and fax bills soared, I grew to know London and its underground rail system better than ever before and I went down dozens and dozens of blind alleys. Job advertisements were the worst waste of time. Over nine months I replied to 134 such ads, of which nine produced an interview and not one led to an offer. The best that can be said for all this activity is that it kept me busy, gave me a sense of purpose and created a feeling of momentum, however illusory.

I began the "campaign," as I soon came to think of it, by drawing up a list of all the people I could think of who knew me professionally and might have a job to offer or a lead to pursue. It was long – more than 80 names were on it – but not so long. Large areas of commercial life such as industry, public relations and the City were under-represented, reflecting the bias of my work as a roving foreign correspondent. Another difficulty was that too few of those I knew best actually employed people. I started cold-calling, usually receiving a sympathetic response but within limits. It reminded me painfully of the many similar calls I had taken from aspirant young journalists down the years. Letter-writing – often as many as five a day with CV and references included – consumed much of my time early on. Later I cut back on this activity to allow more time to chase up leads and attend interviews. Having been a journalist made it all a bit easier; I was used to unearthing information, digging up contact details, calling people out of the blue, being rebuffed, being flexible and using my initiative. And, as I wrote many times, I was a "pragmatic self-starter." It was true, and it helped. I had few illusions, but I did have the drive and determination to persist.

October 3, 1996

TO WHOM IT MAY CONCERN:

I have known and worked with Robin Knight for 10 years and can attest
both to his talents as a journalist and his qualities as a human
being. On the former, Robin is a complete reporter in the
contemporary sense of the word. He not only can gather information
with the best of them, fulfilling the traditional role of the
reporter, he can also analyze what he reports with enormous skill and
nuance. Furthermore, he writes with vigor and clarity and even, when
required, a touch of poetry.
    Talent, of course, is nothing without character and integrity, and
Robin Knight is imbued with both in abundance. In a business where
skepticism, a requirement of the craft, too often slips into
dangerous cynicism, Robin has managed to keep his head and his
humanity.
    It is a pleasure to recommend him without reservation.

Michael Ruby
Former Editor
U.S. News & World Report
Washington, D.C.
202-955-2608

2400 N Street, N.W., Washington, DC 20037-1196
202-955-2000

One of the references I used in my job search

Help came from various quarters. A friend in America recommended a 1960s book by Henry Boll, a Harvard Business School professor, titled *'Executive Job Search'* and kindly mailed me a copy. I found it invaluable.

It laid out a coherent strategy and plan of action for finding a new job, highlighted pitfalls and suggested ideas I would not have considered including one that was to prove crucial – to follow up all unanswered letters and applications two to three months later. Time and again this second shot produced a reaction. Other people passed my CV around. A couple of old friends took the trouble to recount their own experience of job hunting. Several head hunters explained how they worked and gave me good advice. One of them encouraged me to set up on my own, defined what I had to offer and organised a fee-charging schedule. Rather late in the day I came across a good outplacement expert and wished I had had him with me all along. Searching for a job, I found, can be a very lonely business and the more support one has, the better.

To begin with the job search consumed my day, everyday. I could never relax and the pressure to sort out the future was endless. "The only consolation I can offer you," wrote Chris Ma (another ex-deputy editor of *US News*, also fired) in mid-February "is that when you get to the other side you will feel how well rid of *USN&WR* you are." He was right, but at the time, in early 1997, it was difficult to grasp this essential truth. Not least of the challenges related to our marriage. Jeannie took my redundancy very hard. Her bitterness, if anything, exceeded mine – she had always had a stronger sense of fair play than I did. Our joint context had changed utterly, for ever, and with it the whole basis of our relationship, or so it felt sometimes. It helped greatly, though, that we had always talked to each other about everything and were each others' best friend. Throughout the nine months she was always there for me when it mattered most. As in Moscow and at other difficult times, adversity in the end brought us closer together and emphasised our strengths as a couple. I like to feel, looking back, that we emerged from this dark tunnel better people and better partners for each other.

Still, the situation took its toll. My lowest points were not the torrent of rejection letters that arrived each day with the post but other sorts of casual humiliation – building up for an important (to me) interview which was cancelled without anyone bothering to tell me; being asked what I did for a living; having to sign on every second week at the local Job Centre to protect my national insurance contributions; being unable to plan ahead. Jean's lowest points reflected her inability, as she saw it, to help. "I just felt so frustrated all the time. I felt so hopeless and useless," she told me later. Her busy job at the ITC assisted us both,

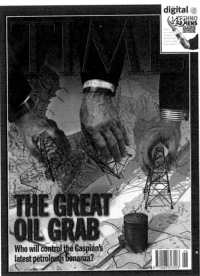

42 *Joe Fromm in 2000.* **43** *A cover story for Time magazine, June 29, 1998.*
44 *With Paul Charles of BP Trinidad in the Port of Spain Oval 1998.*

Previous page: **45** *The former Time Atlantic Editor Chris Redman in his kitchen at Petre – and it's not true!* **46** *En route to inspect a BP Hope school in Hunan province, China 2000.*

Above: **47** *The corporate responsibility issue of The BP Magazine which I inspired and edited in 2001.*

48

49

Previous page: **48** *The BP global press office at a quiz night in 2002 – Roddy Kennedy second left front row.* **49** *At Posof on the Turkish – Georgian border on an inspection of the BTC project.*

Above: **50** *With Jeannie, Mother and Father attending niece Louisa's wedding at Wolverton parish church in 2005.*

Previous page 51 A 40th Reunion Dinner at TCD in the summer of 2006. 52 KnightWrite Ltd at work in 2007.

Above: 53 An issue of BP Shipping's "The Flag" online magazine which I edited in 2008.

54 *At Trevose Head June 2009 on a MUGS golf weekend.* **55** *Chairman of Governors Michael Allsop presents me with a gift on my retirement as a governor of Pangbourne College in 2009.*

giving her a daily purpose and me the space to recover. And in other ways, as I slowly came to realise, we had much for which to be grateful. We were both healthy, the house was paid for, we had no debts and there was money in the bank. I reckoned we could keep afloat for a couple of years on the earned income we had. Nor were we alone. Literally scores of people all over the world tried to assist me in various ways in this period. That, truly, was humbling.

I listed these positive factors in April at a particularly low moment when I sought to reassure myself. I'm glad now that I did. My reactions to unemployment were totally conventional. I felt angry, rejected and humiliated. I hated the idea of no longer being the main breadwinner. The uncertainty of the situation ate into my normally positive outlook. I dwelt unduly on the past. I'm sure I was tricky to live with, however hard I tried not to be. Eventually it was interacting with others not directly involved, such as head hunters and outplacement experts, which got me out of the mire. But it was my strong and enduring relationship with Jeannie that kept me going and gave me the will to succeed. Neither of us has ever felt truly secure again. We know now from painful experience how fragile is the stability, prosperity and security that we have in our lives, and how easily and quickly they can disappear.

As the months passed, and more and more initiatives fell by the wayside, it dawned on me that I might never find another full-time job. Something had to change. In March I began freelancing. I am so glad that I did. It kept me sane and it gave me a new sense of purpose. Some of the assignments I undertook were mundane, and the dreary chore of chasing unpaid invoices and endlessly selling myself never came easy. But the first time a cheque arrived in the post it felt as though I had won the National Lottery. I began to recover my self-confidence, reach out and reacquire a life beyond job-hunting. I even turned down assignments. Along the way I spent a month at a big law firm writing a management report for the partners – an eye-opener into how disorganised large businesses can be and how poorly they communicate. I wrote annual reports. I helped with media relations campaigns run by PR firms on behalf of international clients. In particular, I began a six-year association with *Time* magazine which was to prove both happy and rewarding.

Almost the first letter I had written looking for a new job in September 1996 was to Christopher Redman, editor of *Time's* Atlantic edition. I knew him slightly and I knew that *Time* had turned to him, another Brit working for an American newsmagazine, earlier in the year to transform the way Time Atlantic was edited and produced. I was not to know it, but my timing was awful; Chris had just recruited a dozen journalists and two dozen others to beef up the London operation, and had hit his budget ceiling. When my letter arrived, his hands were tied. For three months I heard nothing but friends in the *Time* London bureau suggested that I keep plugging away. So I did and eventually, seven months after my first approach, I was rewarded with an assignment in late April to write a supplement on the global travel industry. This sprawled into a 4,000-word, seven-page spread. An accompanying page of advertorial for Longines, which involved a visit to the company's factory in Switzerland, put me in touch with *Time's* special projects team. In turn this led to several other supplements including one on Kenya and another on Japan and the euro.

Before long Chris had made me a contributing editor and got my name on the *Time* masthead. In the newsmagazine world *Time* was always the prestige outfit, and for nearly 30 years I had envied its style and resources while trying to compete on a shoestring. So it was a satisfying moment at one of the lowest points in my career when I saw my by-line in the magazine for the first time. Later, Chris offered me the job of *Time* bureau chief in Nairobi but I turned it down for a combination of reasons including the feeling that, at 54, I was simply too long in the tooth to be criss-crossing the continent on a weekly basis and revisiting the disasters that were Africa. Instead I cornered the market in personalised book reviews, writing 25 essays for *Time* over the next few years and always keeping in mind Gore Vidal's justification for being a critic – "What matters is what I think, not what others think of me – and I am willing to say what I think."

Later, when I joined BP, the two organisations agreed an unusual arrangement under which I was allowed to continue writing for *Time* while avoiding anything relating to the oil and gas industry. This worked fine until one day in June 1998 when Chris twisted my arm to write a piece about "The Great Oil Grab" – the rush to exploit the Caspian region's hydrocarbon resources, then being led by BP. I encouraged *Time* to take a more sceptical view of the prospects than that prevailing in BP, which led to one or two raised eyebrows inside the company. But nothing further happened and I went on contributing to *Time* until 2003 when one of Redman's successors abruptly dispensed with my services. Shortly afterwards this visionary was recalled to New York, promoted and then fired in his turn – such is the revolving door at the top. Sad though I was to stop book-reviewing, which I found particularly satisfying, the whole episode had been a life-saver. Despite nearly 30 years in the business and an international profile, no one else offered me so much as a string. I will always remember my *Time* interlude with the greatest fondness – and a sense of pride. At the very least it showed that my demise at *US News* had nothing to do with my ability as a writer and reporter.

Meanwhile the job hunt sputtered on. Psychologically, as the summer of 1997 began, I was nearing the end of my sustained, systematic commitment to job-searching. Months and months of rejections, letter-writing, interviews, wasted trips and unreturned phone calls had got me nowhere. I had started to build up an alternative lifestyle as a freelancer and begun to rationalise my altered status. I didn't like it; it was simply not how I imagined I would end my working life. But I saw no alternative and knew that I had done all I reasonably could have done to nail down a "proper" job. In May a few offers did materialise, including a short term contract at the European Bank for Reconstruction & Development as a speech writer. By mid-June I had more freelance work on my desk than I could handle and felt sure it had to be the way ahead. Then, out of the blue, my luck changed.

In my mildly superstitious mind Friday the 13th had always been a day on which to be careful. Friday, 13th June, 1997 was no different – or so it seemed at first. That morning I was due to meet Roddy Kennedy, head of media relations at British Petroleum. Months earlier I had written to Richard Newton, BP's director of corporate communications, and received no reply. Applying the Boll strategy, I wrote again in May and eventually, after another delay, was invited to meet Kennedy "for a chat over coffee." On the phone he had been frank – "I have nothing for you" – but if someone was prepared to see me, I was always prepared to see them in the hope of developing a relationship. So off I trotted to Finsbury Circus and the odd, curved Lutyens building where BP was then headquartered.

I got to Britannic House early and hung around the lobby for half an hour before being shown to a small smoking area tucked under the stairs on the ground floor. Kennedy, it turned out, was an ex-*Daily Express* journalist in his early 50s, Irish and seemingly laid-back. After about ten minutes he got up, walked away and summoned another smoker to meet me. An idea appeared to be forming in his mind as our conversation proceeded. I left after an hour wondering if, at last, I had impressed someone who was actually in a position to offer me a job. Kennedy had not been specific, but next day (a Saturday) I sent him my full "sales kit" and some clippings selected carefully to display my versatility, business knowledge and (important this, as I discovered later) pragmatism about environmental issues. A couple of days later he responded, asking me to turn a speech by the chief executive John Browne into an article for a coffee table magazine. This I did. Then an agonising wait ensued before a week or so later I was invited back to BP HQ. This time Roddy took me all over Britannic House, introduced me to numerous people, including his bemused deputy who seemed to know nothing about me, showed me a desk in the press office and made me a verbal offer.

I accepted on the spot. Two weeks later in early July a contract arrived to be signed. Roddy told me later that it had been John Browne who encouraged him to offer me a full-time job as BP's Editorial Writer – in effect for the next six years since the company's retirement age was then 60. No one of my "seniority" (a nice word) had been hired by BP for years. The offer was an apparently generous one including pension rights, a car and the chance to acquire BP shares, and was way beyond anything I was ever likely to achieve as a freelancer. Yet the package was not the whole story. In deciding to accept the offer and turn my back on journalism, I was making a fresh start in a new world in a company with global reach and, it appeared, the imagination to reach out to someone with my narrow background at a late stage in my working life. After the never-ending foot-dragging I had endured with companies like Shell and Lehman Brothers, BP's decisiveness was hugely attractive.

I never did find out quite what attracted Kennedy to me at that initial meeting. He turned out to be an often exasperating mix of charm and candour, evasiveness and calculation – a born corporate survivor who enjoyed John Browne's confidence and was well on his way to becoming a BP institution when I met him. Maybe it was simply being in the right place at the right time; Roddy never enjoyed writing and was becoming irked by the constant need to produce articles in Browne's name as the CEO's public profile rose. Whatever it was, I remain duly grateful. Back at the end of September 1996 I had been a prominent UK-based foreign correspondent. Then it all fell apart. Subsequently I had been rejected for positions as humdrum as an assistant regional public affairs manager for the National Trust, a literature officer for the City of London and a "historical research assistant" for NM Rothschild as well as other more elevated positions. High or low, quality outfit or rickety, short or long term, it didn't matter. BP apart, the only serious offer I got in 282 days of ceaseless effort was by networking with friends at *Time*.

Towards the end of this tortuous journey Jean and I were invited by my old contact Admiral Crowe, the US ambassador, to a dinner at Winfield House for the departing embassy press counsellor Mike O'Brien. At the time I thought of this glittering affair as the end of an era. It seems even more so in retrospect. Mike was retiring from the US Foreign Service after 25 years, and the ambassador was marking the occasion as well as bidding farewell to a loyal aide. Around the table was a mixture of Mike's relatives, friends and embassy colleagues. There was a lot of good humoured back-and-forth joshing and some speeches. Even Jeannie added her pennyworth. It was how I would have liked to have ended my own journalistic career, but never did. So this nostalgic, happy last visit to the residence of the American ambassador in London had to serve as a substitute until years later when BP did the honours.

Changing jobs, let alone careers, is always hazardous. Doing so under pressure in one's mid-50s was near-impossible in the tight labour market conditions of the late 1990s, and has not got easier since. A friend who had been made redundant three times in a 40-year career once tried to reassure me by saying that, on reflection, each redundancy had been for the best. I would more or less share that view now. The acrimony of my departure from *US News* never left me, yet it served a purpose. If I had lost the respect of those running the magazine, in turn I had lost respect for the magazine. It took time, but in the end I ceased to want to work for *US News*. Being fired made me develop new skills, think more about what I had to offer as a person, experience some of the downsides of life and confront my own failings. The self sufficiency I prized stood me in good stead. But equally my relationship with Jeannie grew and in adversity I discovered, like many before me, who my real friends were. In the end I was lucky. But perhaps you really do make your own luck in life?

11

Petroleum and Beyond

"Never regret thy fall, O Icarus of the fearless flight, For the greatest tragedy of them all, Is never to feel the burning light."

OSCAR WILDE

If there was a single defining moment in my 12-year association with BP it was a day at the end of July 2002 when the *Financial Times* began serialising what became known as the Sun King profiles of group chief executive John Browne. With hindsight, this three-part series – remarkable for its length, detail and fawning account of Browne's leadership – represented the high water mark of the company's extraordinary transformation since the dark days of the early 1990s when it had all but capsized. Things were never to be quite the same in BP from then on.

Externally, the Sun King series was greeted by a deafening silence. For most journalists, let alone readers, it was too positive, too sycophantic. Overkill, really. I remember we had just two calls about the articles in the press office. Internally, all hell broke loose, set off by hissy complaints from BP's burly Irish chairman Peter Sutherland and the waspish company secretary Judith Hanratty. With some prescience, given what happened later, they objected in particular to Browne's claim that the board had asked him to stay on until he reached the age of 60 six years later. This was stretching the point, and John knew it. In addition many of the directors disliked the characterisation of BP as Browne's fiefdom – the *FT's* portrayal not Browne's, it was true, but too accurate for comfort. John took it all in his small, neat stride and promptly went away on holiday. People like me tried to ignore the raging bulls and prepared to move into another pet Browne project – the company's Scandinavian-style new headquarters building at 1, St James's Square.

Life at BP throughout my years on the staff from 1997-2003, and later as an insider-outsider contractor, was always like this – a roller coaster of highs and lows, triumphs and disasters, macho arm-wrestling at the top, sudden opportunities and abrupt changes. It was never boring, often somewhat hazardous personally, sometimes illuminating and, it has to be said, too rarely fulfilling. As a small cog in a very large corporate machine – albeit one with unusual access to the uppermost echelons despite my ill-defined status – I was lucky to be associated with some of the most talented businessmen of their generation and an amazing period in BP's roller-coaster history.

Many positive BP memories remain in my mind, but few of them are tied directly to the dirty business of actually producing oil and gas. Inspecting lines of children at a secondary school sponsored by the company in southern China, having rowed across a lake and tramped through muddy paddy fields to get there. Climbing the Great Wall of China. Visiting a plant nursery protected by a camouflaged machine gun post in Colombia's Andean foothills. Strolling across the rutted Port of Spain Oval cricket ground in Trinidad. Marooned in western Siberia after a terrorist bombing. Watching the sun rise across the vast Outback horizon in northwest Australia. Picnicking one balmy weekend in remote mountains in eastern Georgia. Helping children to understand computers in a dusty village in Azerbaijan. Seeing the spot where NATO missiles were positioned in north-eastern Turkey during the 1962 Cuban crisis. Attending a hilarious training course with bemused German employees on cross cultural (mis)understanding near Dusseldorf. Touring the World Trade Center site two weeks after the 9/11 bombings. Inspecting a derelict naval base on Sakhalin Island in Russia's Far East one drab Sunday afternoon in autumn. Examining a dhow being built by traditional methods on the shores of the Persian Gulf. Experiencing the magic of Isfahan in Iran, the pastoral beauty of the Wisconsin countryside and the magnificence of Sydney harbour. A rich diet indeed, all courtesy of BP and its global operations.

Yet, equally, there was much professional frustration, and I never felt BP made any serious attempt to make full use of whatever talents I had. When it was all over Roddy Kennedy flattered me by saying I was too good for the sort of work I had been doing – his typically disarming way of finessing my numerous complaints, but maybe there was a grain of truth in it. Little or nothing I wrote or produced – and there was a great deal in a dozen or more years including articles, brochures, books, speeches, web site material and every kind of internal and external report

– ever had much lasting impact. Feedback was minimal, and few things I did proved critical to BP's fortunes. Much of the time I was left to my own devices and created my own opportunities, and right to the end of my years with BP I felt like an interloper parachuted in from Mars to perform chores others did not wish to do – someone eminently dispensable if, or when, things went wrong or budgets had to be slashed.

This may seem a rough judgement because, by and large, I enjoyed my time with BP and I was well treated. But the enjoyment was of the voyeuristic kind one gets from going to a zoo. And the rewards, as I discovered gradually, were at the bottom end of the BP scale.

Right from the start I was made to realise that life at the heart of a large multinational company is not for the faint-hearted. Most situations involved a balancing act. If you were too opinionated, or if you failed to deliver, you would be sidelined. Even when you were successful in BP terms this might happen, as it did to several good people I knew whose faces suddenly did not fit for one reason or another. Much of the time everything in the company seemed to be in a state of flux dependent on the whims of one or two people, many decisions were made on the hoof (often in chance encounters in corridors, which worked to my advantage as I was rarely invited to formal meetings), and about the only long-term certainty arose from personal links to more senior people – of which I had none when I arrived at the imposing, but hopelessly designed, imperial-era headquarters building on Finsbury Circus in the heart of the city of London.

One way or another, settling in at BP proved to be quite a challenge. Until I began to work at BP's head office, I had relied on my own initiative and operated on my own throughout my career – a typical foreign correspondent. Now I joined a huge global organisation which put team-playing and collective endeavour above all else – or said it did. My job was ill-defined and Kennedy, my nominal boss and head of media relations, was a maverick advocate of hands-off management. Hierarchies criss-crossed BP and I didn't fit into any of them. I was a lot older than most of those working around me, following a spectacular cull of BP's workforce earlier in the 1990s, while the low grade I had been assigned in no way reflected the high-level responsibilities thrust on me. There was new technology to absorb, company policies to grasp, personalities to consider and plenty of vultures waiting for me to slip up. In Britannic House (and later in St James's Square) the sepulchral quiet of the senior management floors suggested hard work, but you never really knew. People constantly came and went, trailing luggage in their wake as though transiting an airport terminal. On the fourth floor, where the top executives were grouped in deliberate proximity, even to leave a footmark on the pristine peach carpet felt sacrilegious. All around this oddly-shaped building, little groups would gather in huddles in small meeting rooms encased by glass. From time to time a phone might ring, but otherwise silence reigned and only the press office showed much sign of life.

Ostensibly I had been hired to write articles in John Browne's name – a humble enough activity, but one that thrust me into a political situation at the heart of the company with many others vying for the great man's time or wanting to influence his opinions or simply to obstruct a new interloper. One or two of the executives around Browne seemed to think I was some sort of fifth columnist brought in by him or Kennedy to undermine them; at the court of the Sun King, alliances shifted regularly and no one felt secure for long, not even executive directors. In the group press office, where I had a desk away in a distant corner, people who had been together for years regarded me as an unwelcome distraction. There was also a general envy factor at work. It turned out that I was one of the first people hired in the corporate centre on a full-time basis following the blood-letting of the early 1990s when BP nearly went under and numbers were downsized from 140,000 in 1992 to 56,500 in 1997. It was not a particularly happy inheritance.

Initially, I was oblivious to all this and simply happy to have a job and even to commute from west London to the City on the dreadful London underground system (in 1998 I got my own back by keeping a diary of the daily indignities on the tube. An abridged version was published by the *Evening Standard* and *The Week*). Before long I discovered that writing for Browne involved no more than half a dozen pieces a year so, with a prod from Kennedy, I branched out and eventually unearthed many other "clients" at senior level across the company. This led to interesting assignments all over the world, in countries such as Australia, Azerbaijan, China, Colombia, Georgia, Trinidad and the USA, and an unexpected approximation of the life of a foreign correspondent. Along the way I made friends with a few like-minded spirits and, for the first and last time in my working life, felt that I had the resources to do the job properly. BP never paid me generously – Kennedy's idiosyncratic management philosophy involved keeping his budget as low as possible, to avoid attracting attention from the many bean counters and consultants crawling around the company, and also to give himself maximum flexibility. But equally, he never resisted when I announced I was off to Shanghai or Bogota or New York on some assignment or other. Within a couple of years of being ejected from *US News* I was almost glad to have made the break from struggling newsweekly journalism.

BP itself was in reasonable shape when I turned up, having grown productivity (its perennial Achilles heel) by 8% a year since 1992 and net income per employee by eight times. This was largely Browne's achievement and that of his polished predecessor David Simon. By 1997 the company was making $2 billion a year profit. Yet it remained a medium-sized outfit by oil industry standards, with limited prospects and years of slow development stretching ahead that were unlikely to position it to challenge the Exxons and Shells of the sector. "Organic growth" of this type was never going to motivate an ambitious, competitive go-getter like Browne. So began BP's amazing transformation through nine mergers and takeovers in five years starting with the $50 billion Amoco deal in 1998. To be involved in this volcanic eruption, however tangentially, was such a dramatic change in my fortunes that I often wondered how it had happened. In reality I was just lucky to be in the right place at the right time.

By 2002 BP was making $13 billion a year and was one of the largest companies in the world, and by 2008 annual profits had risen to a staggering $26 billion. Along the way there had been huge upheavals, large numbers of casualties including 20,000 or more Amoco employees, and innumerable controversies such as a series of missed production targets in 2002, Russian blackmail and Browne's dramatic demise. Throughout this extraordinary period BP set the pace in the publicly-quoted oil and gas sector, in industry as a whole and across much of the corporate world, and was always prepared to give a lead on the touchstone social issues which tended to involve me such as corporate responsibility, business ethics, community relations and environmental protection.

This stellar record was manna from heaven most of the time. One thing I never suffered from during my BP years was a lack of positive source material. Often the hardest part in writing for external audiences (and internal ones), was to get the balance right between highlighting BP's real achievements, avoiding hubris or boastfulness and retaining a sense of balance and proportion. Then, post-Browne and with many outstanding problems (or challenges, as BP insisted on calling them) to resolve, the inevitable reaction set in. By 2009, when I ceased contributing on a regular basis, BP had become a very different corporate animal – less ambitious, less sure-footed, less innovative, more cautious, more introspective and far less engaged with the world around it. And that was before the Gulf of Mexico disaster in 2010 and the debacle with Rosneft in 2011.

As this account might suggest, John Browne was the beating heart of everything that mattered. Short, softly spoken and always impeccably groomed in crisp white shirts, sharply pressed trousers and militarily polished toecaps, he was a hard-driving BP lifer with entrepreneurial dynamism and a visionary grasp of strategy. Among all but his closest colleagues he kept his emotions strictly in check, avoided confrontation, left others to wield the knife and never, to my knowledge, lost his temper. Goal-oriented, as befitted an engineer by training, he loathed speculation and was instinctively rooted in what he termed "reality" – in practice, anything that could be measured. Only half in jest did some of his colleagues joke that in John's ideal world he would, Dr Strangelove-like, wake up to a bank of live television screens linked to all BP's 120 business units around the world and immediately start cross-examining the local managers. Yet his lifelong interest in the arts, love of fine wines, hideaway apartment in Venice and knowledge of obscure things like Safavid architecture suggested a softer side.

While Browne's mother was alive (she died in 2000) his personal life as a middle aged bachelor seemed unexceptional, and he was able to get away with claiming (to pushy journalists) that he had had his heart broken by an American (female) academic. "In the end," he once told an interviewer, "if I'd wanted to get married, I would have." Inside BP many people in the corporate centre spotted the essential ambiguity of that comment, but the sexuality of the chief executive was never going to be a factor in how he was regarded. Society had moved on. John, sadly, never believed this, so condemning himself to years of loneliness and subterfuge. Following his mother's death his circle of acquaintances widened and eventually one of them, a young Canadian he met through a gay dating website (and later took on business trips and to high-level dinners), demanded a payoff. Failing to get one, he went to the press, a legal battle over publication ensued, John made a false statement in court and his resignation became inevitable. Years earlier he had been advised by a wise colleague to come out and define himself in public. But this most buttoned-up of Englishmen, working in one of the most macho of industries, just could not bring himself to do it and so suffered humiliation and disgrace. To anyone who had ever had anything to do with him, it was a tragedy of Shakespearian dimensions.

As a business leader Browne saw his role in ambitious terms – setting direction, challenging the status quo, inspiring confidence and keeping his immediate colleagues off balance. His bottom line always was performance, and his gruelling quarterly reviews of potential successors – "strategy tutorials" according to one victim – were legendary. In my time at BP there was no bigger crime than to fail to give the boss warning that an agreed objective would not be met – deeply ironic in view of the series of missed targets which presaged his fall from grace in 2002. In truth, John wanted to control everything, even insisting on occasion that if he was unable to do something no one else would either – itself a surprising hint of insecurity. Critics (often rivals like the heads of Exxon and Mobil) suggested that he was arrogant and overly self-confident, and took delight in off-the-record sniping. As they knew full well, only on rare occasions did Browne consult beyond his immediate circle. Yet when he did open up, the results surprised him as when he sought ideas from the company's extended leadership group of 350 executives about how best to reduce carbon emissions in BP. To his amazement he received more than 300 responses – including one suggesting that BP abolish company cars and make everyone cycle to work. His reaction to me was to smile wanly and say, "I hear what they're saying, Robin. But BP isn't a democracy – more a quasi-democracy."

In running the company, Browne set out an avowedly expansionist game plan and stuck to it through thick and thin, arguably for too long. To his detractors inside BP (and he had some), he was an elitist who had too little time for staffers outside a core clique. In public he came across rather diffidently, often noting the limited power of chief executives and the need for the BPs of the world to operate to higher standards than the law required. "Humility is a very good notion because it is the counterpoint to power," he told me once with a straight face, before going on to repeat his view that it is always better for large corporations to engage with society than to stand apart. The concept of mutual advantage was a particular favourite – in his words "the only way of creating enduring business" – and he never missed a chance to stress the importance of aligning BP as closely as possible with consumers and communities. At one stage he latched on to something that he (or a consultant) termed "radical openness." To the likes of communicators this was marvellous news, in theory. But it proved impossible to apply in practice without compromising commercial secrecy and embarrassing BP.

Externally, the Browne era is identified more than anything else with BP's green agenda dating from a speech John gave at Stanford University in 1997 just before I joined the company. In this presentation he became the first leading oil executive to accept publicly the reality of global warming and to commit his company to do something about it. Inside the industry a torrent of criticism ensued which John rather enjoyed. Eventually all kinds of changes followed, many of them unforeseen. Browne had, in effect, released a genie from the bottle that has never been put back since. His rationale, as ever, was purely pragmatic and business-driven – the weight of evidence, the implication of the science for the hydrocarbon industry, a belief that oil companies had to associate more closely with society if they were to survive, and a desire to modernise the business. Beyond that he never fully embraced an environmentalist agenda, and in the end came to resent the way BP was held to a higher standard by NGO critics than companies which continued their policies of denial.

Throughout my BP years the environmental agenda vied only with the corporate responsibility agenda in its importance to the new BP brand Browne was building and to company communicators like me. Large numbers of idealistic young graduates flocked to BP because of its apparent social awareness and flexibility on issues like climate change, and we were besieged by well-wishers, including governments, wanting the company to support this or that initiative. In writing articles or speeches at that time, the environmental theme was always front and centre, and BP often seemed more akin to a campaigning NGO than to a hard-nosed, profit-driven oil company. Some sort of reality check became necessary in the new millennium. My own modest contribution was to write a speech for a senior executive in 2001 spelling out the limits of corporate influence. By then the horse had well and truly bolted, and such reality-based messages were lost in the clamour for ever-expanding commitments.

All this implies that BP was a bit of a one-man show, and even the ever-loyal Kennedy once admitted in an unguarded moment that John had the presence to engender "a certain amount of trepidation" within BP. This was not invariably the case, but the longer Browne remained chief executive the narrower his trusted inner circle became, the more a "feudal court feeling" took over and the more his one-time peers were squeezed out or drifted away. By 2003, when I retired formally, there was almost no one at the top except the chairman of the board with sufficient authority to challenge him. By then all his close aides were young executives beholden to him, the directors had little influence (and remained largely unchanged for that reason) and Browne increasingly went outside the company when he felt the need for advice, even on one occasion using a management consultancy to counter allegations that he had become autocratic.

Ultimately, of course, it was John's unacknowledged homosexuality, and the way he tried to conceal it, which wrecked his BP career and dimmed his reputation. But long before that mistake, mishaps that could and should have been avoided by timely input from other senior people in the company – missed production targets, the unwise and poorly thought through re-branding slogan ("Beyond Petroleum" – a gift to every oil company critic), naïve blunders in Russia, too close association with New Labour, the Thunderhorse platform disaster in the Gulf of Mexico, safety lapses in Alaska and the truly awful Texas City refinery explosion that killed 15 people in March, 2005 – had dulled the brilliant gloss of the earlier Browne years.

My own relations with John Browne were always a pleasure. If I had problems, which I sometimes did, it was because others around him grew suspicious of my open door access and determined to limit it, which was what happened. Initially I was given 15-20 minute slots on a regular basis to go through articles in his name. He would map out his ideas, we would have a discussion and I would go away and turn the ideas into a finished piece which he would then clear. On these occasions there was little small talk. Everything was matter-of-fact business-driven – why are we doing this; how will it benefit BP; who is the audience; what is the outlet?

Once I tried to encourage John to pick up an initiative being floated by the British government to involve global businesses in the UK overseas aid programme. He would have none of it. "A company like BP can only lead on two or three issues at a time," I remember him saying. "We can educate. We can train people and give them skills and raise capacity. We can create hope of a better future. But we're not an aid agency and we're not a lending agency." It is a classic definition of sophisticated business self-interest. Over time, as his confidence in me grew, there was less of this sort of back-and-forth until, after the schemers had had their way and my access had been curtailed, I used to initiate and write articles in John's name without seeing him at all. Then something urgent or especially high profile would come up and I would get a summons, often in the early evening when he was relaxing over a glass of white wine and a large cigar.

Looking back, what I recall most about Browne is his courtesy, his reticence in social gatherings, his focused determination and his world class risk-taking. Where the latter came from is a mystery since nothing in his background (his father was a mid-level BP executive, his Jewish mother came from Romania while John himself pursued a conventional middle class education through public school and Cambridge) would suggest a man prepared to gamble one of Britain's largest companies on the success of a series of daring takeovers. Yet appearances were deceptive. Browne made his name in BP as a performance-driven cost cutter *par excellence* and his later persona as a cool, rational and thoughtful chief executive who never forgot a name or failed to do his homework somewhat belied his opportunism and business ruthlessness. One evening, years later, I was at a reception in the Long Room at Lord's cricket ground, giving my name to the person at the entrance when a soft voice piped up behind me – "How are you Robin? What are you doing?" It was John Browne, at least six years since we had met and keen to discuss the fortunes of BP Shipping where I was then contracted (he sanctioned the $5 billion revival of BP's fleet in 2000). In the meantime his own fortunes had changed dramatically (he was running an oil and gas investment fund and undertaking worthy public service assignments), but he remained the same impressive, focused and cultured man he always had been – a true leader.

With hindsight, the verdict on his career at BP must be that he hung around too long, ignoring many hints from the likes of chairman Sutherland that it was time to go, and deliberately dragging his heels on the matter of a successor. John also was never sufficiently interested in the nitty-gritty of running a business day-to-day, preferring the adrenalin-rush of deal-making and headline-grabbing "synergies" (cost-cutting to lesser mortals). So events took over and he was sunk by a series of mistakes, personal and professional, which exposed him as perhaps not the great business visionary that he once seemed. To worsen his fall from grace, his eventual successor (a young protégé who owed his rise entirely to Browne) dumped on him from a great height, spending his first 18 months in charge depicting BP, internally and externally, as a mismanaged mess in need of urgent remedial action. It was all unedifying, and could so easily have been avoided if John had taken the toughest management decision of all – to exit on his own terms before he was forced out. But it was not to be.

The group immediately around Browne in the late 1990s was also a notable combination, with many in it going on to flourish outside BP. John's deputy, Rodney Chase, would best be described as his enforcer. Stocky, bull-necked and chippy, he took no prisoners and was the sort of manager who would throw his weight around because his refurbished office turned out to be less impressive than that of a supposed rival (the whole space had to be redesigned at considerable cost). Impatient and impulsive, Chase was sure he was right and was exactly the wrong sort of person to tangle with the green lobby – something he always wanted to do. In press interviews he was a disaster waiting to happen, ever ready to walk out or to lose his temper. In difficult political situations, such as the Greenpeace protest in the North Sea in 1997 or the Arco takeover in 1999, he proved to be headstrong to a fault, refusing to listen to advice and easily wrong-footed by smarter opponents. Browne rated him, apparently, as someone with a thick skin who delivered, but kept him on a tight rein and refused to appoint him head of BP in North America.

My own dealings with Chase were limited to one surreal exchange at the end of 1999. Early one morning just before Christmas he wanted to contact Kennedy urgently after a gossip item in that day's papers claimed that BP directors like himself had been grounded for the millennium on John Browne's orders – true, out of concern about the possible effects of the so-called millennium bug. This little piece, no more than a hundred words long, seriously offended Chase's highly developed *amour-propre* not least because a friend called him while he was shaving to read it out and tease him – not a good move. Roddy, true to form, could not be reached (he was on a train travelling to work, with his mobile switched off) and I was one of only two people present in the press office. So I informed Chase's secretary that she would have to wait for Roddy to return her call – a message she re-calibrated to Chase to inform him that the press office was saying he would have to wait. A few minutes later this red-faced pit bull stormed into our glass cage demanding to know who was telling him to wait. Eventually I calmed him down a bit, and later offered to resign if it helped the press office. The suggestion was declined, at what cost to Kennedy I never knew. Such, sometimes, were the absurd downsides of corporate life in BP HQ, where egos the size of elephants flourished alongside massive insecurities.

Much of my early years in BP were taken up by one-on-one work with Chris Gibson-Smith –appointed the company's first executive director with responsibility for issues like sustainability and business ethics in 1997. Later, after he was eased out by Browne in 2001 on the grounds that he was insufficiently engaged in the real business (harsh, since Chris's terms of reference excluded direct operational responsibilities), he went on to prove his business credentials by becoming head of the National Air Traffic Services (where he saved NATS from bankruptcy), a director of Lloyds TSB bank, chairman of the London Stock Exchange and a member of the most expensive golf club in the UK – the latter not something Browne, with his avowed dislike of golf and all sport, would have approved of at all.

A geologist by training, Gibson-Smith fancied himself as an intellectual. Over time this led him into sensitive areas which Browne considered his own territory – not a career-enhancing move. "My style is softer and wider (than Browne's). It's different," he once reflected loftily to a stunned interviewer, stroking his *coiffured* hair as he spoke and stealing a glance of himself through the large picture windows overlooking Finsbury Circus. On a trip together to China, I saw another side to Chris when he fought a dogged rearguard action with Browne and BP's capital expenditure committee in London over a possible investment in that country. He lost, but went up in my estimation for having the guts to take on such a task which he could easily have ducked. In reality, much of what he did and said in BP at this time was incomprehensible to others, especially to those who nominally reported to him, and he was notorious for straying off message to such an extent that the press office began issuing authorised versions of his speeches.

Yet I was able to establish a rapport with him, discuss concepts back and forth (he was the only senior BP executive I met who was interested in abstract ideas), translate his confusing pronouncements into plain English and write some worthwhile pieces for him including, in 1998, BP's first extended definition of its attitude to sustainable development (in a speech titled "Future growth and sustainability").

On one occasion I managed to include a reference to Benjamin Disraeli in a speech Chris gave to the World Bank, which was something of a coup. But in general, once I got the hang of it, I found that corporate speech-writing was a thankless chore. Writing was the easy part. The hard thing was to get into the mind of the person giving the speech, to study their speech patterns and foibles and to find out whether they could tell a joke. All this had to be done unobtrusively, without offending the speaker and always realising that there would be little job satisfaction at the end however well the speech went on the day. I soon gave up attending any speech I had written; the performance was usually too painful. Instead I came to realise that a positive result was when there was little or no fall-out. Occasionally a journalist might follow up a point but, by and large, external reaction even about the touchiest subjects was non-existent. This applied inside BP, too, including an occasion when I wrote a speech on corruption and business delivered by a senior BP executive at a conference sponsored by *The Guardian* newspaper. In the Browne era this type of risky interaction with the outside world was actively encouraged. The trick was not to fall off the high wire.

Dealing with the press, fortunately, was never central to what I did in BP, although my background, and the fact that I had a desk in the group press office and sometimes had to answer press calls in the absence of anyone else, meant that I was always conscious of the media dimension to the company's activities. This tended to leave me schizophrenic. On the one hand I realised from the outset that BP preferred to adopt a reactive posture in relation to its media coverage, public relations and external information in general. All outside interest from wherever it came tended to be re-directed to the top, business unit leaders worldwide were urged to keep a low profile and many topics were off limits. Any public indiscretion was dealt with quite harshly, and press-related initiatives were few and far between unless they involved a well-timed (from BP's viewpoint) interview with John Browne or (very occasionally) the chairman. On the other hand, BP had inherent contradictions built into its DNA, valuing risk-taking and informality and myriad relationships with outsiders, all of which got in the way of the Exxon-style monolithic front it hoped to display to the world. The wave of mergers and takeovers simply added to these contradictory pressures since few of the senior newcomers I met ever understood BP or took what they were told about it too literally.

My own role was so amorphous that before long I had created my own terms of reference. Within a couple of years I was swamped with work, and in November 1999 I had 21 separate assignments on the go at the same time. It is interesting now to look back at their global scope. They included speeches for BP managers in China, South Africa, Switzerland and Finland, a paper for BP Egypt to submit to the government, an article about BP for a Brazilian magazine, a brochure for BP's Chairman's Awards, a letter from John Browne to Arco shareholders, three newspaper articles in Browne's name, Browne's introductory words for a corporate video on leadership, BP's 1998 Operating Review for the 1999 Annual Report and an article for *Shield* (forerunner of *The BP Magazine*). In addition I was conducting a review of all BP publications for Kennedy.

Direction for most of these assignments was minimal. At the time this seemed relatively sensible and, of course, it suited me but in truth the Browne-era BP was never sufficiently clear about the image that it wished to project to the outside world. Socially responsible or commercially driven? Sensitive to the opinions of its customers and shareholders or certain it knew what it was doing? Leading change or following it? The desire for positive "progressive" publicity clashed constantly with the anodyne corporate messages and jargon crafted by the company's lawyers and accountants. Commercial secrecy and transparency proved to be hopeless bedfellows, and for all the good intentions to break down internal hierarchies that were touched off by the advent of the digital era, communication remained a largely top-down affair even as Browne was encouraging creativity, accountability and the notion of wider corporate responsibility.

Where the media was concerned, BP held all the cards. Finding myself on the other side of the fence for the first time in my life, I was amazed at how poor and skin-deep much of the press coverage of BP was, with a few honourable exceptions. By and large, major news organisations had given up employing specialists to cover the energy sector by the late 1990s. The result was that few reporters were equipped to handle heavyweights like Browne or Sutherland on their own terms, let alone engineers and technicians, unless something broke unexpectedly and the company was forced on to the back foot. BP's media relations at this time were often described as "slick" or "polished" or some such euphemism. In reality, so shallow had the digging around the company become, that all that had to be done was to keep the lid on negative news and deliver Browne for interview occasionally. Given the number of malcontents (especially ex-employees) around, the contradictions in BP's regular analyst presentations, the flux created by so many takeovers in such a short time, the often controversial role BP played in places like Russia and Azerbaijan, the inbuilt unpredictability of the oil and gas business and the close links that developed between campaigning NGOs and the UK press in the 1990s, it was a miracle there were not more media crises than there were.

For this the quixotic Roddy Kennedy, head of media relations for 17 years to 2009, must take much of the credit. He was, in truth, the most unconventional, eccentric corporate spokesman and public relations professional that I came across in my entire working life – which maybe is why he employed me. Mischievous, manipulative, widely read and formidably well informed about everything inside BP thanks to his endless shuffling along corridors and innumerable whispered conversations over a cigarette in the smoking room, he was shameless in playing the favourites game with reporters, turning his deceptive charm on and off as occasion demanded and stonewalling for months or even years at a time. The secret of Kennedy's longevity lay, it seemed to me, in two factors – his ability to cultivate and keep close relationships with those at the top of BP, in particular Browne, Sutherland and David Simon; and his masterly inaction. "Very often, doing nothing is the best course of action. Always take plenty of time before you act," he told an interviewer towards the end of his career. For once, he meant what he was saying. But he was also shrewd, calculating and above all totally loyal to an organisation that had given a poorly educated teenage immigrant from Ireland his big chance in life.

Canny in a crisis, Kennedy's finest moment at BP probably came after the Texas City refinery explosions in 2005. Single-handedly, and against the advice of everyone else at the top in BP, he persuaded Browne to apologise immediately in public for the accident and to pledge to settle the fall-out as quickly and generously as possible regardless of cost or liability – which, broadly speaking, is what happened. Another key moment in his career came when he was forced by Peter Sutherland to witness the chairman's decisive retirement interview with Browne. On a somewhat lesser, but more typical, level – and characteristic of his amazing powers of persuasion – in 2001 he managed to get *The Sun* newspaper to run an editorial arguing that BP's record profits should be a cause for national celebration. The same day *The Mirror* ran a headline excoriating the "oil pigs" of BP. His nadir, without doubt, was the day he had to accompany Browne out of BP headquarters following John's ignominious resignation in 2006 – a humiliating scene captured by photographers standing in St. James's Square that appeared on every front page the next day.

As a manager Roddy was impossible. Secretive, disorganised and a lifelong sceptic of all management fads and every NGO-led fixation, including global warming, he was allowed by his superiors to go his own esoteric way and took only minimal interest in the work of his small team or its future. Much of the time, in true spokesman style, he relied heavily on other people's discretion. His outrageous statements were legendary. "Any press officer resigning on a point of principle must be having a nervous breakdown" springs to mind, as does "We eschew formal planning of all kind" and "If you want my considered opinion this whole 'Beyond Petroleum' thing is a complete and utter waste of time." If he had a lifestyle declaration it was this one – "Keep it as vague as possible so that you can change it later." Sutherland once described Roddy as akin to a "Borgia Pope," and his Machiavellian ploys were indeed formidable and calculated. For years he refused to devise a succession policy, instead designating three different people to take over and then letting each one of them fall by the wayside. Most of his staff was misfits (like me) or people he intuitively felt had talent and deserved a second chance. In turn, they gave him their undivided, if often baffled, loyalty – a shrewd arrangement which suited all parties, but meant that the considerable resources devoted by BP to dealing with the world's media were rarely utilised to the full.

Those who worked for Roddy quickly found themselves in a sink-or-swim situation. Quite a few failed this test. At the end of 2001, sensing that all was not as it should be with the company's allegedly expensive communications set up, Browne created a corporate function to cut costs, manage reputation and ensure that everyone understood clearly what BP was doing and why. It had little or no impact on the press office; if anything, Roddy gained authority in the resultant upheaval and budget-slashing. He also continued to circumvent the defined lines of reporting and to undermine those corporate initiatives he disliked (above all, the 'Beyond Petroleum' strap line). After I "retired" in 2003, I was asked to critique BP's external communications. An outside expert had already written a blueprint for the future of the group press office and a second opinion was required. In theory the consultant's report, advocating a centralized structure, a more pro-active agenda and a high profile rapid rebuttal strategy, made sense. Yet it failed totally to take into account the formidable, entrenched Kennedy factor and died a death, unnoticed and unmourned, and helped on its way by my scepticism that anything would change so long as Roddy hung around.

Part of Kennedy's success, indeed a major element, involved keeping skeletons firmly in the cupboard. At times this became a major preoccupation; indeed, the longer I was at BP, the more skeletons there seemed to be to control. In this, the company was not alone. The oil industry is about as old as modern industries go, and from the outset it has been driven by security concerns as much as by the need for energy. Risk-taking is built into its genes. For many poor countries it is the key to wealth and any hope of development. Massive technical changes have transformed the sector's exploration and production activities in recent years, diminishing many of the negative side-effects involved in the business, including its impact on the environment. Yet almost nothing the industry does is free of controversy. The whiff of corruption is never far away, the regulatory framework varies hugely worldwide and is always subject to negotiation, so-called civil society dogs every initiative and it is axiomatic that nothing lasting can be achieved without government involvement. Along with the arms industry, it is by far the most politicised business in the world today.

This, of course, is a classic recipe for skullduggery, secrecy, pay-offs, cover-ups and historical revisionism. In my experience no two accounts of any new development undertaken by BP ever coincided, to such an extent that it was pointless to try to get to the bottom of decisions such as exiting country X or entering country Y or renegotiating agreement Z or selling or buying a particular asset. Rationales, like balance sheets, changed like the wind, often overnight. All a late-comer like me could do was to rely on common sense and a few good contacts who would describe things as they found them. My exposure to such murky situations was generally limited (the several confidentiality agreements I signed all related to commercial deals). They were, nonetheless, revealing of much else that went on around me.

Take South Africa, possibly the most damaging episode (to BP) that I came across and one that interested me personally. In November 1997, soon after I began working for the company, BP South Africa (BPSA) voluntarily drew up a submission to the Truth and Reconciliation Commission headed by Archbishop Desmond Tutu which was trying to draw a line under the apartheid era. This report provided chapter and verse about BP's prolonged involvement in circumventing the oil embargo imposed on South Africa by the United Nations in 1979. Its findings included a string of embarrassing revelations about the company's close ties with the South African military, its 20-year denial that it had broken UN sanctions, the role of UK-appointed directors in this deception and the fact that BPSA had supplied the apartheid authorities with details about its own staff. The submission ended by apologising to the people of South Africa and asking for their forgiveness. This remarkable document, which has still to be published, was meant to form part of a collective submission by all the international oil companies that remained in South Africa during the sanctions era. At the last minute there was a collective change of heart, and none of them complied – in part because John Browne learned what was afoot and withdrew BP's cooperation. The Commission in South Africa protested feebly, but that was the last anyone heard of this corporate *mea culpa*.

In this instance, BP had dug itself in a hole as early as October 1968 when the South African government began pressuring BPSA, and executives in London did nothing. In other cases it was seemingly well-intentioned initiatives which caused the problems. Early in 2003, for example, John Browne voluntarily revealed the tax and profit sharing terms of BP's licenses in Angola as part of a drive for greater transparency in dealings with undemocratic Third World states. The move backfired spectacularly when the outraged Angolan government threatened to revoke BP's licenses and no other company – in particular Shell and its chief executive Mark Moody-Stuart (with whom Browne had been discussing the issue for months) – followed suit. BP backed down and then, as it made 19 sizeable offshore oil and gas discoveries, adopted a posture of head-in-the-sand silence and supine compliance with Luanda's every whim.

Angola, together with Azerbaijan and Colombia, were prime targets of another of Browne's favoured projects – an edict in 2001 prohibiting all political contributions. Four years before, when I joined the company, I had been told that such payments were acceptable outside the UK "in local terms, of modest size (and) properly recorded." In 2002 I visited Sakhalin Island off Russia's Far East coast to compile a feature article for *The BP Magazine.* The company was trying to secure potentially lucrative offshore prospecting rights. The Sakhalin governor, starved of resources by Moscow, was demanding that $10 million be paid by BP into his personally-run "development fund." In London a suitable letter of response had to be devised which did not offend the spirit of Browne's recent edict. With appropriate contortions, this was achieved and eventually a payment of $5 million was made to help fund the upgrade of an old gas pipeline that transported energy to Sakhalin's largest city, Yuzhno-Sakhalinsk.

"Facilitation payments" were a third area of controversy. In 2002 a new definition of these payments was drawn up by BP to distinguish them from bribes "which typically involve paying someone to do something improper or illegal." Prior to this, the only test in the company had been the "red face" one – could BP live with the embarrassment of seeing such payments reported in the press? Immediately, arguments broke out among confused managers inquiring where to draw the line. Were hotel tips acceptable? Paying for a fast-track service to ensure Browne was not kept waiting for hours in airport customs? Meeting local authorities half way on security issues around BP facilities? Through a friendship with the head of BP in China I joined the Asia regional ethics committee, one of several such groupings set up to adjudicate borderline cases. I recall one particular case that involved a request to fund the purchase of weapons for the police in Chongqing in central China, where BP owned and operated a large chemical plant. The request was refused. Instead the purchase of "non-lethal" motorcycles was approved.

The root of the problem for BP, as a wise colleague put it to me once, was that "a low standard industry with a high standard BP is never going to work in the long term." Yet it was difficult to know what would work. In some places like Tanzania, where the government extracted $8 million from BP's local bank account and then tried to fine the company to cover up its own corruption, it was hard to understand why BP kept quiet. On other occasions, such as when Venezuela's dictator Hugo Chavez came calling while on a visit to London and tried to pressure BP and Shell – both big investors in Venezuela at the time – to help break a strike by state-employed oil industry workers (he was turned down), it is easier to understand why silence was the best course. In Colombia, where BP continued to be attacked by NGOs and leftwing journalists for alleged collusion with paramilitary forces long after effective measures had been introduced to prevent this happening, nothing the company could ever say or do stopped the flow of innuendo. In those circumstances silence definitely was the best tactic.

Over time I came to regard many of the campaigning NGOs taking aim at BP with real suspicion – even those, like WWF and Save the Children, apparently happy to work with the company when it suited them. Throughout the decade or more that I was associated with BP a string of highly misleading claims was made and rarely, if ever, retracted by NGOs when facts on the ground clearly contradicted the original assertion. The company, it was alleged at one time or another while I was working with BP, was involved in arms dealing in Colombia, providing weapons to security forces in Indonesia, colluding in the suppression of Tibet by the Chinese government, victimising Kurds in Turkey, exploiting children in Angola and stoking up ethnic violence in Sudan to name a few of the worst canards. At the start of 2004 one NGO actually compiled a list of 44 separate human rights allegations against the company and posted them on its web site. Not one of them was true.

Browne's pursuit of the moral high ground on matters like the environment, political contributions and facilitation payments made things worse, however laudable his basic aim. Thereafter NGOs invariably held BP to a higher standard than companies like Exxon and Total. In an article I wrote for John in April 2001, he attempted to redress the balance in the *Financial Times* and tried to soften the adversarial nature of some of the links BP had with NGOs by stressing the importance of mutual advantage in associations between large companies and "civil society." It achieved nothing. By the time he resigned from BP the company's relations with the NGO community in the UK had degenerated to such an extent that the term "corporate social responsibility" had become a no no. Browne's heirs did little to rectify matters.

An equally relevant question is what BP might have done more or better to burnish these ties. Seen from inside, much of the NGO criticism of the company was a grotesque, and quite deliberate, misrepresentation of the facts designed to provoke rather than to inform. Nothing exemplified this more than the huge controversy surrounding a deal in 2003-05 to build a $4 billion, 1,768km-long oil pipeline through the Caucasus to link Baku on the Caspian Sea with Ceyhan on Turkey's Mediterranean coast – the so-called BTC project. From the outset a group of campaigning NGOs determined to fight the link tooth and nail. Their hostility derived from a combination of human rights, environmental and social concerns, arrogance (the same grouping had previously prevented a dam being built in Turkey) and an abiding mistrust of big business. The project's mistaken decision, endorsed by Browne, to seek a relatively small amount of "public" money from multilateral lending institutions, simply exacerbated matters and gave the campaigners leverage and spurious authenticity.

Regardless of the rights and wrongs of the strategic arguments for the pipeline – even at the time the Clinton administration's claim that the project would lessen Russian influence in the Caucasus region and bolster western energy security seemed overblown given the amounts of hydrocarbons involved – the criticisms of what turned out to be a massive infrastructure benefit for a poverty-stricken region were hard to credit. One statement by the NGO grouping at the end of 2003 suggested, for example, that the BTC link would contravene international law, cause severe economic hardship, destabilise the entire Caspian region, violate communities' human rights, wipe out Kurdish villages, trash the planet, worsen climate change and involve a loss of sovereignty for every country hosting the route. Vast amounts of time and effort had to be devoted inside BP to counter such wild arguments and also to find ways to ensure that every community affected by the project benefited.

I visited BTC construction sites in all three countries (Azerbaijan, Georgia and Turkey) on a number of occasions, edited a quarterly publication put out during the construction phase and attended many meetings and events related to the project. Today I recall with admiration the dedicated idealists who worked with BP on its social initiatives in the region during this fascinating time, and sincerely hope that their work had lasting impact. Whatever else they did, though, these ventures – some of them quite extraordinary for an oil company, such as improving cattle fertility and seed quality and entrepreneurial skills in remote villages – demonstrated to a very neglected part of the world for the first time in living memory how it is possible for human beings to change their lives for the better. Given the legacy of the Soviet era which had stifled initiative, punished enterprise, corrupted relationships and undermined the rule of law, it was never going to be easy to turn things around in this part of the world – a malign inheritance that BP also ran into in Russia during the 1997-2009 period. But at least the company tried.

There were, of course, other factors at work in Russia, and of all the external situations I experienced at BP none was handled with less deftness by John Browne. For whatever reason he simply could not, or would not, get to grips with the reality of post-communist Russia – its history and culture, its prevailing attitudes, the proud record of its oil and gas sector and the Wild East character of the country following the collapse of the Soviet system. If he was given impartial and well-informed advice by specialists inside or outside the company, he tended to ignore it. At heart, for all his diplomatic words in public, Browne persuaded himself that he was negotiating with a bankrupt second-rate country, a broken system and a corrupt business elite and he believed he could outsmart them. It was a grave miscalculation.

My first inkling of trouble ahead came one day only months after I began working in Britannic House in 1997 when I noticed a low-slung, armour-plated Mercedes parked outside the building. An early oligarch named Vladimir Potanin had come calling to agree a $571 million deal with BP to sell it a 10 per cent stake in a mid-sized Russian oil company called Sidanco. At the time BP totally lacked experience or knowledge of Russia, the Russian business context and Russian politics. I must have been the only person in BP headquarters at the time that had actually lived and worked in Moscow and spoke some Russian, but no one was interested. From the sidelines I watched the Sidanco deal unravel within a year and Browne ill-advisedly give the brush off to Tyumen Oil (later TNK), one of his Russian partners. BP then found itself outmanoeuvred at every turn and eventually, in 2000, gave up the fight.

Browne, to be fair, saw this surrender as a (rather costly) learning experience and tactical retreat and by 2003 was itching to make another attempt to buy into the reserve-rich, but vulnerable, Russian oil and gas industry. Publicly, at least, he claimed to understand the reasons for the Sidanco fiasco. As one of his aides put it to me: "We learned the hard way. We made the mistake of expecting the Russians to step aside and let us run things. We just walked in expecting everybody to fall over. That's not how it worked." Having digested this unpalatable lesson, John pulled off what he regarded as a masterstroke – a $7 billion deal in February 2003 to buy a 50 per cent stake in Russia's third largest oil company – TNK no less. This extraordinary turnaround, blessed by Vladimir Putin and Tony Blair, was a unique 50:50 deal (which Putin had the gumption to say at the outset would never work) which boosted BP's reserves by one-third and was intended to be a new, fair and safe model for foreign investment in Russia. Yet BP then repeated many of its previous mistakes, in particular believing that the size of the deal, and its perceived importance to Russia's external relationships and image, would somehow protect the company from future trouble and that ultimate reliance on an arbitration procedure based on Swedish law would protect BP more than the TNK oligarchs.

Today it must be doubtful that any western company would replicate such terms despite the successes of the deal in reviving discounted assets and generating huge cash flows for BP over a sustained period. Right from Day One many of the Sidanco difficulties resurfaced. The BP negotiating team, led by Chase, antagonised its Russian interlocutors with its high-handed behaviour and failed to tie up dozens of loose ends, above all what should follow when the initial five-year joint ownership agreement lapsed. Objectives were left vague. And no one could agree who should run the merged organisation. Browne's eventual choice to represent BP as chief executive was a buttoned-down ex-Amoco American called Bob Dudley, who spoke little Russian and came to rely on a coterie of former BP executives seconded to the new company. Few of them showed much long term commitment to Russia or Russians or real interest or understanding of the Russian psyche or the troubled Soviet inheritance. For their part, the Russian oligarch shareholders regarded Dudley's plans to create a modern, western-style oil company as inimical to their interests. These were directed solely to milking TNK-BP of as much cash as possible as fast as possible. TNK employees and their future counted for little or nothing. As for western notions of corporate governance, they were seen as fanciful, even counter-productive, in the anything-goes business environment of the time where who you knew in Russia was far more important than what was legally possible or desirable.

By this stage, however, John Browne thought he understood the Kremlin's tacit rules and the best way to do business in contemporary Russia – a gesture or donation here, a private discussion in the Kremlin or a fix there, and all would be fine. To an amazing degree he was impressed by Putin and went around BP extolling the Russian leader's "competence." He also appeared to believe that the legal system in Russia had some autonomy outside politics. In truth he fooled himself, or was poorly advised by a succession of superannuated western "experts" who were lined up to take the BP shilling. As Putin and his ex-KGB allies moved to regain control over Russia's hydrocarbon sector by fair means or foul in 2003-04, the scales slowly dropped from everyone's eyes. By then John was losing the confidence of the board and had few cards to play and it was left to his hapless successor, Tony Hayward, to pick up the pieces as best he could. When Hayward in his turn was forced out following the Gulf of Mexico disaster, through a supreme irony his replacement turned out to be Bob Dudley, who promptly proceeded to antagonise his former adversaries in TNK-BP once more by trying to conclude a share swap deal with the state-owned Rosneft company in violation, so a Swedish arbitration tribunal ruled, of BP's original deal with the TNK oligarchs. Not surprisingly, they were rather upset. If it hadn't happened, no one would have believed such a tale of sustained miscalculation and self-inflicted wounds.

My own involvement in these engagements proved to be a fascinating exercise in futility. A week or two after I left BP in June 2003, a friend on the TNK-BP integration team called and asked me to join him for a few months in Moscow, focusing on communication issues. Until the final deal was sealed in November I travelled back and forth from London, helping to devise a strategy both for the signing ceremony and for the first year of the new entity. Day after day we worked long hours trying to craft a way forward. It was like wading through treacle. One obstacle proved insurmountable. All communications in the Russian managerial context are top down – a legacy of the past. But Dudley favoured a new, inclusive style. So we were told to come up with a plan to sell TNK-BP to its employees, and consult local managers and officials that involved numerous town hall meetings around the country. No Russian we met in TNK-BP had ever heard of town hall meetings, and the Russian owners had never met their employees. I also had real doubts about letting Dudley loose in such circumstances, given his reliance on interpreters, which would simply have reinforced his outsider status. Meetings on the problem got nowhere, not least because the TNK side often failed to show. Young, post-Soviet local designers turned up as requested with great ideas and found them all rejected by the prevailing Soviet mentality. After months of trying, we failed to achieve consensus on anything. In the end, to prevent a fiasco on signing day, BP's plans were steamrollered through to the undisguised fury of the Russian side, several of whom promptly quit TNK-BP. A few townhall meetings were held but only revealed the wide gulf between East and West.

This small but revealing episode proved to be a harbinger of all the trouble that lay ahead. Even as we were debating communications strategy Dudley was in a fight about such mundane matters as office space, telephones and headed notepaper. Already his key opponents in TNK-BP had identified themselves, especially the combative German Khan (also a shareholder in TNK-BP), who seemed to specialise in throwing things at people who he disliked. Dudley, a straightforward and mild-mannered engineer from the American Midwest, was no match for such rough-house tactics though he had stamina and guts by the planeload. Meantime, out in the boondocks in places like western Siberia, BP's technical secondees were isolated and easily sidelined. Here and there potential allies, mostly young Russians who had been educated in the West, were unearthed. But a year later, when I returned to compile TNK-BP's first corporate brochure and to help define the company's brand identity, cultural and personal tensions were palpable to the extent of Russians refusing to see or work with me once they discovered I came from BP.

In the following four years the underlying friction never went away despite TNK-BP's many operational achievements. Almost my last serious BP contribution, at the end of 2008, was to write an article for *The BP Magazine* summing up BP's five-year record in Russia. On a practical level progress had been made. More relevant, though, was the no-holds-barred struggle for control among the shareholders which raged through most of 2008. This culminated with Dudley fleeing Russia to avoid arrest, most of the remaining BP secondees exiting after him and

Russian managers taking operational control – albeit with BP still hanging on. TNK-BP could have been a constructive and successful model for East-West business cooperation. Instead it stands as an example of how not to do it – undone as much by the failure of westerners to understand how best to coexist with the complicated, wounded bear that is post-communist Russia as by Russian xenophobia, closed minds and historic mistrust of the West.

In a way it was apt that Russia should provide me with my last important memory of my dozen years working in and with BP. If there is one emotion looking back it is frustration – that this great company pigeon-holed people, and that those at the top were insufficiently flexible to reach down into what was a vast organisation chock-full of talented employees. Perhaps it is significant that the person who asked me to work with him in Moscow also was an outsider. All too often BP seemed to reject those who had not risen through its oily ranks or were not engineers or geologists by training. The only routine exceptions were retired ambassadors and members of MI6 recruited for their supposed ability to open doors and influence the right people – like Muammar Gaddafi.

The result was that a gilded individual like Tony Hayward could reach the uppermost ranks of the company in the 1990s with a distinctly uneven track record, little or no experience of the world outside BP and a tin-ear for communications, secure in the knowledge (like Browne before him) that he was one of the chosen few. An abiding early memory of Hayward – later to be stigmatised by the horrendous Deepwater Horizon disaster in the Gulf of Mexico in 2010 which so nearly capsized the company – was the day he slid into the press office in 2002 for his first session of high-level media training. A cynical, superior smirk creased his youthful face. Afterwards one of the trainers confessed that he had never had to deal with anyone near the top of BP quite so detached from the whole learning process. In fact, as later became apparent, some people never learn. In Hayward's case his flippant manner and persistent refusal to take corporate communications, the media and external relations seriously ultimately cost BP and himself very dearly. Bob Dudley was neither a visionary nor a born leader. But at least he understood the multi-dimensional nature of a global business and the importance of clear, thought-out rational communication.

As I look back now I recall the first lines of a poem by AP Herbert:

"Oil! / Beneficent oil/ Mankind's most precious treasure in the soil! / Oil! / Disgusting oil, / Father of blood and sweat and tears and toil!" In view of the volcanic ups and downs that occurred in BP during my involvement with the company, the crises, the petty politicking and the huge egos lurking behind every office door, one does wonder if it was all worth it. I believe it was. After three decades in journalism it was stimulating to see life from the other side of the fence and to work in an organisation with global reach and money to spend. A few of the things I did for BP deserve to be remembered, including an issue of *The BP Magazine* which I edited in 2001 devoted to the company's work in the community around the world, and writing the first speeches given by senior BP managers on three important and sensitive issues – sustainable development, business corruption and the lessons learned from the Texas City refinery explosion in 2005. I'm glad that I was able to produce a report on the "secrets" of western technological progress for the governor of Guangdong province in southern China (perhaps he read it), and write two books for the company. For 11 years I was the leading internal contributor to *The BP Magazine.* At one time or another I overhauled BP's magazines, went to the US to appease disgruntled ex-Amoco communications staff, helped to revive BP Shipping's identity and wrote the BP Azerbaijan Sustainability Report for eight consecutive years. Given where I started at the age of 54, it was a reasonable record even if it did leave me feeling that I could have done so much more. C'est la vie.

12

Loose Ends

"It's only those who do nothing who make no mistakes, I suppose."
JOSEPH CONRAD

On being made to retire by BP in mid-2003 when I reached the company's then official retirement age of 60, I was determined to go on working for a few more years if I could. I had acquired some marketable skills, we needed the money and I felt more than healthy and determined enough to reinvent myself for a third time. So I persuaded BP to offer me several short term writing contracts, set up my own company Knightwrite Ltd. and for the next eight years undertook a variety of freelance corporate communications work for various parts of BP, Rolls Royce and other large UK-based companies.

While my contacts remained good, Knightwrite flourished. Inevitably, as time passed, the gloss dulled on many of these relationships as people moved on or corporate priorities altered or the generations changed. By that point, after working virtually without a break for 40 years, I was losing the motivation to continue chasing the next buck and the next contract. The symbolic denouement took place one morning in the spring of 2009 on a park bench under the big, leafy trees which surround Richmond Green in west London – a bizarre setting to be fired for the third time in my life. On this occasion the executioner was a mid-level bean counter at BP Shipping whom I had never met. I had begun working there with two BP chums, Pablo Urrutia and Simon Lisiecki, three and a half years earlier when we set up an imaginative in-house online monthly magazine called *The Flag* which was distributed far and wide to ships and crew via the internet. In 2008 I spent most of the year working full-time at Shipping as Pablo's posting in the UK came to an end and he returned to Colombia. Then the shipping cycle turned down, a cautious new chief executive took over, BP group budgets were cut back all over the world and that was the end of me. The only compensation was that I was part of a wider slash-and-burn trend as the recession, induced by the global banking crisis of 2007-08, took hold. "In business right now cash is king and the only way ambitious managers progress is by driving down costs," I wrote in a letter published in *The Daily Telegraph* in April 2009. "Every sort of contractor is being squeezed from the top of the supply chain to the bottom, in the UK and around the world." Too true; a couple of years later BP actually had the cheek to ask Knightwrite for a discount!

Freelancing and contract work, though, served its purpose well as a rewarding bridge between full-time working and full-time retirement, and for a number of years it gave me some enjoyable late-career reporting and writing opportunities including choice assignments in Australia, China, Iran, Russia and Azerbaijan. In Australia I toured the vast country from Karratha in the far northwest to the Olympic Stadium in Sydney in the southeast in 2005, gathering material for a series of articles for BP publications. In China I found myself in Guangdong province sipping a local blush wine and lunching with an intimidating, bald Army officer known as Colonel O who wanted BP money to transform a nearby reservoir into a scaled-down version of Venice. Having survived that encounter, I was paddled across a lake in a rowing boat to visit a nearby school sponsored by BP. When I got there, a little dishevelled from a hike across sodden paddy fields, hundreds of pupils were lined up on the playground awaiting my inspection as a marching band played. In Iran I was part of a forlorn attempt by BP to edge its way back into its country-of-origin via the unlikely vehicle of a past-and-present photo exhibition in Tehran. This costly gesture went nowhere, but at least it allowed me to visit Ayatollah Khomeni's shrine outside the capital, talk to veterans of the Iran-Iraq war at a cemetery nearby, discuss politics with well-educated (and schizophrenic) professors and young women, see the memorable Islamic architecture of Isfahan and fly south to Qeshm Island in the Gulf where I watched dhows being crafted on a sandy seashore by carpenters using skills unchanged for centuries – and somehow pull all this vivid material together in an article for *The BP Magazine* which showcased this fascinating, if volatile, country without upsetting the applecart for BP.

Various visits to Russia from 2003-07 mostly involved describing the on-scene reality of the new TNK-BP alliance as best I could without making matters worse than they were. Sadly, right from the start of this troubled relationship suspicion proved to be the name of the game although there were exceptions on both sides, especially at the technical level. On one occasion, before the TNK oligarchs really began to flex their muscles, I was invited to western Siberia to see what was being done to revive the giant Samotlor oil field, and was in Tyumen when female Chechen suicide bombers blew up two planes in mid-air over Russia in August, 2004. Instructions reached me from Moscow to stay put until airline travellers' safety could be "guaranteed." The prospect of weeks stuck in the taiga did not appeal and, reckoning that security would be good after such a cataclysmic incident, I flew back to Domodedovo Airport shortly after accompanied only by a cheery Russian Army general.

Azerbaijan, too, generated many visits and assignments in the 2002-06 period as the BP-sponsored Baku-Tbilisi-Ceyhan oil pipeline was strung more than a thousand miles across the rugged hinterland of Azerbaijan, Georgia and Turkey. This enormous project caused the biggest disappointment of my BP years when an illustrated coffee-table book in four languages, which I had authored and helped to design over a six month period to celebrate the completion of the pipeline, was pulled by the head of the venture just days before the printing presses were due to roll. His spurious reasoning was that the all-embracing product I had delivered was not the "lite" picture postcard fluff that he had commissioned. As usual, when things went wrong in BP, support was nowhere to be found when it was most needed. The book's sponsors, all of whom had been flatteringly complimentary up to that point, went to ground. Some £60,000 disappeared down the drain, together with an opportunity to provide a fitting testimonial to what was by any yardstick an amazing engineering achievement completed safely, on time, in remote conditions lacking all infrastructure, with minimal environmental damage and within the original budget. Such, unfortunately, can be life in global corporations with more money than sense.

By that stage in my career there were always non-work compensations to be found if I searched hard enough. Throughout this period I was involved with secondary education as a governor of Pangbourne College, the successor institution to the school in Berkshire which I had attended rather uncomfortably as a teenager. To say that this was a surprising development is to understate the matter very considerably. For a quarter of a century after leaving the NCP I had no contact of any sort with the College. In 1969, as the British merchant navy collapsed, the governing body decided to turn Pangbourne into a civilian school with a difference. From then on few of the pupils, as they were now called, went to sea or into the armed services although they continued to wear the naval uniform, march on the parade ground and generally behave as though they were still cadets in the Royal Naval Reserve. Numbers stabilised and slowly rose under the inspired leadership of the College's first civilian headmaster, Peter Points – the ideal mix of the old (he was an ex-Royal Marine officer) and the new (as a mainstream schoolmaster). Peter stayed for 20 years, transforming Pangbourne in his own robust, demanding image. It was the close relationship I developed with him as editor of the *OP Magazine* which introduced me to everyone who was anyone connected to the new College. This led to an invitation to join the governing board in 1994 where I acted as the "tame rottweiler" of the chairman, the ever-tolerant and understanding Vice Admiral Sir John Webster, himself an OP. In reality all this involved was asking the difficult questions that no one else seemed inclined to do at board meetings – behaving true to form, in other words.

In the 1990s Pangbourne evolved again under the headship of Anthony Hudson, moving away from its naval roots to a softer, less hierarchical learning institution with time for such alien attributes as feelings and emotions. Early on in his tenure Anthony convinced the governors (including me, somewhat reluctantly) that the time had come for the school to go coeducational. Over the next 20 years the girls – originally recruited to try to boost numbers and examination results and smooth some of the rough edges off the school – outperformed the boys in many respects and proved to be a huge success. Anthony was a born motivator and marketer, and he also succeeded in raising £2 million single-handedly to build the beautiful Falklands Islands Memorial Chapel in the heart of the College campus – a magnificent personal achievement which reached an apogee in 2007 when the entire British Establishment, led by Queen Elizabeth, prime minister Tony Blair, senior members of the government, all the Service chiefs and, of course, Margaret Thatcher, descended on Pangbourne for a nationally televised Service of Thanksgiving to mark the 25th anniversary of the Falklands conflict – a proud moment indeed for anyone connected with the school.

Such highlights made the routine dross of quarterly board meetings, at which the main topics often were unpaid debts or the dowdy state of the school fabric or the persistent failure of Pangbourne – very much a mixed ability institution – to move up the dreaded GCSE and 'A' level league tables, that much more palatable. Like many smaller private schools in Britain, the College suffered from an underlying lack of capital. It had virtually no endowments to call on, so any major new project involved either selling off parts of the 240-acre campus, increasing the bank overdraft or launching an appeal. Meanwhile, in the wider world, society was demanding ever-higher standards of creature comforts, academic qualifications and campus security. Squaring this circle was never easy. Yet with its unusual history, distinct ethos, committed staff, loyal parents and notable *esprit de corps*, Pangbourne always had a lot going for it, and even in the depths of recession numbers held up well given the sky-high fees involved.

Ultimately, as I found out for myself over time, the rhythm and development of any good school centres on the personality, character and leadership of the head teacher. "Perhaps schools (and newspapers) are the last examples of dictatorship in action," I wrote soon after becoming a governor. "Everything revolves around the top." This was most vividly emphasised to me in 2007-08 when the Charity Commissioners, prompted by chippy left-wingers in the Labour Party, selected Pangbourne as one of the first five independent schools to be "audited" to justify their prized charitable status. By this time the College was led by an outstanding personality in Thomas Garnier – an ex-naval officer appointed to the headship in 2005 at the tender age of 36 and destined for great things wherever he worked. Thomas correctly viewed the subsequent intrusive, scatter-gun "audit" as an opportunity rather than a threat, and the school sailed through the anomalous test with minimal changes to its activities and character.

I remained a governor at Pangbourne for three five-year terms retiring in 2008, by which time the idea of more board discussions about property issues, run-ins with the West Berkshire planning authorities and Ofsted inspections had begun to pale. Much of the time I was little more than a reasonably well-informed overseer – part of a group of fifteen or so people with varying skills and educational know-how who set "policy" but left it to the Headmaster and Bursar and others to implement. My input mostly involved asking tricky questions, pressing for a more professional approach to marketing and external communications and helping to resolve reputational issues rather than education per se. Private schools, I discovered, only reluctantly accepted the idea that they had a valuable brand to nurture and protect and needed to be sold professionally. After years of my lobbying, the board eventually caved in and appointed an excellent marketing director in 2006. Trying to incentivise the teachers' salary structure – another board preoccupation – proved to be a bridge too far, even for me. Every now and then tough decisions did have to be taken, but mostly we directed matters with a light touch and kept a watching brief from the sidelines over what, by that stage, had become a multi-million pound business. On Founder's Day 2009 I was honoured to be presented with a beautiful glass vase to mark my time on the board. It was the satisfying culmination of an unexpected, and unsought, 15-year stint at the heart of the school that must have made the sceptical captain superintendents of my day turn in their graves – not least because, following my resignation, I was asked by the governors to compile an illustrated history of Pangbourne College to mark the school's centenary in 2017.

As my sixties wore on regular writing remained central to my life whether it was paid assignments, contributions to journals, book reviews or the occasional freelance piece for a literary magazine. Across the Atlantic, my old newsmagazine stamping grounds were becoming a meltdown zone, and the chances of anyone like me having the sort of career that I had enjoyed had already become non-existent. *Newsweek* and *Business Week* were sold for derisory amounts, *Time* was slimmed down drastically, while *US News & World Report* contracted from 50 issues a year in the 1990s to 36 issues a year at the start of the new millennium and 26 issues a year in the mid-2000s, before finally ending its print edition in late-2010. According to the hapless editor at the time, "This puts us in a strong position to continue building the *US News* brand in the new media world."

Such wretched, self-serving cant merely reflected the reality that the era of the weekly current affairs publication (with the honourable exception, in the English-speaking world, of *The Economist*) had more or less drawn to a conclusion eighty to ninety years after it began. Efforts to remake mass circulation newsmagazines began in earnest in the US in the mid-1980s. But they tended to be unsatisfactory because the key conundrum around the rationale for such complex and costly publications – who wanted to buy them and why – proved impossible to resolve at a time of declining advertising revenues and static circulations. At root newsmagazines were always a means by which a group of elite writers, reporters and photographers combined with a clear rationale every week to create an attractive physical product of value to millions of literate readers seeking a regular update on the world around them. In the era of 24-hour news services, bloggers, instant messaging, talk shows, specialist publications and vastly better daily newspaper coverage and distribution that need all-but evaporated. Turning such publications into online brands seemed unlikely to alter this core reality. For two generations after World War II the newsmagazine had the analytical/trend/predictive field of journalism largely to itself. Today such journalism is commonplace – a staple in all print and digital media.

If that has been hard enough for someone like me to swallow, the demise since the mid-1990s of the classic foreign correspondent – someone permanently based abroad who is charged with keeping readers up-to-date on news and trends in a country or a region – has been even more discomforting to observe. Almost without exception, as costs have risen and revenues have fallen, magazines and newspapers have chosen to close bureaus abroad and rely instead on wire services or young cheap stringers or instant experts flown in to cover big events like earthquakes or revolutions. Day-to-day, websites now cover narrowly selected areas of the global market – celebrities, sports, entertainment, business. Within seconds of a wire service putting out a story, it is parroted by TV channels and newspapers and online outlets in all corners of the planet – it saves them hiring their own journalists. In the process the appearance of foreign reporting is preserved but all context and expertise is lost, ignorance of life deeper than television headlines grows, valuable news sources disappear, repressive governments cheer and lunatic conspiracy theories (especially in the Mideast and America) take root which, over time, have the potential to cause large parts of the world to spiral into a nationalistic maelstrom similar to that of the 1930s.

I was often asked about the lifestyle, role and justification for foreign correspondents when I was one. Just the mere words "foreign correspondent" seemed to tweak an interest, evoking connotations of glamorous derring-do. In terms of lifestyle, it was an easy question to answer. Wherever a foreign correspondent is based, his or her life is enriched and sometimes tested by continuous exposure to new customs and assumptions, by the new friendships and associations which can be made and by the opportunity to observe as a fly on the wall how the billions of people on this planet pursue quite singular ways of conducting the business of life – all of which may be reflected in one's reporting. Being a foreign correspondent can be exhilarating, rewarding and worthwhile, with far more highs than lows – a job that allows an uncommitted outsider privileged *entrée* into different societies at varying levels and with varying impact. At its worst, it can be risky and frustrating, lonely and unhealthy. In my experience there was never much in between – certainly not boredom nor repetitiveness nor the dulling shackles of management hierarchies. Occasionally one can be a witness to great events and be among the first to try to make sense of them for others, but that is the exception. More often, particularly as a weekly journalist, one is digging beneath the local daily news to discover the factors that lie behind a situation or peering forward, both of which can only be done by utilising that most traditional weapon in any journalist's armoury – in-depth, persistent, on-the-scene interviewing and reporting.

Each foreign correspondent will have a subtly different perspective on this challenge – some stimulated by exposing wrongs, others focused more on the conventional political process, still others energised by conflicts or business trends or cultural events or even (dare it be said) the chance to eat at fine restaurants on an expense account. Targeting the offbeat and quirky in a foreign society usually required too much explanation to work well, especially in the irony-free context of American life; by the time a tongue-in-cheek piece had survived the editorial meat-grinder at *US News,* all colour and flavour tended to have been lost. In my time, though perhaps less so today, exactly where one placed the emphasis was a matter of personality and temperament as much as the character or focus of the publication or its editorial bent. But whatever one's approach, the responsibility is always the same. For a reporter given the great privilege of living and working abroad at someone else's expense, the primary accountability has to be to one's readers and, alongside them, one's editors. Advances in technology may have helped to bridge the gulf between the person in the field and editors back at base and made parts of the job easier; when I first visited Washington in 1970, rewrite editors at *US News* cut and glued stories on bits of yellow paper to take account of breaking news and editorial whim. Yet with the greater and more immediate contact that has followed the arrival of satellite phones and laptops, there has also come more micromanagement, many more day-to-day filing demands and much less chance to display individual initiative.

Where foreign coverage is concerned, editors all over the world remain strangely inhibited in setting clear guidelines. My view always has been that if funds are short, resources should be concentrated on countries and situations of most direct relevance to the reader at home – particularly since no magazine or newspaper today can possibly cover every foreign event of significance. Foreign reportage is not essentially about facts or education; there are plenty of universities and research institutes around to do that. Nor is it about forecasting, although television reporters routinely overlook that in their rush to appear significant. Instead it is, or should be, about alerting the reader, listener or viewer to interesting or significant trends which might otherwise go unnoticed, to events which conceivably might affect outsiders' lives in the nearish future and to developments of any sort with the potential to cross borders. Foreign correspondents – or the good ones – need the ability to interpret the unusual and make it readable and understandable. They need a keen eye for the significant detail or quotation or piece of colour that often makes all the difference in a report from abroad. They need a magpie mind for facts and figures, and the ability to synthesize complex issues accurately and succinctly. They need the sort of character that is capable of persuading local personalities to spare them time – not easy if the publication in question is barely known in the host country. Occasionally they need to be courageous. They must be self-reliant, resourceful and tenacious. And given the global time zone differences involved in their work, they also need the stamina of an ox.

Some, it is true, believe they are charged with an "idealistic aim to convey the importance of history in the making" as Ray Moseley (who was doing the job for the *Chicago Tribune* in his late 60s) puts it delicately in his memoir *In Foreign Fields*. I'm not sure that I ever belonged to this superior caste. First and last my primary motive always was to inform my readers (assuming there were some) as clearly as possible about the reality of life or events elsewhere in the world, without fear or favour – although idealism sometimes was useful body armour when sitting across a table from a glowering dictator. To me, the best journalism wherever it originates should primarily seek to establish the truth – understanding all the time that in the modern world this is an uphill task. "On the face of it, it is an insane way to live," Ray added in his book – and foreign correspondents do pay a high price in terms of professional and personal relationships. Yet most would agree with Moseley that it is worth it, if only to "try to lure the non-committed into an engagement with the outside world that goes beyond superficiality and fleeting notice."

It's conventional at this point to suggest that one has no regrets, but one of the things that becoming a foreign correspondent obstructs is any kind of logical or sensible career path. It happened to me, and I do regret that. Out of sight, out of mind, all too often is the long term fate of any individual posted abroad for any length of time, sometimes, it must be admitted, to mutual satisfaction. Exactly how one fits into an organisation's hierarchy is never clear and, as the years pass, younger, sleeker models back at base tend to overtake on the inside before you know it has happened. How many former foreign correspondents do I know who failed to fit in at any level when they returned to their home base? Too many to count, sadly.

As a Brit working for an American publication, and latterly as a 50-plus business neophyte and one-man gun-for-hire roaming largely unsupervised through a global corporation, I was fated to be an outsider. Yet I always wanted to run something, particularly as an editor, and only achieved that once or twice and only for short periods. The one real chance I had, through *The Times* foreign editor offer, would never have worked. The person who got the job lasted little more than a year before the paper went through another paroxysm and a new-broom editor took over. I was lucky not to be left high and dry. In retrospect, perhaps I should have left *US News* after my stint in Africa when I was in my late 30s, returned to London and taken my chances with *The Financial Times* which, even at that point a dozen or so years after its initial offer, indicated that it would have been happy to take me on. Who knows what would have happened? Instead, Italy and the Mediterranean region beckoned alluringly, and the chance went begging. That is the trouble with regrets. Usually one has no one but oneself to blame for missed opportunities with the result that looking back becomes an exercise in self-flagellation.

Journalism, though, is not a dead end. Many of the people I rubbed shoulders with on the road went on to interesting and varied second careers. Joe Fromm remained with *US News* until 1986, and then carved out a new life as a consultant in Washington, advising the US government and others on military-strategic issues. Marv Stone became deputy director of the US Information Agency and later ran a US government fund set up in the late 1980s to promote democracy in Eastern Europe. John Harvey-Lee, a human cork if ever there was one, bobbed up again after his dismissal by *US News* and worked in the Foreign Office in London escorting journalist visitors around Britain. Benjamin Pogrund was left high-and-dry when the plug was pulled on the *Rand Daily Mail* by its weak-kneed owners in 1985 following unrelenting hostility from the apartheid regime. He moved to London for a time, before settling in Jerusalem where he devoted his energies to promoting Arab-Israeli understanding. James Buxton transferred to Edinburgh with the *Financial Times* and became the paper's respected Scotland correspondent. Jeff Trimble left *US News* in 1997, joined *Radio Free Europe / Radio Liberty* in Washington and rose to the dizzy heights of executive director of the Broadcasting Board of Governors – the official body that oversees publicly funded international broadcasting in the United States. John Walcott ran the large Knight Ridder/McClatchy Newspapers Washington bureau for 15 years. The Rubys wrote and edited books from their home in Arizona after Mike retired from the *Milwaukee Journal Sentinel*. John Marks flirted with television current affairs programmes at *CBS* and wrote several well-received novels. Chris Redman filed on luxury products and other esoteric upmarket activities for *Time* and *Fortune* and bought a beautiful farmhouse on a hill in Gers in rural southwest France. Simon Lisiecki left BP, went back to Alaska and studied carpentry. Roddy Kennedy had an impressive home built for himself in rural Hertfordshire and stopped spinning after escorting two successive ex-chief executives out of the front door of BP's headquarters.

Jeannie, my rock and anchor throughout my working life, departed with honour from the ITC in 2005 – one of the last people to leave the organisation before it was absorbed into Ofcom. She never looked back. Without her constant support and encouragement, and ever-sensible advice, I would not have survived and even flourished for as long as I did at *US News* or BP or Knightwrite. Putting a value on such a contribution is impossible. How many times did she wisely counsel caution? How many times did she stoically rally to the flag? How many times did she put her own interests second to mine without hesitation? We have both travelled a very long way as individuals and as a couple since our marriage in 1972 and, for certain, our lives would have taken different routes had we not met. All I can be sure of today is that for me the journey would have been far less fun, far less worthwhile, far less happy and far less fulfilling.

In retirement (or nearly so) I returned to the golf course in 2003, soon after joining the friendly Huntercombe club on the edge of the Chilterns – a true "hidden gem" in the bucolic Oxfordshire countryside – and several wandering golf societies full of convivial types. For this I am thankful to a fellow governor at Pangbourne, David Griffiths, who opened doors for me and kept telling me to hit the ball down the middle of the fairway in his lilting Welsh voice. Each summer I take up a favourite position on the ground level in front of the members' bar in the pavilion at Lord's cricket ground – a rare privilege which comes from being a Life Member of the MCC. Having travelled so much, the urge to combat more security and passport checks at London's Heathrow Airport has dimmed. But when the spirit moves us or a good opportunity arises – to visit China with Jean, or to go on a cruise together or to see old friends abroad – the effort usually is worth it as the wider world unfolds in all its variety. Then I wonder once again at my great good luck in having done it all before so many times.

My generation in Britain has, indeed, been a fortunate one. By the time I reached adulthood the dreary chore of rebuilding the country after the Second World War was almost complete. The second half of the 1960s followed, with its explosion of opportunity, creativity and social reform which relaxed life so much and broke down most of the old English class system. I was given a generous grant by the state and was able to go to university – the first person in my family ever to do so. When I graduated, employers queued up to offer work. Throughout my life the material world improved, almost beyond recognition. Today food and clothing are better and cheaper than anything my grandparents knew. So are restaurants and hotels and cars and ships and planes. A train will take you from London to Paris is less than three hours. The Thames, in front of me as I write this, has surged back to life. Fishing goes on up and down the riverbank, swimmers sometimes crawl past in sponsored contests and not long ago the Port of London Authority thought it worth its while to re-cobble the centuries-old landing stage nearby at Fisherman's Wharf. People are healthier and living much longer. Cancer is on the retreat and heart transplants have become almost commonplace.

Relationships, between and among men and women and children, are unrecognisable compared to fifty years ago. "When did you last hear the word 'Sir' outside a school?" someone asked me the other day. I couldn't recall. Women have made huge and deserved advances in almost every sphere of life. Bullying is taken seriously in schools. The arts – especially film and museum exhibitions – have become ever-more imaginative, dynamic and accessible. So has the theatre – who remembers the wretched Lord Chamberlain? Communism is on its last legs and democracy, though a fragile flower in many parts of the world, continues to spread its wings. Wars still scar the planet but on a far lesser scale than the horrific conflicts which decimated both my grandparents' and parents' generations – and my generation in Europe has escaped largely unscathed.

I was fortunate, too, in becoming an international journalist when the global print media counted, twittering was for the birds and a foreign correspondent could walk in the front door at 10 Downing Street as though he or she mattered. Being paid to report life around the world for so long was a wonderful privilege as well as (mostly) fun. No one that I knew went in to journalism to become rich and all too often, as this memoir makes clear, I had to get by on very thin rations. But the egalitarian lifestyle suited my temperament, and the work rewarded me in many ways that had nothing to do with money. My efforts only rarely made headlines; indeed I remember once being dismissed offhandedly by a self-important academic media guide produced in Canada, of all places, as offering "conventional examinations of political and social trends written mostly in newsmagazinese" – clearly a damned-by-faint-praise assessment dreamt up in an ivory tower by people who had never worked for a news magazine and disparaged them. That's one of the core difficulties with journalism – it is highly subjective. Everyone has a view about it, entry is difficult, few people manage to make it to a serious level, and the rest sit on the sidelines pontificating about things they never had the ability and/or opportunity to do themselves. As it happens, that acid put-down missed the mark where news magazines are concerned. In such a collective activity, the message always matters far more than the messenger.

These reflections maybe seem pollyannish; whingeing is the default mechanism of the new millennium as prosperity softens critical faculties and the idea takes hold in many western societies that life ought to be risk-free and nothing should ever go wrong and someone else always is "responsible." But one of the few compensations for growing older is that it gives a sharper sense of perspective. All sorts of things might have worked out differently for me, some better, some worse. Overall, I feel, a fair balance has been struck and the lonely furrow I ploughed from an early age has been reflected, one way or another, in everything I have done since. I am not complaining. My life has, indeed, been "a road less travelled," and the happier for it.

Appendix

I began writing opinion columns in *US News & World Report* in the late-1980s. Until then the magazine had shunned such pieces and prevented its reporters from expressing opinions in print except in the form of structured question-and-answer interviews. The two articles reprinted from 1978 and 1982 are as close as it went. Then the publication was sold, new people came in and editorial policy changed.

To begin with I was reluctant to get on a soap box, but as the conflicts in the Balkans worsened in the early-1990s it seemed the best weapon I had to prod opinion-formers in Washington into action. Later, at BP, I was encouraged to make full use of the Talking Point pulpit in the staff magazine Horizon; few others in the company seemed keen to stick their necks out like that. In between, *Time* encouraged me to express opinions in the many book reviews that I wrote for the magazine.

All the columns reproduced here ran originally as one pagers of about 700-750 words – an ideal length for an argument containing two or three core points. Reader reaction was baffling – one never knew what would arouse a response. "A test the West is failing" in 1993 led to a flood of abusive mail to *US News* decrying my interventionist stance. The BP piece on "Ageism" in 2003 produced guffaws from my colleagues. Three years later the chief executive John Browne, then nearing 60 himself, made the same argument in a public speech and before long the company's mandatory retirement had been abolished.

Analysis

Detente: Why

View From Moscow—a Report by
Robin Knight of Our Bureau in Russia

COMMUNIST LEADERS here in Moscow are puzzled and dismayed by what they see as an inconsistent and unpredictable—even hostile—policy pursued by the Carter administration toward the Soviet Union.

Soviet officials allege that the American President made agreements with Moscow late last year that he has since repudiated. They refer in particular to a strategic-arms-limitation understanding reached in September and a joint Mideast declaration issued in October.

Further, Kremlin leaders view Carter's human-rights policy as nothing less than a challenge to Communist rule in the Soviet Union and therefore a violation of "the spirit of détente."

These grievances, valid or not, are to a considerable extent responsible for the suspicious and unyielding attitude that Soviet decision makers show toward the Carter administration.

In recent weeks, a new factor influencing the Kremlin's approach to détente has surfaced: a growing conviction among Soviet leaders that the administration in Washington is weak. The evidence as Moscow sees it: Carter's inability to devise a Mideast settlement, to push an energy bill through Congress—or even to counter Soviet-Cuban moves in Africa or protect Soviet dissidents whose cause the U.S. had championed.

Despite U.S. strength—. Moscow now seems to have concluded that President Carter is unable to match his tough talk with tough action abroad. However, this in no way implies that Soviet leaders are ignoring or discounting intrinsic American military and technological strength. Rather, it is what is seen as Carter's political weakness that encourages the Kremlin to adopt a more aggressive posture in world affairs. This in turn imposes further strains on détente.

Nowhere is this aggressiveness more evident than in the latest Soviet moves in the Strategic Arms Limitation Talks, which Moscow sees as the linchpin of détente. Officials in Moscow are clearly worried by the slow progress in negotiations and by congressional opposition to the deal they assumed had been accepted by President Carter.

But Moscow's strategy in attempting to break the impasse is anything but conciliatory. In mid-February, the newspaper *Pravda* published a rare full-page editorial on SALT, with this uncompromising message: Concessions by the U.S., not the Soviet Union, are imperative if there is to be an arms agreement.

The editorial went to considerable lengths to demonstrate continuing Soviet intransigence on the critical issues that have stymied the negotiations for nearly three years—what, if any, limitations should be applied to the Russian Backfire bomber and the American cruise missile.

Diplomatic observers in Moscow say that this hard-line approach is calculated to serve notice on Washington, and the Senate in particular, that the Kremlin refuses to be pushed any further in the arms negotiations. Another objective is to intimidate the American people by raising the specter of another uncontrolled arms race.

Soviet policymakers seem to be operating on the assumption that the U.S. values an arms agreement now more than does the Kremlin. That view stems in part from Carter's refusal to react strongly to Soviet and Cuban intervention in the Horn of Africa.

While the White House has warned of the potentially dangerous consequences of what Russia is doing in Ethiopia, it is noted in Moscow that American officials have carefully avoided any linkage between the Ethiopia-Somali war and the SALT negotiations.

There are other reasons why Soviet leaders appear unimpressed by U.S. warnings of the price they may have to pay for meddling in Africa and for their uncooperative stand in the Mideast. In private, officials point to the history of the Angola episode, where Russia and Cuba intervened, and, in effect, ask: "Why should we worry?"

It is true, the Russians say, that in the short run the Angola adventure brought a temporary standstill in détente. But, viewed from a somewhat longer perspective, these officials now point out that Soviet-American relations seemed to suffer no lasting damage from that one episode. The U.S. returned to the SALT negotiating table, and a Marxist regime remains in power in Angola.

Although the Soviet-American disagreements over major issues are sharp, Western diplomats in Moscow say there is little danger that the superpowers will drift into a new cold war.

Pressing the challenge. All that is happening now—the ongoing arms buildup, the reach for global power, the crackdown on human-rights dissidents—is consistent with détente as defined in Moscow. That definition allows the Kremlin to enjoy the benefits of arms agreements and access to Western technology without restricting its freedom to challenge the U.S. by all means, short of nuclear war.

Diplomatic observers here say that the lack of a coherent and consistent policy of détente in Washington encourages the Soviets to go on pressing their global challenge against the U.S. with even greater vigor.

Letter from Italy

Despite Discord, Strong Ties Still Bind Alliance

Almost ignored in present-day tensions between the U.S. and Western Europe are the historic links that unite America with its European allies. One forceful symbol of those ties is the Sicily-Rome American Cemetery near the World War II beachhead at Anzio. Robin Knight, chief of the magazine's Rome bureau, visited the grounds, then wrote the following memo to his editors in Washington.

Nearly 8,000 Americans killed in Italy during World War II are buried at Nettuno.

NETTUNO, Italy
You enter the American cemetery at Nettuno through a broad iron gate that opens up a peaceful parkland vista of wide, green lawns, a tranquil pool full of lilies—and the graves of 7,862 U.S. servicemen who died fighting in Italy during World War II.

This is a moving memorial to the dead. But it is more. In a unique way, it is a living demonstration of the ties that bind America and Europe to this day—ties cemented in blood and sacrifice almost 40 years ago, yet as real and enduring today as they ever were on the beaches of Sicily and Anzio.

For months now, the transatlantic air has been thick with the clamorous noise of discord over pipelines, steel, animal feed and interest rates. In Moscow, it must seem that at long last the Western Alliance is unraveling.

There is a different story, one that tends to be overlooked in a world obsessed with crises, conflicts and arguments. It is a story of shared values, mutual commitments, common ideals and continuing cooperation. It operates below the level of day-to-day current affairs. Frequently it is ignored or neglected. But it exists.

Often the signs of this amity are subtle and easily overlooked. To take one example: When Britain went to war with Argentina, its government and people instinctively turned to Washington and to Americans for support. How the Reagan administration responded soon became as important as how the Argentines fought.

Here in Italy, every official sinew has been strained in the last month or so to avoid a break with the U.S. over the Siberian gas pipeline. In the end, a limited break has occurred. But what is more important—the basic Italian desire to stay close to America, or the isolated instance of divergence?

Questions may reasonably be asked, however: "Where are these areas of shared values and continuing cooperation? How do they express themselves?"

The one answer that matters is that almost all disputes within the Western Alliance remain open to reasoned debate. Whether it is steel, corn, defense spending or East-West ties that provoke discord, eventually the problems will be sorted out by negotiation.

Agreeing to disagree. Dissent is contained within the alliance. Trade sanctions, threats, and challenges play little part in the Allies' mutual relations. Often there is agreement to disagree. But in the end, every member of the alliance acknowledges an underlying need to get on with the others.

Indeed, it is symptomatic of this basic closeness that whenever transatlantic links fray to the point of danger, there is a collective drawing back as leaders instinctively seek to minimize differences, close gaps, reassure each other that it is only a family row.

At this very moment, there are separate Canadian, Italian and German proposals before the North Atlantic Treaty Organization aimed at strengthening consultation and understanding. Spain has just joined the grouping. And even Greece, keen to walk out of NATO nine months ago, now prefers membership to uncertain isolation.

Those arguing that present disagreements are unique in range, depth or both also fall wide of the mark.

Almost from its inception, NATO has had divisions, often more serious than today's. Who recalls now the split that opened up after the Anglo-French-Israeli attack on Egypt in 1956? Or that France alone among the Allies backed the U.S. during the 1962 Cuban missile crisis? Or that the 1971 dollar devaluation caused far greater European anguish than the current dispute over American interest-rate policy?

What has changed since the mid-1950s is that U.S. power is no longer paramount. Economically, Europe is now the equal of America. Militarily, too, there has been a leveling, although U.S. might is still dominant.

Relatively speaking, American power has declined. The United States remains one of the world's superpowers. However, it must deal not only with a militarily assertive Soviet Union, but also with increasingly vocal and important allies. More and more, they are inclined to act alone—in the Mideast, toward Moscow, in the Third World—whenever they perceive vital national interests are at stake.

Inevitably, this makes interalliance disputes harder to resolve. But the mutual will to do so is as strong as ever.

Meantime, more than 300,000 U.S. troops remain stationed in Western Europe to help defend the Continent. Business ties are so intertwined that it is difficult, as President Reagan is finding, to define purely "American" or "German" or "British" companies any more.

In a real, living way, three decades of cooperation have made one community of two regions separated by 3,000 miles and several centuries of history.

Not far from Nettuno are other cemeteries built after the war that ended 37 years ago. These contain the bodies of British, Canadian, French, Polish and other Allied troops killed during the Italian campaign fighting alongside American GI's. Since those days, Allied unity has altered, the enemy has changed, the world has moved on.

But walking around these haunting graves, one is reminded once again of what we all share in common—values that temporary exasperations and differences do not obscure or diminish. □

Just you move over, 'Enry 'Iggins

A new regard for profits and talent cracks Britain's old class system

Not so long ago, the signposts marking a Briton's place in one of the world's most class-conscious societies were clear. The upper crust was educated at Eton and Oxford, vacationed on Mustique and spoke like Henry Higgins. Those in the middle attended "minor" private schools, vacationed in Chiantishire (a k a Tuscany) and mimicked the BBC. The lower orders made do with state education, spent a week in Blackpool and talked like Eliza Doolittle.

No more: It's becoming harder to pigeonhole the British. Income, taste and education, rather than birthright, now set most Britons apart from each other. As Margaret Thatcher prepares to celebrate 10 years in power next month, her most enduring legacy could be a country in which individualism is replacing collectivism, initiative has cachet regardless of background, and the landed gentry, like everyone else, must justify its existence.

A national crisis of confidence when Thatcher took power in 1979 gave her the elbowroom to shake up a hidebound society. Ever the outsider, she seized her chance with relish. Growing prosperity and mobility, and the wider horizons they opened, also played a part.

Class, in the Victorian sense of arbitrary and unjust privilege, can still be found. Debutantes come out each summer, hordes of Hooray Henrys (wealthy young men) have turned polo at Windsor into a socially exclusive art form, and hereditary peers still dominate the House of Lords. Medical researchers even reported recently that upper-class men are growing taller more quickly than their lower-class brethren.

Yet meritocracy marches on. Take the deb season. In the 1950s, it attracted 500 upper-crust young ladies on the prowl for husbands. Nowadays, the number of predators is down two thirds, the girls no longer are presented at court, and lavish balls have been superseded by utilitarian cocktail parties. Jobs, not spouses, are what preoccupy the scions of the British aristocracy these days.

Royal soap opera. Or take the monarchy. Perhaps it's the presence of a rival show at 10 Downing Street. Perhaps it is the exhibitionist antics of the younger royals. Maybe it is constant exposure on television, or the blanket coverage given by London's tabloid press. Whatever the reason, the royal family has gone down-market in the 1980s to the point that it sometimes resembles soap opera as much as grand opera.

Even London's fusty clubs seem infected. Few of them, it's true, are prepared to put nameplates on their front doors or to admit women. But P. G. Wodehouse's world of Drones, the club with drowsy members called Egg, Beans and Crumpet, is almost extinct. Instead, membership is booming as upwardly mobile yuppies invade, saunas and squash courts are *de rigueur*, and checkbooks, not pedigrees, have become the passports to entry. Ten years on, the bowler hat, once the insignia of the upper class, is worn mainly by racecourse spivs.

Fueled by seven consecutive years' growth, by tax cuts and by a sharp decline in union power, a generation of classless entrepreneurs has leapt to prominence, united only by its contempt for legendary British amateurishness and its faith in the new gospel of profit. Inherited money may still dominate a list of Britain's 200 richest men and women, but 86 of the entries made their fortunes themselves. The youngest is a 32-year-old former store assistant, Sophie Mirman (now reckoned to be worth $50 million), who opened a chain of sock shops in 1983.

To Thatcher's many critics among the "chattering classes," the leftish intellectuals agnostic about the Thatcher revolution, the emphasis on money is sapping Britain's spirit and producing a selfish free-for-all. It is an ironic argument, given the nation's past failures, but it also is one that puts these intellectuals uncomfortably in bed with doctors, lawyers, diehard Tories, the Church of England and other relics. Instead of paying attention to such snipers, Thatcher has formed a new meritocracy. "Britain is no longer run by an Establishment," argues John Lloyd of the *Financial Times*. "In its place is a Disestablishment comprising men and women whose values, assumptions and habits are those of outsiders."

A new English disease. This metamorphosis is most evident on the streets, where deference to one's betters and "knowing your place" are things of the past. "Even quite recently, somebody with the right accent could quell unruly conduct," Peregrine Worsthorne, the patrician editor of the *Sunday Telegraph,* wrote more in sorrow than in anger the other day. He is not alone in mourning the erosion of civility in British life. Strikes were once the English disease. Today, it is "yobs" and "lager louts," gangs of antisocial youths prone to mindless violence.

Old hat. *For some, it's still royal Ascot*

As the rhetoric of class warfare fades, the political loser has been the Labor Party. Its bedrock, the unionized working class, is now badly splintered. Four in 10 blue-collar voters back the Tories, and only half of those born to working-class parents are in working-class jobs later life. "Quite simply, the Conservative advance . . . has been entirely within the working class," says Ivor Crewe, one of Britain's leading pollsters. Meantime, new agenda items—women's rights, ethnic issues, the environment, nuclear energy—are cutting across traditional left-right, blue-collar-white-collar divisions, fragmenting the center and making British politics more fluid and less predictable.

There are signs that Labor's eclipse may be ending. One reason is plain boredom. Another is a sense, reinforced by a huge and widening trade gap, that Britain still cannot compete with rivals such as Japan, and that its economic turnaround is less than complete.

More fundamental, a decade of Thatcherism has done nothing to diminish the gap between haves and have-nots. Few Britons, even in the country's current go-go mood, are at ease with this. A clear majority believes taxes should be raised to support such enduring symbols of the welfare state as the National Health Service. The British, in short, remain addicted to "fairness" even as they worship mammon. Therein, perhaps, lies the Achilles' heel of Thatcher's classless vision. ■

by Robin Knight in London

Does NATO have middle-age myopia?

While the alliance negotiates, members are reducing their commitments

Once again, NATO is in turmoil over symbolism. Bickering about short-range nuclear missiles, topic A at the alliance's 40th-birthday party this week, veils deeper threats to long-term security. The weapons of first resort in nuclear war are, of course, important. But in the 1990s, NATO will be in far greater danger of disarming itself out of domestic budget and social concerns, and the politics of East-West relations, than of disintegrating over nuclear strategy alone.

As the 1980s end, the defense spending of the 16 members is static or falling. Equipment and manpower costs soar; force cuts have begun in some countries, and demographic trends make it unlikely that any will meet troop commitments by the mid-1990s. Mounting environmental and social unrest in West Germany, the heart of the alliance, has forced cutbacks in military exercises. A series of accidents has curtailed training for combat aircraft. The consequences already are apparent in both the combat readiness and the politics of the alliance. Plans to fight a 30-day war before resorting to nuclear weapons are now more a dream than a strategy. The idea of a credible West European force, the so-called European pillar, matching that of the U.S. seems more illusory than ever.

Military expenditures are the most immediate worry. This year, every NATO member has projected cutbacks in spending, manpower or procurement only months after an internal study urged increases all around. Canada set the standard in April by announcing a $2.7 billion reduction over the next five years, just 20 months after revealing an ambitious expansion program. Belgium, the Netherlands, Italy, Norway, Denmark and Britain have set standstill budgets, which inflation will translate into cuts. In the U.S., the Bush administration has slashed $20 billion from its predecessor's final two-year defense plan. In France, the Rocard government is pruning military outlays by $6.5 billion over the next four years. The French at least justify the cuts with a conceptual change, emphasizing training to rejuvenate what is now a large, run-down conscript Army.

Home-bred concerns. Most of the cuts lack military rationale. Norway, for example, is shifting priorities from defense of its remote northern border with the Soviet Union, always costly, to softer, cheaper options in the south. Endless left-right political deadlock in Denmark has created a stalemate on defense commitments. Britain is now feeling prosperous enough to be repaying its national debt, yet Prime Minister Thatcher recently produced a budget with a slight cut in military spending for this year and further declines in 1990-91. The impact of the cuts of new equipment, which is squeezed most, means a shrinking British Royal Navy, no new German battle tank, no Canadian submarine force, no modernization of Belgian and Dutch helicopter forces, no replacement of 11 F-16s lost to attrition by Norwegian forces.

Such retrenchment is not fatal in isolation. But it means far more as strategic emphasis moves toward non-nuclear forces and high-tech weapons, especially when coupled with develop-

ing manpower shortages. Nowhere is the latter weakness more debilitating than in teenager-deficient West Germany.

By 1994, the number in the German military-age reservoir will be half that of 1985. The Bundeswehr needs 250,000 new men a year to keep its strength at 490,000. Since the Kohl government's reversal of a decision to extend the draft, it will be lucky to stay above 400,000. Recent plans indicate that seven brigades will be disbanded, armored brigades cut to 70 percent of strength and most other brigades to 50 percent. Today, the Bundeswehr is forbidden to use more than 2,000 men in maneuvers at one time. Tank crews are limited to 400 miles and one live-firing exercise a year. A growing distaste for all things military has contributed to a severe cutback in training. Deferment for conscientious objectors is becoming easier, and last year one exercise was called off when local residents objected.

Chancellor Helmut Kohl's Germans are not alone in expecting birth control to do what arms control so far hasn't. Britain, under tougher-talking Margaret Thatcher, is facing a 20 percent decline in its pool of military recruits over the next five years; force levels are already down 5 percent from 1985. Italy has cut its conscript intake by 20,000 this year. In Belgium, a decision to withdraw 1,400 troops from the 29,000 in West Germany has led in turn to claims that the force is now incapable of fulfilling its mission and should be withdrawn altogether.

Like it or not, and few NATO commanders do, these underlying realities are forcing the alliance to re-examine its doctrine of flexible response. The doctrine, which has sustained the alliance since 1967, calls for graduated escalation from forward conventional defense to local nuclear warfare against attack by superior Soviet forces.

Shared concern. *Thatcher and Kohl both cut costs*

trends are all contrary. They suggest for the future a tripwire German-manned defense at the frontier with the East, with a mobile allied corps based well back from the border, fewer American and British troops in West Germany, heavier reliance on reserves, an offshore nuclear capability and ultimate dependence on the U.S. strategic-missile force. A central problem is that the trends are being shaped by narrow national budgetary and social concerns rather than rational study by the alliance.

Domestic and alliance concerns are never entirely separate, of course. Governments are concerned first of all with political survival, and that can be determined by sometimes-shifting attitudes toward the alliance. But some governments are taking at face value, and acting upon, the peace offensive of Mikhail Gorbachev, while anticipating success in East-West negotiations, only now beginning, to reduce conventional forces. The internal and external forces feed on each other: Détente undermining defense spending, missile cuts weakening core strategy and blurring the case for nuclear weapons, arms-control offers reducing the sense of threat and making it harder for the alliance to train for war. The more distant the most recent war in Europe, the harder it becomes to guard against another. Gorbachev cannot have expected the West's home-bred problems to do so much of his work for him. ■

by Robin Knight

■ WORLD REPORT

STEVE RAYMER – © NATIONAL GEOGRAPHIC SOCIETY

Dwindling asset. *Oil and natural gas production, which fueled much of Siberia's growth, is dropping.*

Northern exposure

The bills are due for 30 years of communist exploitation

There is a saying in Siberia: "When you chop the forests, you cut down more than trees." Somewhat belatedly, this truism is coming home to roost for the 3 million people who live in the mineral-rich but inhospitable steppes of western Siberia. After three decades of relentless and largely uncontrolled exploitation, the bills are coming due in one of the world's last great natural frontiers.

The best of times in western Siberia would be the worst of times anywhere else. Temperatures routinely reach 40 below zero in winter. Roads are few, swamps cover half the territory and winter is eight months long. The rest of the time mosquitoes a couple of inches long rule the skies. Although most of the region lies in the permafrost zone, blocks of barrackslike apartments were built to the same slipshod Soviet specifications as those in subtropical Crimean resorts.

Not long ago people were either sent here by Moscow or drawn here by the lure of wealth, the promise of jobs or the optimistic belief that in the vastness of Siberia, individualism still counted. Today, like shipwrecked sailors, many Siberians feel they are being left high and dry by the changes sweeping across Russia.

Oil and gas production, which fueled the region's development, is falling sharply, and world prices are too low to justify the massive new investments needed to modernize the oil industry and find new reserves. Rivers and aquifers are so polluted that drinking the water in some cities is a health hazard, but there is no money to clean up the mess. The communist system that funneled scarce consumer goods to Siberia has collapsed, and prices are skyrocketing.

Communism is gone but the malady lingers on. Political and economic power remains in the hands of a local "mafia"—industry bosses and ambitious apparatchiks in their early 40s who until recently formed the second rank of the Communist Party leadership. Nominally Moscow's representatives, these men serve mostly themselves and stay in power by scratching each other's backs. Corruption is running riot, a sense of alienation is palpable and all the ingredients exist for serious unrest if prices go any higher, food gets any scarcer or work becomes even harder to find. A Wild West, anything-goes mentality is taking

LETTER FROM SIBERIA

hold, and there is nothing to suggest that the worst is over.

It is enough to make even Siberia's rugged inhabitants nostalgic for the good old days of stagnation under Leonid Brezhnev. "People used to eat caviar by the spoonful then," reminisces Victor Gorbachev, a newspaper editor in Tyumen and no relation to the former Soviet leader. "We lived well."

In the ivory towers of Western embassies in Moscow, diplomats calculate Russian President Boris Yeltsin's chances of surviving this winter of discontent and seeing his reforms take root at 70-30 or 80-20. But out in the sticks, people are losing hope. "Sausage has first place, not democracy," says Alla Pozhidayeva, a feisty environmentalist who has been dragged into court by oil generals determined to silence her exposés of their wholesale vandalism.

Russians are stoics; they have to be to endure their country's endless troubles, extreme climate and innumerable false dawns. Yet even stoics have limits. Victor Gorbachev thinks the moment of truth will come in a month or two when "balcony stockpiles" of hoarded food are exhausted. Oil industry chiefs say Siberia will reach the breaking point when energy prices are raised but none of the extra revenue flows back to Siberia. Others argue that low wages and awful conditions will lead to walkouts in the oil fields that will cripple the Russian economy and touch off nationwide strikes.

Outside the Tyumen city hall a pathetic little market suggests that many are already at the point of desperation. Old women and men, some wearing World War II medals, stand silently selling off their possessions. Blocks of ice hold down grubby cloths on which are displayed combs, buttons, bits of half-eaten food, a tattered scarf, individual cigarettes, a shoelace and two socks. A freezing wind is blowing, but few of the poorly clad vendors seem to notice. They have nothing else to sell, nowhere else to go and no safety net to save them. ■

BY ROBIN KNIGHT IN TYUMEN

■ ON BOSNIA

BY ROBIN KNIGHT

A test the West is failing

Two years after the Yugoslav implosion began, the West still cannot decide how to react. Having intervened a bit, Western leaders shrink from intervening a bit more. In Belgrade and Banja Luka, Serbian leaders snort contemptuously. "If [Serbian President Slobodan] Milosevic knows you're not going to use ground troops and not follow through if necessary, there is not enough pressure on him to stop," says George Kenney, the State Department official who resigned over Yugoslav policy.

The Vietnam syndrome, Eurowimps and pusillanimous generals are only part of the reason for Western paralysis. The United States and its allies have failed to stop the Serbs largely because they cannot agree on what is at stake in the Balkans. After the Berlin Wall came down in 1989, the West lost its bearings. It is as if the North Pole is demagnetized: Suddenly, the old compasses are useless.

For centuries, nations intervened abroad for economic or imperialist reasons—to secure trade routes, control raw materials, undercut competitors. The cold war introduced the idea that every place on Earth was "strategic." A move by one side in Ethiopia had to be countered by the other in Somalia. Now no one is certain what matters and what does not, at least when oil or jobs are not at stake.

Transparent cynicism. One approach to this dilemma is simply to intervene where it is easy and to steer clear where it is hard: Invade Panama, bomb Libya, overwhelm Iraq, rescue the Somalis, bomb Iraq again, but avoid the Serbs and their Balkan quagmire, let alone the former Soviet empire. Such transparent cynicism cannot even pass the television test in a world that often finds images more compelling than reality.

Humanity is the first reason Bosnia matters to the West. The United Nations relief operation in Bosnia already is in danger of becoming a fiasco as Serbian harassment continues, the harshest Balkan winter in a decade takes hold and as many as 400,000 lives are jeopardized by cold and hunger. Up front, in the refugee camps and in besieged Sarajevo, there is no argument about the morality of intervention.

Politics is the second reason. Ethnic cleansing is contagious, and it may be especially catching in places such as Russia, the Caucasus, Slovakia and Hungary. The feeble Western response to Serbian aggression angers Muslims and invites Islamic involvement in Europe. And in the

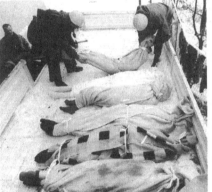

Burial detail. *Exposure killed 10 in a Sarajevo nursing home.*

Balkans, as surely as in Iraq, U.N. resolutions must be enforced or Milosevic and Saddam Hussein and who knows who else will realize that they can thumb their noses at the world with impunity.

The crisis in Bosnia, in other words, is a test not only of the West's values but also of its credibility as democracy's champion. America's and Europe's "too little, too late" half measures damage them as much as the Bosnian Muslims.

Too late? The West has already paid a high price for its empty gestures. The growing trans-Atlantic divide has widened. The global pretensions of the European Community have been punctured. The North Atlantic Treaty Organization and the concept of collective security have been made to look ridiculous. Meantime, an Orthodox axis of Russia, Serbia, Greece and Bulgaria has emerged, endangering Moscow's rapprochement with the West. Decisive action early in 1991 could have averted these developments, and perhaps halted the Serbs. But America and its allies were too busy basking in the reflected glory of their cold war triumph and their gulf war pushover.

Walking away from Bosnia now is not an option, however. Any peace settlement will need a Western guarantee. Humanitarian aid cannot be switched off by the whim of Western policy makers or the guns of Serbian thugs. "Yugoslavia is a symbol of something that will be present everywhere," says Anglo-German historian Ralf Dahrendorf. "I suspect we will live in a world of tribalism, which means intolerance within and enmity without."

Flaccid resolutions designed to make the West feel good by enforcing militarily irrelevant no-fly zones over Bosnia will not turn back a new dark age. Yet misapplied force is likely to be worse than no force at all, only reinforcing the Serbs' siege mentality and sense of martyrdom without producing a change of heart.

Decisive intervention requires a specific, justifiable and attainable goal. The creation of "safe havens" for 1.5 million Muslims in central Bosnia, many analysts contend, might fit the bill. It would be risky: Confrontation with Serbia might follow, the U.N. consensus could fracture and at least 10 times the 6,623 troops now based in the area would be needed, most of them American. But, as advocates of safe havens argue, anything less will expose both the West's timidity and its bankruptcy. ■

Can a nation's death revivify an old idea?

There are two simple truths about the North Atlantic Treaty Organization. One is that it works best when America gives leadership. The other is that it is almost always in "crisis." Last August, Secretary of State Warren Christopher called NATO "the most successful alliance in history." The emphasis was on the past. Today, the crisis is more real than usual.

Last week, as NATO defense ministers gathered by the Baltic Sea, the alliance dipped to a new low as charges of bad faith over Bosnia pinged across the Atlantic. Bosnia is the proximate cause of the tension, revealing a deep divide in strategic interests between Europe and **ONE WEEK** the United States. But the underlying cause is NATO's loss of focus, which has followed the end of the cold war.

The issue now is whether NATO can refocus. Edward Luttwak of the Center for Strategic and International Studies thinks not. In his book *The Endangered American Dream,* he argues that the old order of alliances rooted in a common danger is giving way to random "geo-economic" conflict. War, Luttwak reckons, will be about trade barriers, not territorial imperatives, and, in the end, trade rivalry and defense solidarity are incompatible.

If NATO is to survive such a development—and by any yardstick, America and Europe are already at odds over trade—it needs a sustained dose of leadership that somehow can revive a belief in what the allies have in common. Experience shows that the impetus for renewal can come only from the United States. But so far, the Clinton administration has been too busy to pay much attention to the Atlantic alliance. Asia, says the president, is of greater importance. Meanwhile, defense cuts across the alliance are doing more to reforge NATO than any new strategic concept.

To argue for NATO in such circumstances is like defending mothers-in-law. Yet the case for an alliance of free-market, democratic states is no less compelling today than in 1949. Twice this century, U.S. alienation from Europe has encouraged global conflict. The Communist threat to Western Europe may have vanished, but daily events in the former Soviet Union suggest that Luttwak's view that the risk of total war is gone may be too optimistic. Margaret Thatcher, for one, thinks so. In her newly published autobiography, she argues powerfully for NATO's relevance. She did so again last week: "Whatever is wrong now between the Americans and Europe, and especially Britain, it must be mended." This can only mean striking a better balance between a sustained U.S. commitment to European security and greater European willingness to share the risks of collective peacekeeping.

NATO has failed in the former Yugoslavia because of a lack of political will. But to say that NATO should be allowed to die is like arguing that police should be abolished because crime persists. Hoping to reverse the drift, President Clinton has called a summit for early January, perhaps a last chance for a fresh start. If the chance is ducked, geo-economic conflict among old allies may indeed become a reality. □ BY ROBIN KNIGHT

> **'The case for an alliance of free-market, democratic states is no less compelling today than in 1949.'**

■ **ON EUROPE**   BY ROBIN KNIGHT

Collective insecurity

Bosnia has demeaned all who have touched it. The United Nations operation there is in total disarray, unable to protect the victims or produce a settlement. Europe's desire to police itself in the post-cold-war world has been exposed as a sham. Bad feeling and basic disagreements are sapping the Western alliance. In Bosnia itself, more than 200,000 people have been killed and an additional 3 million made homeless. Serbians have been impoverished and brutalized by their pursuit of "destiny." So have Croats. And, as it did in the 1930s, diplomacy has become synonymous with appeasement.

Bosnia is a leitmotif for the indifferent, cynical, inward-looking '90s. From Belgrade to Moscow, fascist demagogues have been reinforced in their belief that might is right and the West is spineless. The very idea that people of different ethnic origins can coexist peacefully has suffered a heavy, perhaps fatal, blow. In the Islamic world, already facing a flood tide of fundamentalism, Western values have rarely appeared less worthy.

No one, of course, can be sure how an event like the rape of one small Balkan state will influence developments in places as diverse as Russia, South Africa and Algeria. Genocide in Cambodia, after all, did not spell the end of civilization in Southeast Asia. But in one respect, at least, there is little room for argument.

PAUL LOWE   MAGNUM

'Bosnia is a leitmotif for the indifferent, cynical, inward-looking '90s.'

———

Bosnia has sounded the death knell of the Western concept of collective security, which guided and sustained the North Atlantic Treaty Organization throughout its 42-year confrontation with totalitarianism.

Cries and whispers. Until the recent NATO summit in Brussels, the demise of collective security was merely whispered about in the corridors. Nine alliance members have troops in Bosnia, seven do not, but somehow the split was finessed. This is, after all, an "out of area," humanitarian U.N. deployment in a region that poses no obvious threat to NATO's security.

Yet Bosnia has become the model for NATO's future. At Brussels, all eyes focused on whether the alliance should expand eastward. The meeting, however, will be remembered in history not for its timid Partnership for Peace offer to Poland, the Czech Republic, Hungary and Slovakia, but for sanctioning the so-called a la carte option, which permits member states to choose which security issues they consider vital and which they wish to avoid.

Dreamed up by outgoing Secretary of Defense Les Aspin, the concept is grandly called Combined Joint Task Forces, and given their mounting resistance to any foreign entanglements, many Americans will cheer it on. But it may be wise to keep the champagne on ice. For more than four decades, NATO gave the West a common sense of purpose, deterred East-West conflict and imposed a degree of order even on antagonists such as Greece and Turkey. Its success came solely from its solidarity, from the knowledge that an attack on one member was an attack on all. The new go-it-alone doctrine threatens all these underpinnings.

Bosnia, of course, is a symptom rather than the cause of NATO's confusion. But every attempt to generate a more forceful Western strategy simply stimulates more disagreement. Last week it was France's turn to demand that the West impose a peace in the Balkans. Secretary of State Warren Christopher, visiting Paris, balked, arguing that it is unfair to pressure the Bosnian Muslims just when they are making gains on the battlefield. Christopher is right that the diplomatic track in Bosnia has reached a dead end. Yet to do nothing is simply to condone more violence, to sanction more slaughter and to invite more trouble.

Ethnic war on the Yugoslav pattern is now considered the greatest threat to Europe's peace. This idea may be wrong; a revanchist Russia may prove to be even more destructive. But the evidence suggests that the Clinton administration and NATO have already opted out of both scenarios, tacitly accepting the creation of a Russian sphere of influence in the East and adopting a new alliance doctrine that is a formula for impotence in troubled regions such as the Balkans and Central Europe.

If the West is to retrieve the Bosnian situation at this late stage, it must finally define its objectives. The logic of Christopher's stance is that any solution that allows the Serbs to keep what they have conquered is unacceptable. If that is the case, NATO should arm the Muslims, use air power against the Serbs—and prepare for the consequences, including anger from the Russians. A second option is to withdraw U.N. troops, leave the warring parties to slug it out and deliver as much humanitarian aid as possible. Continuing the present policy will only hasten NATO's disintegration without ending the fighting or helping to broker a compromise. ■

■ **ON THE ECONOMY**   BY ROBIN KNIGHT

Gender, jobs and economic survival

North Shields is not the sort of town that many economists often visit. But they should. For here in bleak and wind-swept Tyneside in northeast England a phenomenon of the postindustrial age can be studied in advanced form: the out-of-work blue-collar male. At the local job center, four times as many men as women are registered as unemployed workers, and the male-female jobless differential is widening as the region's old economic mainstays—shipbuilding, coal mining and steelmaking—contract and shrink to the point of economic extinction.

The situation in Tyneside illustrates a trend best seen today in Britain, the Western country closest to deindustrialization and a nation where unemployment hovers near 10 percent despite economic recovery. But according to a recent study by the Paris-based Organization for Economic Co-operation and Development, Britain is not alone as manufacturing employment declines, technological innovation gains momentum and part-time work increases across the Western industrialized world. In the United States, according to the OECD, "nonemployment"—the total number of registered unemployed workers plus those too discouraged to look for jobs—has doubled for men between the ages of 25 and 55 since 1970. In Britain, France and Germany, the nonemployment rate has tripled. Seventy percent of the jobs created in Europe in the second half of the 1980s went to women and new entrants to the labor market. And male participation in the British work force actually fell from 93 percent to 84 percent between 1973 and 1992, while female participation rose from 53 percent to 65 percent. By 1991, one third of unskilled British males were jobless. According to a forecast prepared by Warwick University's Institute of Employment Research, jobs performed by women in Britain will grow by 700,000 in the next five years, while those carried out by men will fall by 200,000.

Part-time job boom. Service-sector jobs in areas like health care, retail, travel, office equipment and telecommunications now account for two thirds of all positions in OECD countries. But an increasing proportion of this work is part time, requiring an average of 15 hours of labor a week. In Britain, 215,000 new part-time jobs were created last year, while the number of full-time jobs fell by 287,000 even though gross domestic product grew 2.5

Men are clinging to traditional jobs in smokestack industries.

percent in the second half of the year. The great majority of these part-time positions were secured by women. Females account for 85 percent of part-time British workers, 66 percent of all part-time employees in the United States and 91 percent of those who labor part time in Germany. Yet in no OECD country do more than 10 percent of the men work part time. Part-time work allows employers to cut costs by reducing permanent payrolls, and women earn less per hour than men in each of the OECD nations. The growth in part-time female employment helps explain why average earning growth in Britain has dropped to 30-year lows.

One way workers might be able to improve their employment prospects is through job training. But training programs across the industrialized world have met with mixed success, although in some cases they have helped get unemployed workers back on the job in economies that are shifting from manufacturing to services. Many government-funded training programs exist in Tyneside, but skepticism about the value of learning is deeply embedded in a culture in which male unemployment has scarred several generations of workers. Over $3 billion in capital investment has flowed into northeast England since the mid-1980s, for example, but most of the new jobs have gone to young, skilled and more educated workers. Early retirement is a way of life in Tyneside and the rest of Britain; only 45 percent of British men over 55 years of age are working today, compared with 70 percent in the 1960s.

The 21st century could be a time of great employment opportunity for Western women, especially those who are highly educated and highly skilled. But in terms of wage equality, there is still a long way to go. Many jobs performed by women are part time and pay poorly. And women are vastly underrepresented in management circles. But the female advance seems inexorable, although Western governments have yet to grapple fully with the transformation in the workplace. And some of the long-term implications are disturbing. As John Tomaney of Newcastle University's Center for Urban and Regional Development Studies puts it: "We've created a huge male underclass in which crime and unemployment are a way of life. Our new economic base is very fragile." ■

■ COMMENTARY

A global moment of truth

From South Korea to South Africa, nations are struggling to come to terms with past horrors. Their shared hope: a better future

A defining moment in the post-communist era is taking place in Chamber 417 of the Seoul District Court in South Korea. Prisoners 3124 and 1042, better known as ex-presidents Chun Doo Hwan and Roh Tae Woo, are accused of treason and mass murder in connection with a coup in December 1979, and the slaughter of pro-democracy students in the city of Kwangju soon after. If found guilty, they face the death penalty. Yet their mere presence in the court highlights a global phenomenon: As ideology weakens and dictatorships crumble, the search for truth has become a potent way of legitimizing the present—and underpinning the future.

Magnus Malan, the general who masterminded white South Africa's resistance to black-majority rule, knows all about this. He is on trial in Durban with 19 others accused of complicity in death-squad killings three years ago. So does Richard Goldstone, chief prosecutor at the International War Crimes Tribunal in The Hague. His task is to orchestrate a day of reckoning for mass killers and those who led them in Bosnia and Rwanda. Ordinary folk are getting the message too. Outside the Seoul court last week, hundreds of demonstrators demanded justice. "We've come here to rip them to pieces," said one. "We've waited 16 years [since the Kwangju massacre] and our suffering has never stopped."

PATRICK CHAUVEL – SYGMA

Crimes against the people. *The 1980 crackdown in Kwangju*

The very process of seeking the truth can prove destabilizing.

It's easy to attribute such courtroom dramas—they are taking place in Eastern Europe and Latin America, too—to the simple, understandable desire for revenge. Indeed, wherever unelected regimes have abused power and broken trust with their own citizens, the search for truth is cathartic. It establishes accountability and eases victims' grief. But the impact often goes deeper, defusing tensions between past and present that, if not resolved, can undermine the new order. "If we sweep things under the carpet," says South African Justice Minister Dullah Omar, "the danger is that reconciliation will be short-lived."

The search for truth, however, is never simple. Goldstone has spent the past two years navigating the labyrinthine complexities of Balkan history and understands that truth is relative; the very process of seeking it can prove destabilizing. Ethiopia, for example, is a country full of broken people after 16 years of Marxist, military-engineered mayhem. More than 100,000 died violently between 1975 and 1991. Today, a newly elected government is adamant that holding mass trials is the key to building a more consensual future. But in this oldest of Christian countries, many believe that punishment should be left to God. In some countries—Russia is one—the truth about the past is so painful for so many that there is no consensus about the need to search. Boris Yeltsin, facing an uphill presidential re-election fight against a resurgent communist opposition, follows closely press accounts of the travails of the former South Korean leaders.

What's more, governments that seek truth frequently lay themselves open to charges of opportunism. South Korea's current president, Kim Young Sam, is a protégé of one of the men on trial in Seoul. But he faces a tricky election soon and has had no compunction in ditching his previous view that the past should be left to the judgment of history. South Africa's new rulers are less compromised. But they also must weigh the demands for justice against society's need to heal its wounds.

One solution is to set up "truth commissions." South Africa's version, based on the Chilean model, begins work next month. Its head, Archbishop Desmond Tutu, says his goal is restitution, not retribution. Tutu's assertion—"You cannot forgive when you do not know what or whom to forgive"—is compelling. But it is not the whole story.

In the heady days after Czechoslovakia's 1989 "velvet revolution," the country's new government eagerly put Tutu's truism into practice. Many Czechs now regret that such an exercise was ever undertaken in a society with a long tradition of bending in the wind. Jan Kavan is one. During years of exile in London, he played a key role in the underground movement, only to find himself denounced as a collaborator by a secret policeman on his return home. The charges against Kavan were never proved. But his new life as a democratic politician was ruined almost before it began. "It's impossible to prove a negative," he later said. "Once you are tarred [with complicity], it sticks." Indeed, as Austrian psychiatrist Alfred Adler cautioned in 1929, "It is possible to lie and even to murder for the truth." Notwithstanding the risks, in a world lacking clear ideological compass points, the truth is more indispensable than ever. ■

BY ROBIN KNIGHT

BOOKS

The Kodak Country

Editor Harold Evans puts together a rousing, roller-coaster history of the American Century

By ROBIN KNIGHT

IT WAS HENRY LUCE, IN A 1941 TIME essay, who first gave prominence to the idea that the 20th century could be the American century. Since then, as expectation turned into the reality of American global hegemony, many others have echoed this theme. Harold Evans, who with his new book *The American Century* (Jonathan Cape; 710 pages) is the latest and perhaps the most creative writer to mine this lode, is different. His goal is unashamedly populist—by presenting information in easily digestible bytes and concentrating on people, he aims to open the dynamic and often heroic story of the United States in this century to new Americans of the multimedia 21st century.

Evans is a British-born journalist and editor of Britain's *Sunday Times* 1967-81 and the *Times* 1981-82. He was president and publisher of Random House 1990-97, and is now editorial director and vice chairman of *U.S. News and World Report*, the *New York Daily News* and *Atlantic Monthly*. This background gives his work an edge it never loses. This is history with bite, history with attitude, history in the raw. Egalitarian and liberal by inclination, Evans delights in debunking myths, tweaking conservatives and using hindsight to his advantage. And above all, he loves the idea of America. "This book," he writes, "is the thanks of an immigrant to the United States, and a celebration of my becoming [in 1993] an American citizen."

Twelve years in the making, *The American Century* covers the period between 1889 and 1989. Significantly, 1889 was the year that popular photography arrived with the Kodak camera, and Evans—with help from Gail Buckland, a professional photo historian—culled 900 memorable images which flesh out 15 punchy, themed essays and scores of self-contained vignettes culled from everyday American life.

But what, exactly, does the author mean by American? Evans offers various clues, but nothing definitive. The characteristic that matters most to him is "the constitutional freedom to speak and write according to conscience." But there are others. "Relentless optimism and self-righteousness;" "A spirit of freedom, equality, honour, individualism and courage—universal values, but ones of central importance in America's perception of itself"; Americans "best understand the paradox that if anything is to be preserved it must change."

TRANSPLANT: The British-born Evans thrives on America

How have Americans lived up to these ideals? Evans believes the century ends with the balance well on the credit side—a huge achievement when judged against the demands of the past 100 years and the many episodes of maleficence, which Evans covers relentlessly. Vietnam is summed up as a debacle caused by hubris. The Great Depression of the 1930s, he argues, stemmed from Americans' "lack of intellectual curiosity and the general pressure for conformity of opinion." The most unsparing chapter in the book—on the civil rights cam-

paigns of the 1950s and 1960s—documents in scathing detail an enduringly dark side of American society. "To spell it out," writes Evans, "the white response to the [civil rights] movement was nearly always indifferent when it wasn't hostile; petty when it wasn't cruel; vicious when it wasn't murderous."

Scandal is another ever-present theme coursing through *The American Century*. The book ends just before the Clinton era. But, as Evans observes, there's nothing new under the sun. Between 1921-23 President Warren Harding conducted an illicit sexual relationship in a White House anteroom, had a lawyer associate who shot himself, allowed cronies to sell political favors and was married to a protective First Lady he nicknamed "the Duchess."

Age (he is 70) and success have not mellowed Evans. Big business gets scarcely a mention. The élite arts and the billion-dollar professional sports industry are similarly shunned. Some of Evans' judgments—on the avoidability of the cold war and on Franklin Roosevelt's attitude to fascism, to name two—seem oddly nuanced. But mostly he writes with a robust, stinging conviction about the downtrodden and about ordinary Americans, whose stories he illuminates with a true reporter's gift for telling detail. There's Izzy Einstein, the Prohibition-era federal agent who was fired in 1925 for being too good at his job. There's Jay Near, a scandal sheet editor, who won a seminal press freedom case in the Supreme Court in 1931. Jason Betzinez, the last Apache—"a humble, friendly man of fiery, independent spirit"—merits a profile. So does Igor Belousovitch—a Russian émigré serving in the U.S. Army who took the first photograph of American and Russian troops linking up on April 25, 1945. The book resonates with victims—from American Indians to women, Okies, and the labor movement.

Contradiction, of course, lies at the heart of the American Dream. Evans notes both that the 20th century ends with "the gap between rich and poor the most extreme in Western civilization," and that "Americans enjoy more happiness and more individual liberty under the law than ever dreamt of in 4,000 years of ordered societies." It is the real achievement of this epic work that both conclusions ring true.   ■

BOOKS

The Daily Courage

Journalist Benjamin Pogrund let the facts speak for themselves, no easy task in apartheid South Africa

By ROBIN KNIGHT

JOURNALISTS' MEMOIRS TEND TO FALL into two categories—those with a story to tell, or those with a score to settle. Benjamin Pogrund, one of South Africa's most courageous reporters during the dark era of apartheid, has added a valuable third dimension in *War of Words* (Seven Stories Press, 380 pages), a vivid account of what it was like to stand on the front line of press freedom during that period. His story conveys his compassion and an enduring belief that if people of differing races and ideologies can only know the

facts, the world will be a better place.

That such optimism has survived a life full of disappointments and betrayals says a great deal for Pogrund's innate fair-minded ness. Liberal by instinct, Jewish by origin and an outsider by temperament, Pogrund also has that "element of anger" which keeps the best reporters in the hunt day after day, year after year. In his case, this was an anger born of determination that the ugly reality behind the neat façade of apartheid be revealed to the widest possible audience. Indeed Harold Evans, the distinguished British editor who ran Pogrund's reports from South Africa in the London *Sunday Times*, believes that his "seminal contribution" was that he reported—straight and dispassionately, without favor or hostility.

In apartheid South Africa, letting the facts speak for themselves was revolutionary, subversive and dangerous. Until Pogrund began reporting on African affairs regularly in the *Rand Daily Mail* in 1958, most of what went on in the townships and tribal "homelands" to which blacks were consigned was ignored by the country's mainstream white-run press. Simply to report police conduct in a riot accurately, as Pogrund did at the Sharpeville massacre in 1960, was a breakthrough. Destroying this blind spot proved lengthy and contentious. But it had lasting effect. In 1985, when the *Mail* bit the dust, the country's leading black paper the *Sowe-*

tan published an enduring epitaph: "It was the first paper to regard [blacks] as human beings. It fought for them. Its blend of inspirational and aggressive writing was the talk of the times."

But that is to jump ahead. The loss-making but hugely influential *Mail* had by then waged a lonely 30-year struggle on behalf of truth and decency against overwhelming odds. Scores of Kafkaesque laws circumscribed its coverage. It was infiltrated by government spies, communists and agent provocateurs. Its management was either inept or craven or both. Yet despite everything, the *Mail* not only survived but set a standard that all other media outlets in South Africa are still judged against.

Pogrund's account of these years and particularly his assessment of two episodes— the 1969 trial when he and *Mail* editor Laurence Gandar were charged with publishing untrue information about prisons, and the opportunistic closure of the *Mail* 16 years later—has a biting, hard-edged quality which elevates this book well beyond the normal biographical rut. Pogrund was put on trial several times, imprisoned once, had his passport removed and was twice investigated by the security police as a threat to the state. His compensation was the lasting respect and affection of many of the "new" South Africa's leaders, including Nelson Mandela.

The temptation now is to leave to history books the saga of the courageous *Rand Daily Mail* and the fate of such individuals as Benjamin Pogrund. But that would be a big mistake. Today the press in South Africa is still white-dominated, but now it is also marginalized and enfeebled—and the roots of this lie in the loss of talent (black and white) and commitment after the closure of the *Mail.*

Racism remains an issue, too; not long ago the press was accused of "subliminal racism"—an ominous, catchall charge that disturbs Pogrund as much as anyone.

In *War of Words* Pogrund never claims the moral high ground and explicitly rejects the idea that he and the *Mail* were fully paid-up members of the anti-apartheid struggle. "That would have been totally unacceptable to the newspaper, and offensive to my own sense of journalism," he writes. Instead, the motivational commitment was to something more enduring—truth and the rule of law. It's a fine line, but it is one that remains as valid as ever for reporters, be they in Serbia, Pakistan, China, Colombia or a dozen other countries where the press still faces a daily struggle to report the facts. ∎

SHARP END: Pogrund, above, reported without fear or favor on major events in South Africa, including the 1960 Sharpeville massacre, right, when police opened fire on peaceful demonstrators

BOOKS

Perpetual Prisoners

A new book journeys to the frozen heart of Russia to find Siberia a wasteland of lost souls

By ROBIN KNIGHT LONDON

FOR THE FIRST TIME IN RUSsia's xenophobic history, foreigners are able to roam more or less at will through Siberia. So what? In the 400 years since Russians began colonizing this land mass that covers one-twelfth of the earth's surface, very little that stirs the soul has come out of its featureless, mosquito-plagued (in summer), icebound (in winter) expanse. "A traveler needs to believe in the significance of where he is," the British writer Colin Thubron observes at one point in *In Siberia* (Chatto & Windus, 320 pages), a finely crafted account of a 25,000-km journey through the region in 1997. "Nothing, it seemed, has ever happened here." Most of Siberia is like that—profoundly isolated, profoundly monotone and profoundly boring.

In Czarist times, Siberia was settled by exiles and convicts from European Russia as a way of ring-fencing dissent. In Stalin's time, it became a byword for cruelty and degradation. Today, as Thubron makes clear, the pendulum has swung back a bit. Now Siberia and its 30 million inhabitants have come to epitomize—in deluded nationalist minds at least—"the Russia that was lost, the citadel of the spirit."

At the start of this heroic project (he was nearing 60 at the time), Thubron half believed this cosy theory himself. "I was trying to find the core to Siberia," he writes. "I could not imagine a Russia without faith." Instead he found himself face to face with something far less palatable—a perversion of progress. "Everything achieved under slavery, it seemed, was being destroyed by freedom," he notes bleakly at the midpoint of his four-month journey. By the end, in an irradiated hellhole called Butugychag in the heart of Stalin's Gulag archipelago, he wearily informs a somewhat skeptical Siberian: "Whatever it's like now, things are better than they were then." Which elicits the supremely bleak Russian response: "People believed things [then]."

Travel writing of this caliber is rare. Thubron journeys for understanding,

not effect. Mostly he confines himself to the margins and lets others talk for him. At times his prose soars, as though the sheer awfulness of what he is seeing spurs him on. In the collapsing hubris of Komsomolsk-na-Amur—Stalin's "City of the Dawn" founded by idealistic young communists in 1932—his eye for detail alights on the grandiose architecture: "The snow was falling along their avenues so that little infidelities of style, the crumbling corbels and collapsing balconies, faded down long vistas of puritan uniformity, almost beautiful."

What Thubron found in the fishing hamlet of Potalovo, south of Norilsk and close to the Arctic Circle, deserves a book in itself. Here a native community, the Entsy, "had declined into barbarism." Unemployment was over 50%, life ex-

ICE AGE: Life in Siberia is a bitter struggle to uphold humanity against the elements

pectancy was down to 45 and the triumph of vodka was complete. Only an indomitable doctor called Nikolai offered any hope. Things had been worse, he claimed. For years the Entsy had been dying of dysentery because of foul drinking water. Now they drank snow water in winter and river water in summer. Siberians are like that, muses Thubron. "They adapt, cut down, muck in, suffer, wait."

Nikolai is just one of a cast of strong, resilient characters who have given

Siberia its life-blood down the centuries. They parade across Thubron's pages like beacons. In Komsomolsk he unearths an ebullient Baptist pastor who was once a KGB officer. On the border with Mongolia he meets an unabashed Stalinist burying her head in local history. He interviews an 87-year-old former political prisoner "bitter for all my life's waste" and in Akademgorodok—the once highflying science city outside Novosibirsk—an academician who rambles about cosmic wave experiments.

Siberia, of course, has always seemed larger than life. Bigger than the U.S. and Western Europe combined, it lends itself to extremes. Temperatures can plunge to -60°C. It is home to three of the world's great rivers (the Ob, Yenisei and Lena) and the world's deepest inland lake (Lake Baikal). It stretches across seven time zones and is traversed by a railroad that stretches for 8,851 km.

Thubron's lasting achievement is to convey this epic scale and yet to do so in a way that brings alive the smallest detail—larches "wasted to leaden filigree,"

in Ulan Ude "the biggest head of Lenin in the world," police barracks in Magadan with "each dungeon sheathed in ice." The book ends gloomily as Thubron visits the detritus of Stalin's prison camp system in northeast Siberia and wonders if he is any closer to defining Siberia than when he set out. But by reporting what he saw and heard in writing of supreme talent and clarity, Thubron has created that most precious artistic blend—a memorable work of scholarship, beauty and enduring value. ∎

Talking Point

Ageism

An issue whose time has come

Companies are wasting their most valuable resource–people–because of an outdated approach to age, retirement and work patterns, argues Robin Knight

AGEISM—BASICALLY discrimination against older workers on grounds of age—is like one of those mystery viruses that periodically appear from nowhere.

It has spread almost unnoticed and now infects wide swathes of society. You can't see it, but many people suffer from it. There are plenty of initiatives designed to eradicate it, but none seem to be working. Indeed, this particular virus is estimated to be costing the British economy $50 billion a year.

Like spitting and smoking, almost everyone says they oppose ageism. But the will and stamina to do something about it seem feeble and there are always more pressing matters—combating teenage unemployment, giving working mums job flexibility, boosting gender and ethnic diversity in the workplace and so on. And anyway, isn't it true that everyone wants to retire early and many have the means to do so? The result is that the issue festers.

Yet times are changing and companies that refuse to recognize this are storing up problems for themselves. Consider a few facts and figures: there is a groundswell under way against ageism. A majority of British workers believe their career prospects are limited by the age of 49. Seven out of 10 Britons of all ages say they believe age discrimination exists. And two thirds think it should be illegal.

Worker shortage: Markets are ageing. In today's Britain, one third of citizens have notched up their half century. Within a generation that proportion will have risen to one-half. Already the over-50s account for more than half of discretionary spending in developed countries.

Yet fewer and fewer older people are working. In the UK in the mid-1960s, nine out of 10 men aged 60-64 had jobs. Now three out of 10 do. By 2025 there will be one economically inactive person aged over 50 for every two people in work. Many countries already face a shortage of workers.

More and more people reaching retirement age cannot afford to give up work. Horrendous stock market conditions in the past three years have wiped out all gains achieved since

Both Mick Jagger and Robin Knight are about to turn 60

1997—a staggering $2.7 trillion of pension assets lost worldwide, equivalent to a drop of more than 20%. In the UK the decline has been nearer one third.

As the conclusion of a huge UK survey called 'Generation Flex', published last year, put it: "Finding solutions to the problems of an ageing population, a disgruntled and disadvantaged older workforce, as well as the problems of financing retirement, is becoming critical."

Private sector: Unfortunately, for the past 20 years too many companies have behaved as though they don't want older workers—downsizing, offering early retirement packages, promoting younger and younger senior managers with an inevitable effect on other staff. In fact, today only 21% of those working in the UK private sector are aged over 50.

Some things are altering. Between now and 2006, European Union member states will be introducing legislation that prevents employers from fixing arbitrary ages at which people must stop doing specific jobs, effectively joining the US, Australia and other countries in barring mandatory retirement. Some companies have begun to actively recruit older workers. Courts in the US and Britain are starting to support employees who sue on grounds of age discrimination. And even the advertising industry has begun to realize that life does not end at 35.

Still, there is a long way to go until we reach utopia—which might be defined as a society where recruitment is based on ability, workers are judged on performance, employers recognize the advantages of mixed age teams, and silly prejudices about older people (they work less hard, take more time off, adapt to technology more slowly) are abandoned.

Legislation is part of the answer—but this takes time to work. A better approach is for those older people who want to work to make their voices heard—and for everyone to get behind these challenges. The time for passive acceptance of an unfair situation is over. After all, we all get older. One day this will be your problem too if nothing changes.

Talking Point

Report Robin Knight

MORE A BLESSING THAN A CURSE?

Oil is blamed for everything from communal violence to failed states, the spread of corruption and environmental degradation. But there is another side to the argument...

IT HAS become fashionable to refer to 'the curse of oil'. The BBC put the phrase on the title of a television programme about the Baku-Ceyhan oil pipeline. *The Economist* devoted an entire piece recently to "Tackling the curse of oil". The *Washington Post* attempted some balance—"How oil can be a blessing instead of a curse." But perhaps the *Financial Times* was most in tune with the prevailing mood with its comment last autumn that oil revenues "frequently and corruptly make their way into the pockets of a rich elite, distorting the economy and the political life of the country cursed with its [oil's] presence."

The tone of present discussion around oil is clear. Far from being seen as essential for the modern economy, oil is viewed in almost distasteful terms—as a commodity that encourages corruption, nationalism, conflict, misgovernment and environmental damage. This critique has its roots in some eye-catching 'facts', spouted by every campaigner against the oil industry. Venezuela, for instance, has earned more than $600 billion in oil revenues since the mid-1970s. But real income per head has fallen by 15% since then. Oil must be at the root of the dreadful under-performance.

Missing earnings: In Angola one in every four dollars in oil earnings goes 'missing', according to statistics published by a non-governmental organization. At the same time one in four Angolan children dies before the age of five from a preventable disease. Find the missing oil revenues and infant mortality rates in Angola will improve dramatically. Or take Transparency International's (TI's) benchmark 'corruption perceptions' survey, which ranks countries according to the extent they are perceived to be corrupt. Many of the worst offenders are oil producers. *Ipso facto*, say the critics, oil must be to blame. So—get rid of oil, cut back official revenues and you reduce corruption.

Sadly, this kind of analysis has taken a grip on Western opinion formers. It's never noted, for example, that plenty of oil producers—including the United Arab Emirates, Qatar and Kuwait as well as Norway, the UK, the US, Canada and Mexico—are to be found in the top third (least corrupt) of TI's 146-country survey. Or that there are plenty of failed states that have no oil.

Nor are the manifold benefits that stem from oil given much of an airing any more. Leave aside the obvious—the heat, light and mobili-

ty that stem from hydrocarbons. As group chief executive Lord Browne pointed out recently, BP alone pays $6.5 billion in taxes each year and supports more than 100,000 jobs worldwide. In the US, development of the Gulf of Mexico over the last 15 years has created more than 40,000 jobs and the multiplier effect of what BP does is thought to be three to four times its initial investment—meaning that in the US the $6 billion invested by the company in 2004 was worth around $20 billion to the national economy.

Small beer, maybe, in the US. But in Azerbaijan, Angola, Colombia, Vietnam, Trinidad and other countries where the company operates, its beneficial role in the national economy is hard to exaggerate. Nor is it confined to revenues. Through training, health and safety standards, community investment and everyday business conduct, companies like BP can have a great effect on collective behaviour. Azerbaijan's recent decision to begin implementing the UK-sponsored extractive industries transparency initiative is only the latest example. Another is the mould-breaking corporate governance reforms being introduced by TNK-BP in Russia.

No one disputes that oil can have negative side effects. Yet surely the emphasis should be on the word 'can'? Clearly, some societies handle the challenges of oil better than others. But challenges exist to be overcome—as Browne puts it, "they do not run beyond human intelligence." The fact that some states fail to rise to the occasion hardly justifies the slur that oil is a curse to be avoided.

BP's standards and conduct can bring great benefits to Vietnam and other countries where it operates

Bibliography

Almond, Mark, *Europe's Backyard War* (William Heinemann, 1994)
Bassow, Walt, *The Moscow Correspondents* (William Morrow & Co, 1988)
Beeston, Richard, *Looking for Trouble* (Brassey's, 1997)
Bergin, Tom, *Spills and Spin* (Business Books, 2011)
Bower, Tom, *The Squeeze* (Harper Press, 2009)
Brown, Archie, *The Rise and Fall of Communism* (Bodley Head, 2009)
Browne, John, *Beyond Business* (Weidenfeld & Nicolson, 2010)
Childs, David, *Honecker's Germany* (Allen & Unwin, 1985)
Coleman, Fred, *The Decline and Fall of the Soviet Empire* (St Martin's Press, 1996)
Combs, Dick, *Inside the Soviet Alternate Universe* (Penn State Press, 2008)
Djilas, Milovan, *Land Without Justice* (Harcourt, Brace & Co, 1958)
Doust, Dudley, *Bradley Brook* (Fairfield Books, 2009)
Drury, Allen, *A Very Strange Society* (Michael Joseph, 1968)
Evans, Harold, *My Paper Chase* (Little Brown, 2009)
Gergen, David, *Eyewitness to Power* (Simon & Schuster, 2000)
Harris, Robert, *Good and Faithful Servant* (Faber & Faber, 1990)
Hess, Stephen, *International News & Foreign Correspondents* (Brookings, 1996)
Kaiser, Robert, *Russia* (Secker & Warburg, 1976)
Kaufman, Michael, *Mad Dreams, Saving Graces* (Random House, 1989)
Klein, Naomi, *No Logo* (Flamingo, 2000)
Lelyveld, Joseph, *Move Your Shadow* (Michael Joseph, 1985)
Levine, Steve, *The Oil and the Glory* (Random House, 2007)
Maitland, Donald, *Diverse Times, Sundry Places* (Alpha Press, 1990)
Marsh, David, *The Germans – Rich, Bothered and Divided* (Century, 1989)
Matlock, Jack, *Autopsy of an Empire* (Random House, 1995)
Mayers, David, *The Ambassadors* (Oxford University Press, 1995)
Meredith, Martin, *The Past is Another Country* (Andre Deutsch, 1979)
Meyer, Christopher, *DC Confidential* (Weidenfeld & Nicolson, 2005)
Moseley, Ray, *In Foreign Fields* (Ray Moseley, 2010)
Ogden, Chris, *Maggie* (Simon & Schuster, 1990)
Pogrund, Benjamin, *War of Words* (Seven Stories Press, 2000)
Richards, Charles, *The New Italians* (Michael Joseph, 1994)
Satter, David, *Age of Delirium* (Alfred Knopf, 1996)
Sebestyen, Victor, *Revolution 1989* (Weidenfeld & Nicolson, 2009)
Siani-Davies, Peter, *The Romanian Revolution* (Cornell University, 2005)
Smith, Hedrick, *The Russians* (Quadrangle/NYT, 1976)
Stephens, Lionel, *Pangbourne College* (Dovecote Press, 1991)
Sudetic, Chuck, *Blood and Vengeance* (Norton, 1998)
Thornley, Yseult (ed), *Unquiet Spirit* (Liberties Press, 2008)
Thubron, Colin, *Among the Russians* (William Heinemann, 1983)
Tuohy, William, *Dangerous Company* (William Morrow & Co, 1987)

Index